HOUSE OF SLAUGHTER™
— THE BUTCHER'S MARK —

Published by

BOOM!
STUDIOS

ROSS RICHIE Chairman & Founder
JEN HARNED CFO
MATT GAGNON Editor-in-Chief
FILIP SABLIK President, Publishing & Marketing
STEPHEN CHRISTY President, Development
LANCE KREITER Vice President, Licensing & Merchandising
BRYCE CARLSON Vice President, Editorial & Creative Strategy
HUNTER GORINSON Vice President, Business Development
JOSH HAYES Vice President, Sales
SIERRA HAHN Executive Editor
ERIC HARBURN Executive Editor
RYAN MATSUNAGA Director, Marketing
STEPHANIE LAZARSKI Director, Operations
ELYSE STRANDBERG Manager, Finance
MICHELLE ANKLEY Manager, Production Design
CHERYL PARKER Manager, Human Resources
DAFNA PLEBAN Senior Editor
ELIZABETH BREI Editor
KATHLEEN WISNESKI Editor
SOPHIE PHILIPS-ROBERTS Editor
ALLYSON GRONOWITZ Associate Editor
GAVIN GRONENTHAL Assistant Editor
GWEN WALLER Assistant Editor
RAMIRO PORTNOY Assistant Editor

KENZIE RZONCA Assistant Editor
REY NETSCHKE Editorial Assistant
MARIE KRUPINA Design Lead
CRYSTAL WHITE Design Lead
GRACE PARK Design Coordinator
MADISON GOYETTE Production Designer
VERONICA GUTIERREZ Production Designer
JESSY GOULD Production Designer
NANCY MOJICA Production Designer
SAMANTHA KNAPP Production Design Assistant
ESTHER KIM Marketing Lead
BREANNA SARPY Marketing Lead, Digital
AMANDA LAWSON Marketing Coordinator
ALEX LORENZEN Marketing Coordinator, Copywriter
GRECIA MARTINEZ Marketing Assistant, Digital
JOSÉ MEZA Consumer Sales Lead
ASHLEY TROUB Consumer Sales Coordinator
HARLEY SALBACKA Sales Coordinator
MEGAN CHRISTOPHER Operations Lead
RODRIGO HERNANDEZ Operations Coordinator
JASON LEE Senior Accountant
FAIZAH BASHIR Business Analyst
AMBER PETERS Staff Accountant
SABRINA LESIN Accounting Assistant

BOOM! STUDIOS

HOUSE OF SLAUGHTER VOL. 1, JUNE 2022. Published by BOOM! Studios, a division of Boom Entertainment, Inc. House of Slaughter is ™ & © 2022 James Tynion IV & Werther Dell'Edera. Originally published in single magazine form as HOUSE OF SLAUGHTER No. 1-5. ™ & © 2021, 2022 James Tynion IV & Werther Dell'Edera. All rights reserved. BOOM! Studios™ and the BOOM! Studios logo are trademarks of Boom Entertainment, Inc., registered in various countries and categories. All characters, events, and institutions depicted herein are fictional. Any similarity between any of the names, characters, persons, events, and/or institutions in this publication to actual names, characters, and persons, whether living or dead, events, and/or institutions is unintended and purely coincidental. BOOM! Studios does not read or accept unsolicited submissions of ideas, stories, or artwork.

BOOM! Studios, 5670 Wilshire Boulevard, Suite 400, Los Angeles, CA, 90036-5679. Printed in Canada. First Printing.

STANDARD EDITION: ISBN: 978-1-68415-816-4, eISBN: 978-1-64668-449-6
DISCOVER NOW EDITION: ISBN: 978-1-68415-831-7
BOOM! STUDIOS EXCLUSIVE EDITION: ISBN: 978-1-68415-865-2

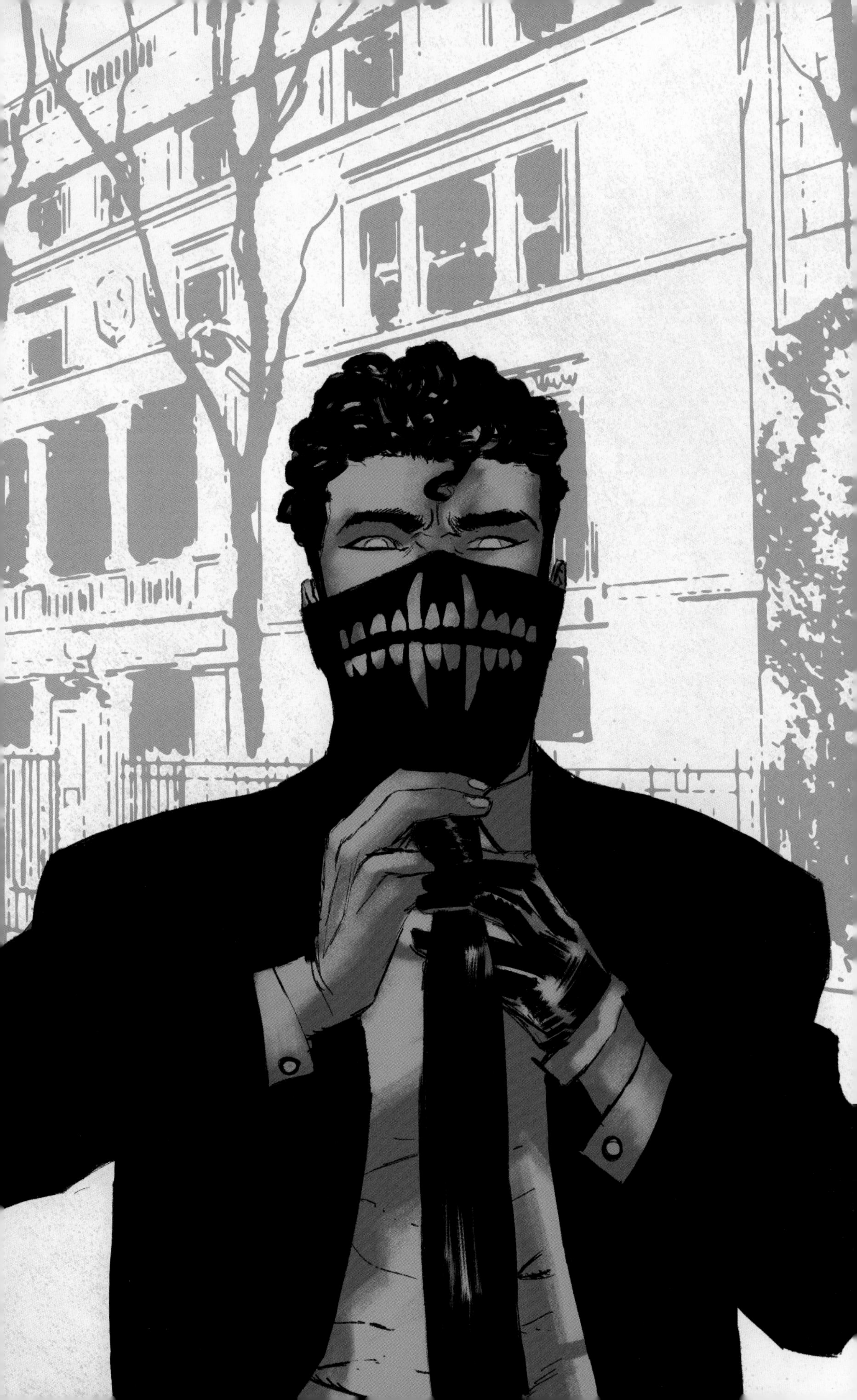

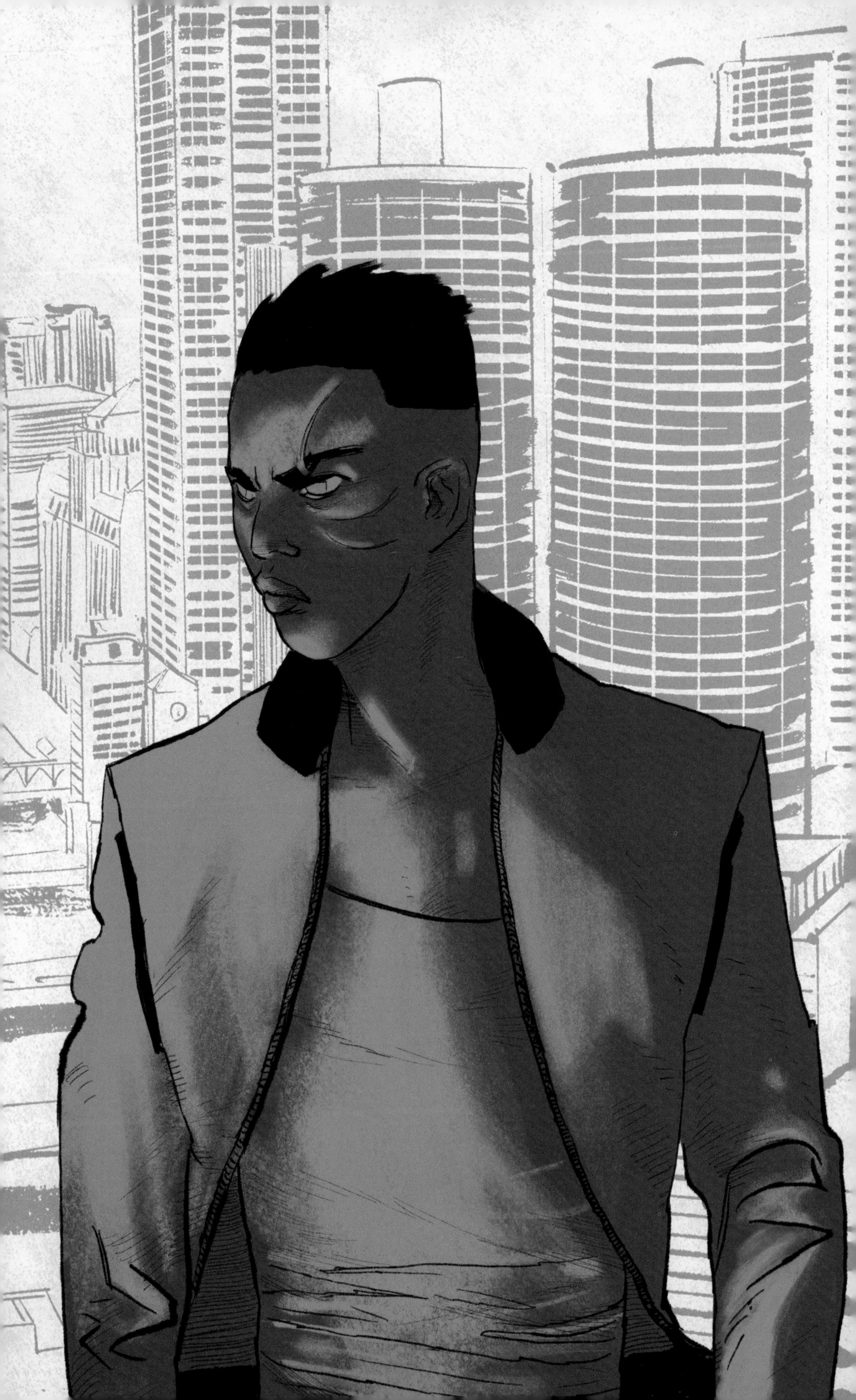

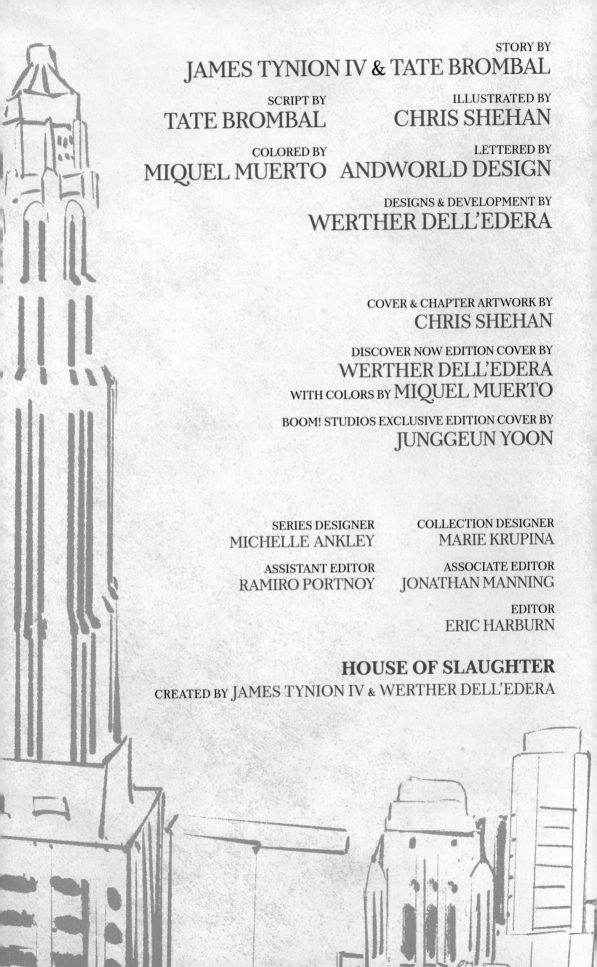

STORY BY
JAMES TYNION IV & TATE BROMBAL

SCRIPT BY
TATE BROMBAL

ILLUSTRATED BY
CHRIS SHEHAN

COLORED BY
MIQUEL MUERTO

LETTERED BY
ANDWORLD DESIGN

DESIGNS & DEVELOPMENT BY
WERTHER DELL'EDERA

COVER & CHAPTER ARTWORK BY
CHRIS SHEHAN

DISCOVER NOW EDITION COVER BY
WERTHER DELL'EDERA
WITH COLORS BY MIQUEL MUERTO

BOOM! STUDIOS EXCLUSIVE EDITION COVER BY
JUNGGEUN YOON

SERIES DESIGNER
MICHELLE ANKLEY

COLLECTION DESIGNER
MARIE KRUPINA

ASSISTANT EDITOR
RAMIRO PORTNOY

ASSOCIATE EDITOR
JONATHAN MANNING

EDITOR
ERIC HARBURN

HOUSE OF SLAUGHTER

CREATED BY JAMES TYNION IV & WERTHER DELL'EDERA

PART ONE

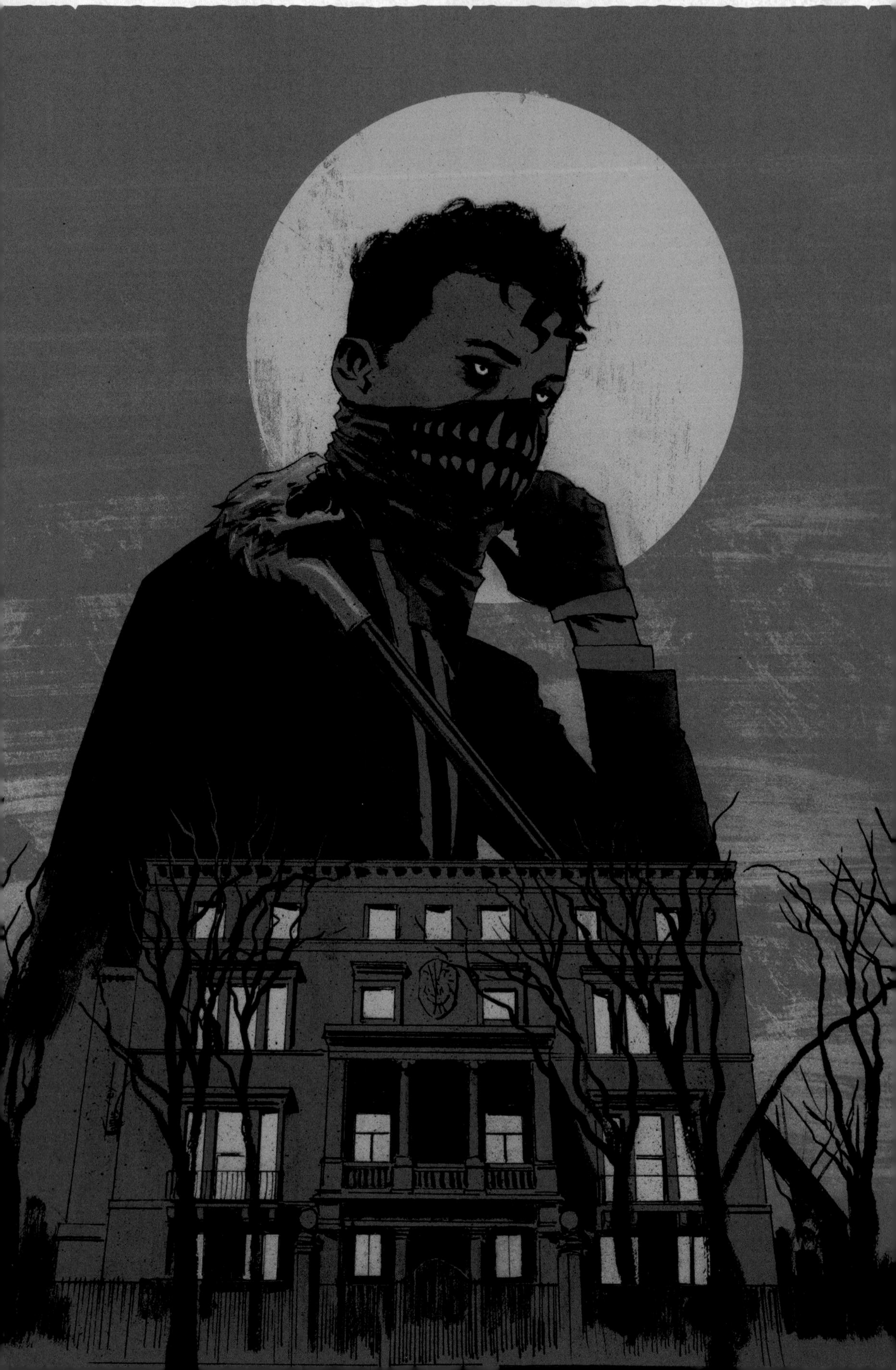

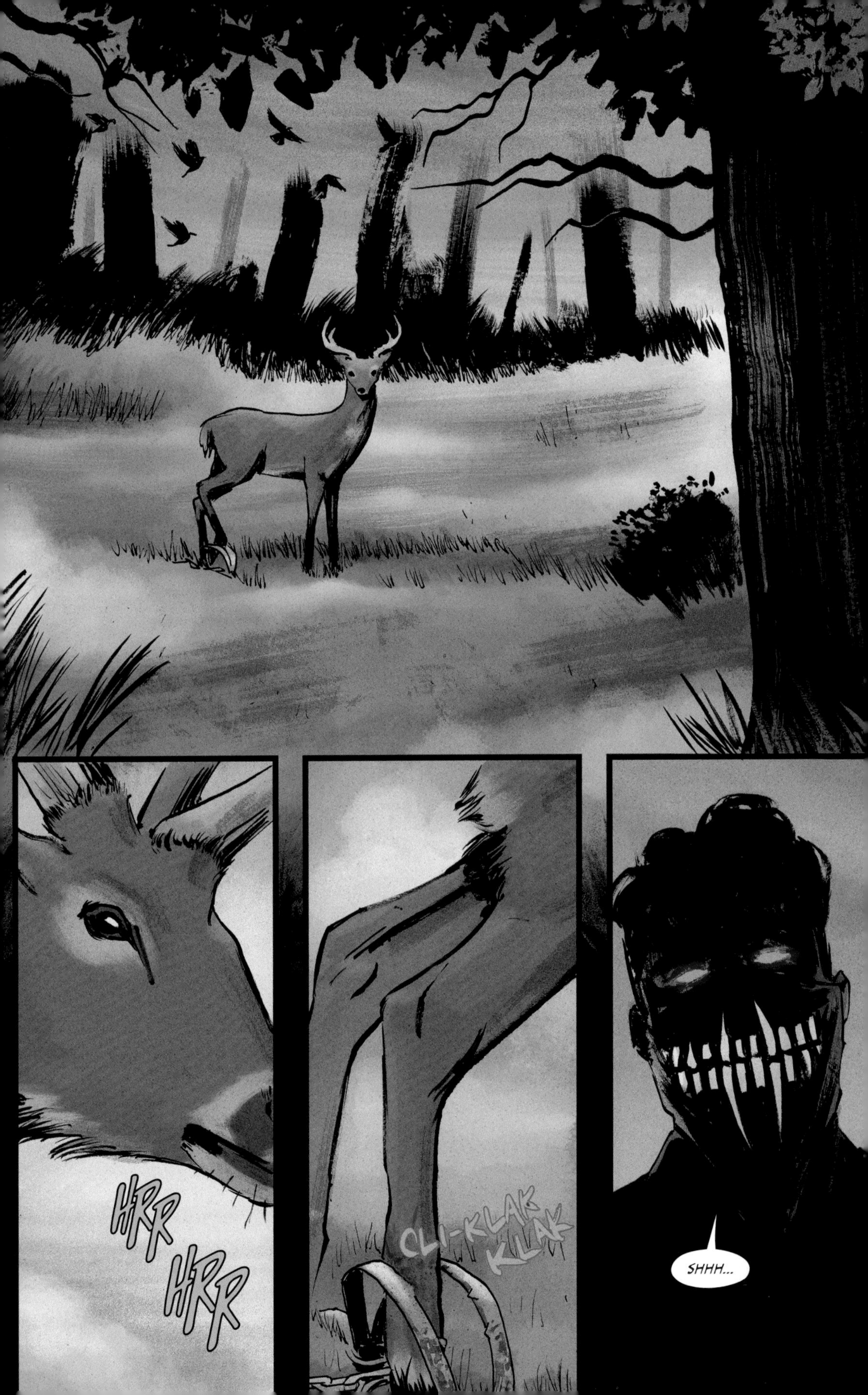
HRR
HRR
CLI-KLAK
KLAK
SHHH...

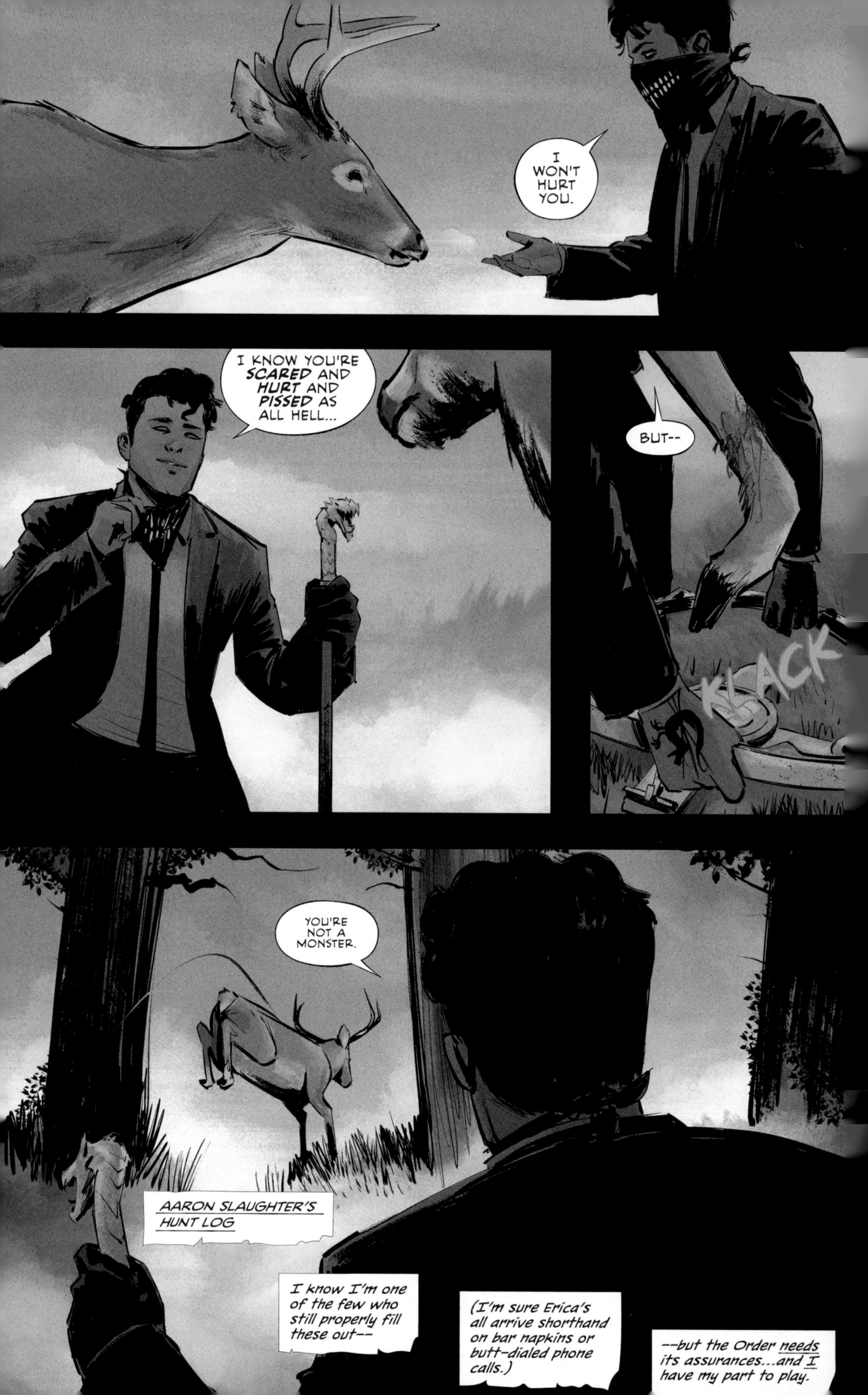
I WON'T HURT YOU.
I KNOW YOU'RE SCARED AND HURT AND PISSED AS ALL HELL...
BUT--
KLACK
YOU'RE NOT A MONSTER.
AARON SLAUGHTER'S HUNT LOG
I know I'm one of the few who still properly fill these out--
(I'm sure Erica's all arrive shorthand on bar napkins or butt-dialed phone calls.)
--but the Order needs its assurances...and I have my part to play.

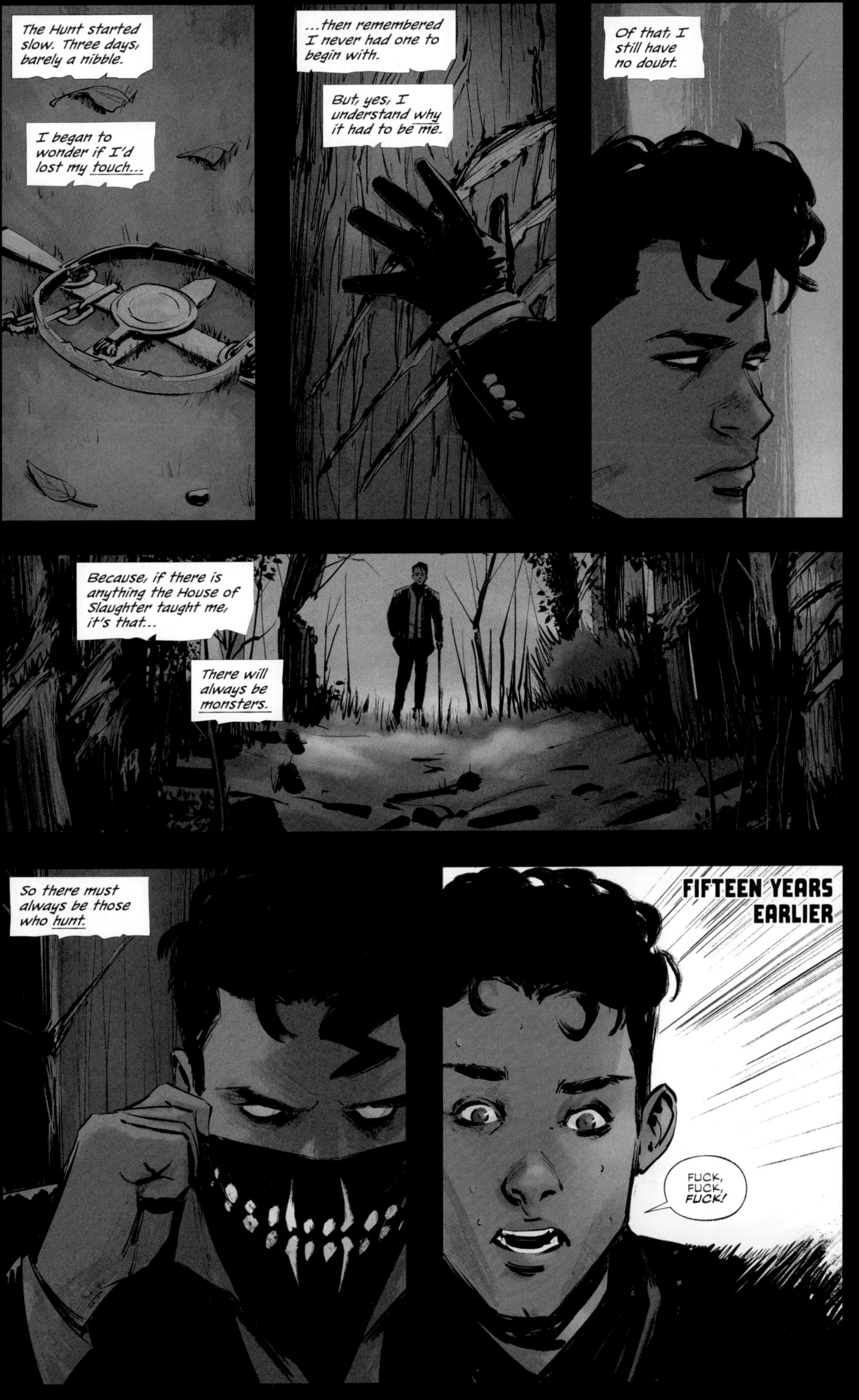
The Hunt started slow. Three days, barely a nibble.
I began to wonder if I'd lost my touch...
...then remembered I never had one to begin with.
But, yes, I understand why it had to be me.
Of that, I still have no doubt.
Because, if there is anything the House of Slaughter taught me, it's that...
There will always be monsters.
So there must always be those who hunt.
FIFTEEN YEARS EARLIER
FUCK, FUCK, FUCK!

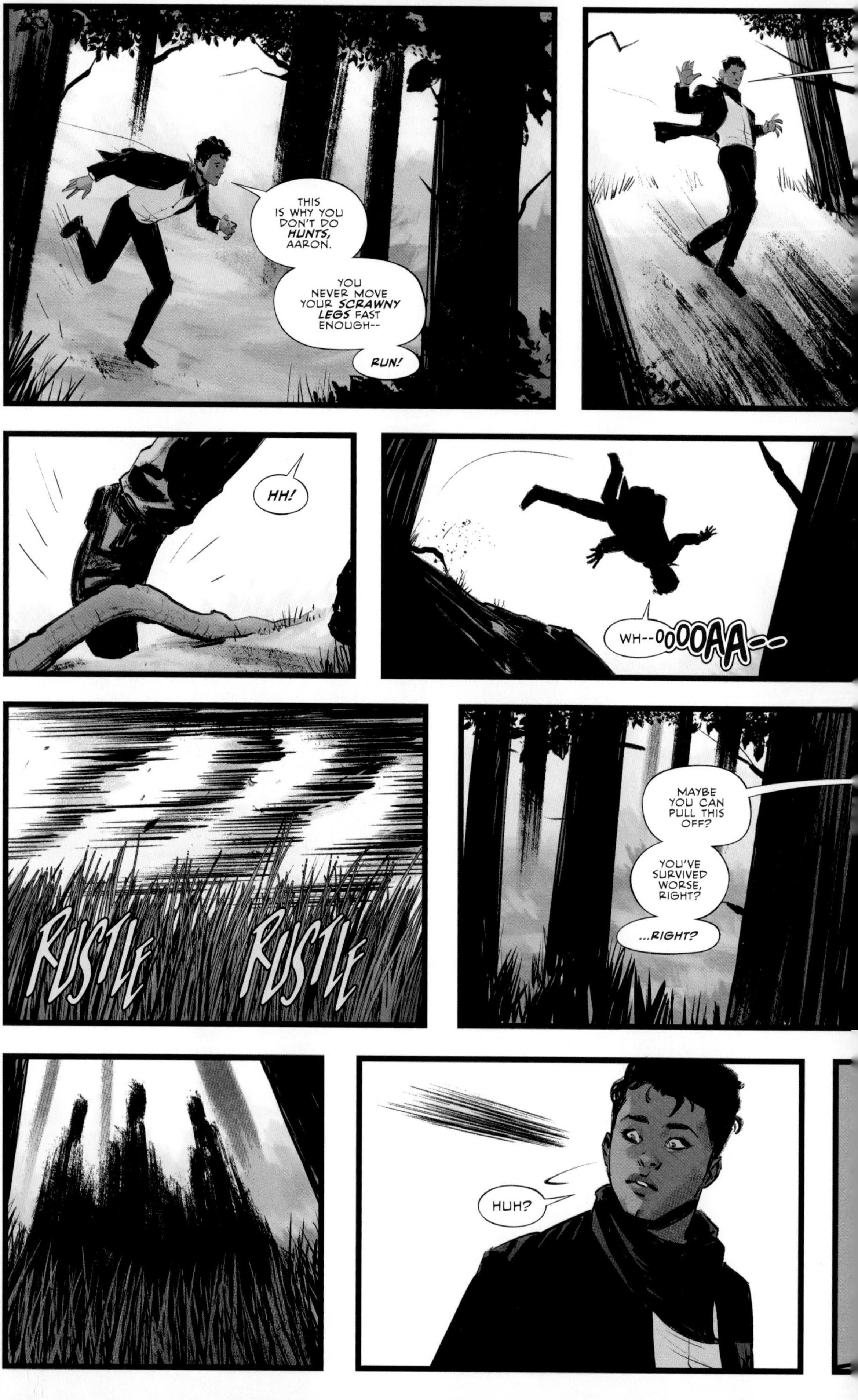
THIS IS WHY YOU DON'T DO HUNTS, AARON.
YOU NEVER MOVE YOUR SCRAWNY LEGS FAST ENOUGH--
RUN!
HH!
WH--OOOOAA--
RUSTLE RUSTLE
MAYBE YOU CAN PULL THIS OFF?
YOU'VE SURVIVED WORSE, RIGHT?
...RIGHT?
HUH?

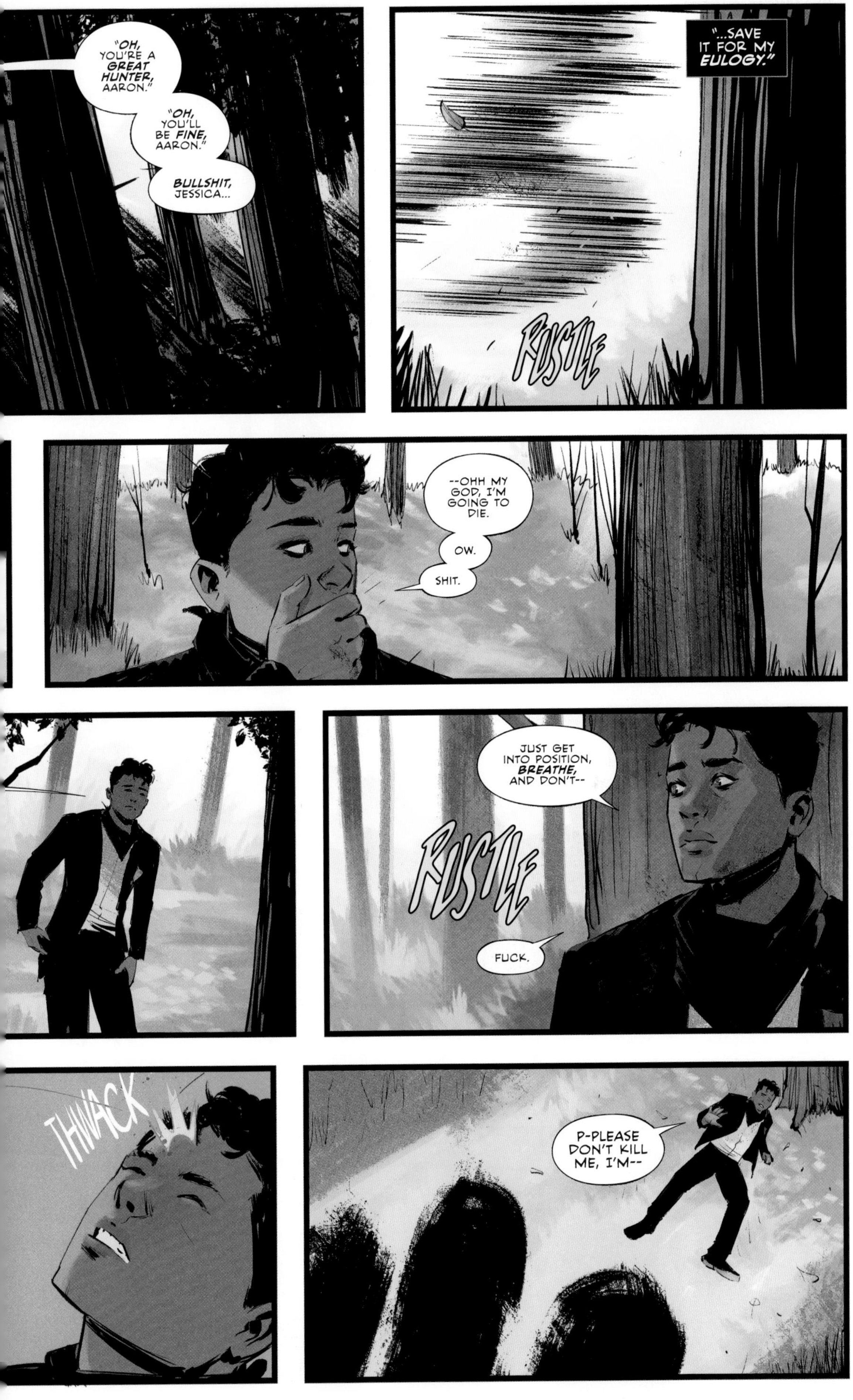
"OH, YOU'RE A GREAT HUNTER, AARON."
"OH, YOU'LL BE FINE, AARON."
BULLSHIT, JESSICA...
"...SAVE IT FOR MY EULOGY."
RUSTLE
--OHH MY GOD, I'M GOING TO DIE.
OW.
SHIT.
JUST GET INTO POSITION, BREATHE, AND DON'T--
RUSTLE
FUCK.
THWACK
P-PLEASE DON'T KILL ME, I'M--

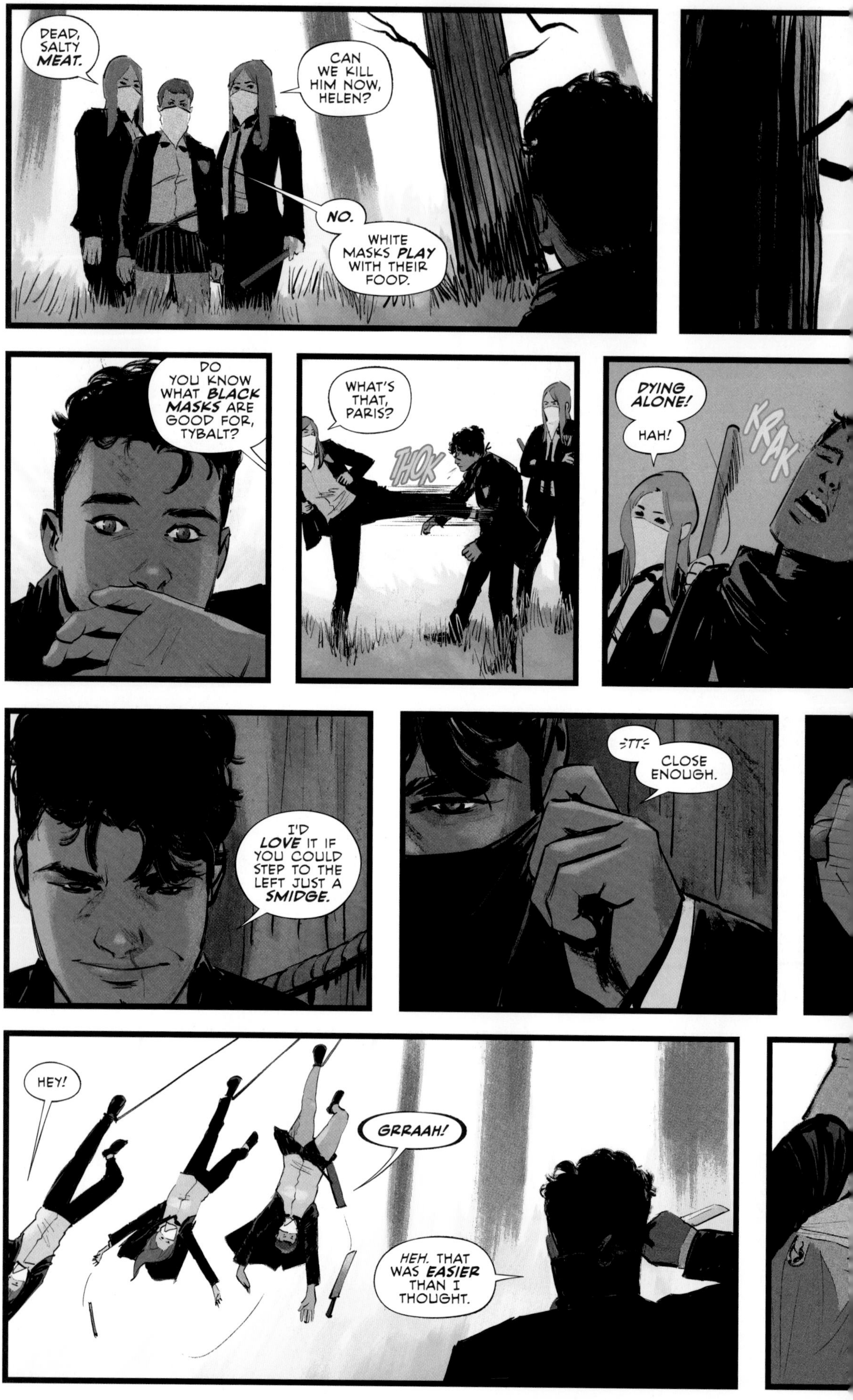
DEAD, SALTY MEAT.
CAN WE KILL HIM NOW, HELEN?
NO.
WHITE MASKS PLAY WITH THEIR FOOD.
DO YOU KNOW WHAT BLACK MASKS ARE GOOD FOR, TYBALT?
WHAT'S THAT, PARIS?
THOK
DYING ALONE!
HAH!
KRAK
I'D LOVE IT IF YOU COULD STEP TO THE LEFT JUST A SMIDGE.
TT
CLOSE ENOUGH.
HEY!
GRRAAH!
HEH. THAT WAS EASIER THAN I THOUGHT.

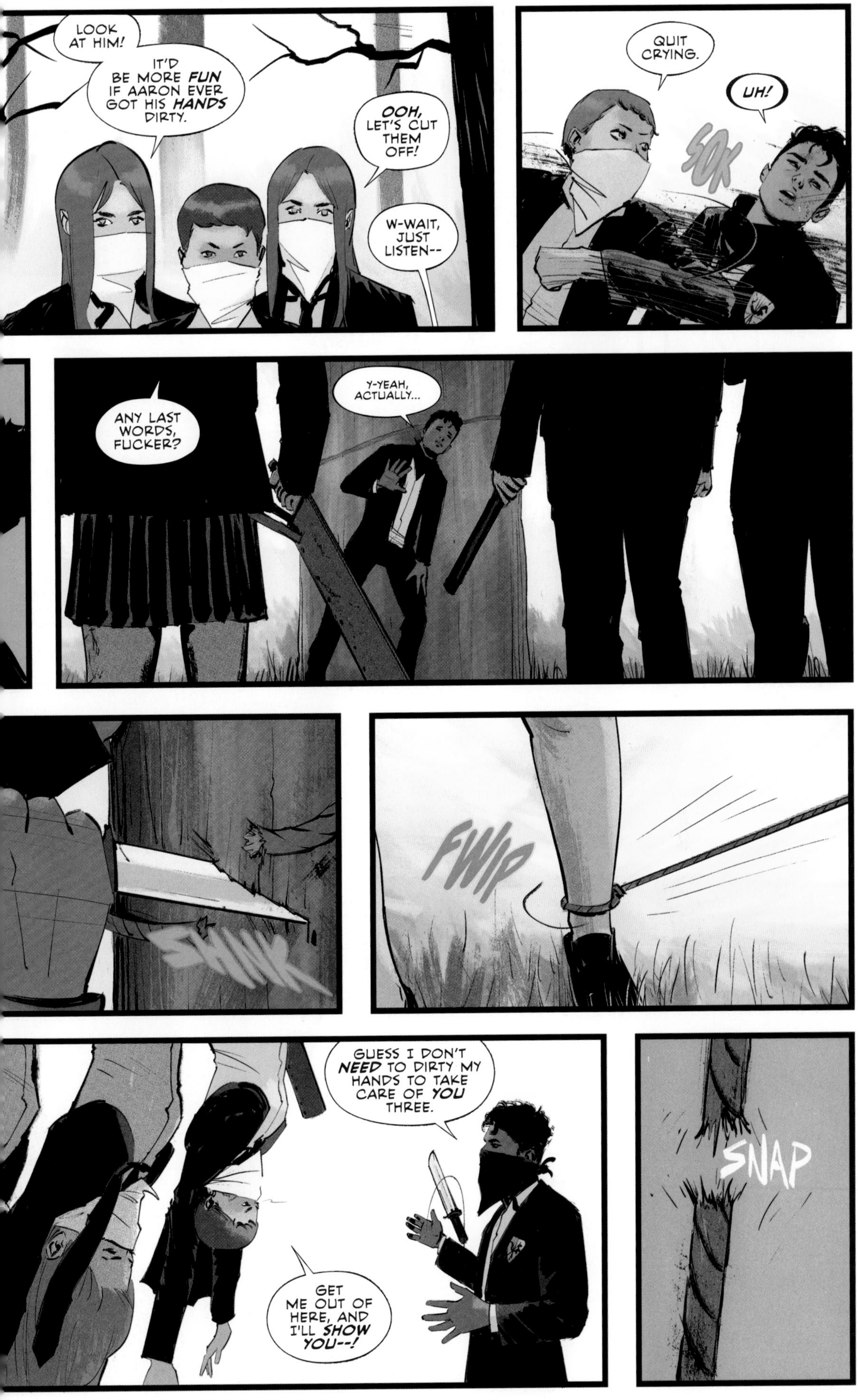
LOOK AT HIM!
IT'D BE MORE FUN IF AARON EVER GOT HIS HANDS DIRTY.
OOH, LET'S CUT THEM OFF!
W-WAIT, JUST LISTEN--
QUIT CRYING.
UH!
SOK
ANY LAST WORDS, FUCKER?
Y-YEAH, ACTUALLY...
SHNK
FWIP
GUESS I DON'T NEED TO DIRTY MY HANDS TO TAKE CARE OF YOU THREE.
GET ME OUT OF HERE, AND I'LL SHOW YOU--!
SNAP

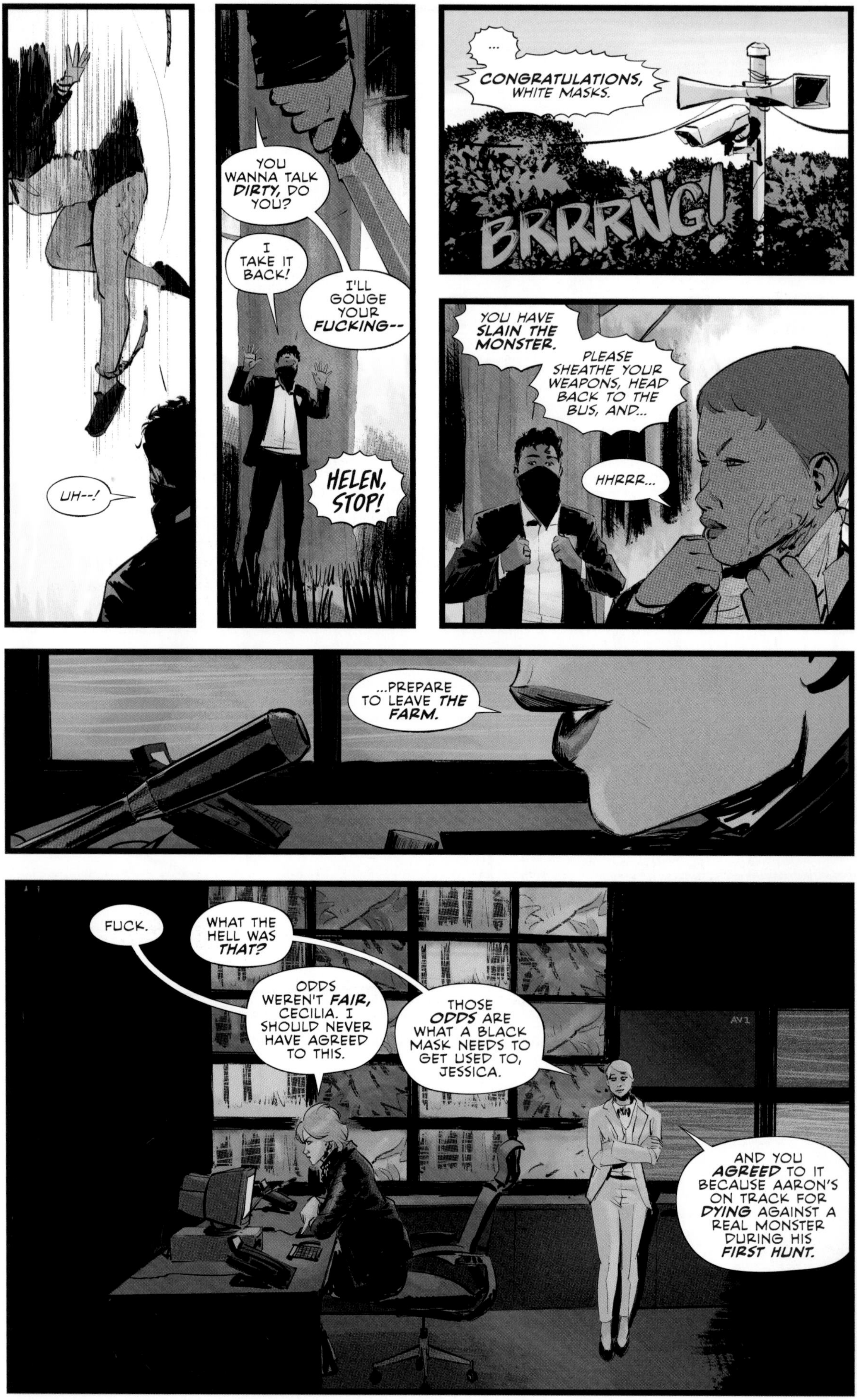
UH--!
YOU WANNA TALK DIRTY, DO YOU?
I TAKE IT BACK!
I'LL GOUGE YOUR FUCKING--
HELEN, STOP!
...
CONGRATULATIONS, WHITE MASKS.
BRRRNG!
YOU HAVE SLAIN THE MONSTER.
PLEASE SHEATHE YOUR WEAPONS, HEAD BACK TO THE BUS, AND...
HHRRR...
...PREPARE TO LEAVE THE FARM.
FUCK.
WHAT THE HELL WAS THAT?
ODDS WEREN'T FAIR, CECILIA. I SHOULD NEVER HAVE AGREED TO THIS.
THOSE ODDS ARE WHAT A BLACK MASK NEEDS TO GET USED TO, JESSICA.
AND YOU AGREED TO IT BECAUSE AARON'S ON TRACK FOR DYING AGAINST A REAL MONSTER DURING HIS FIRST HUNT.

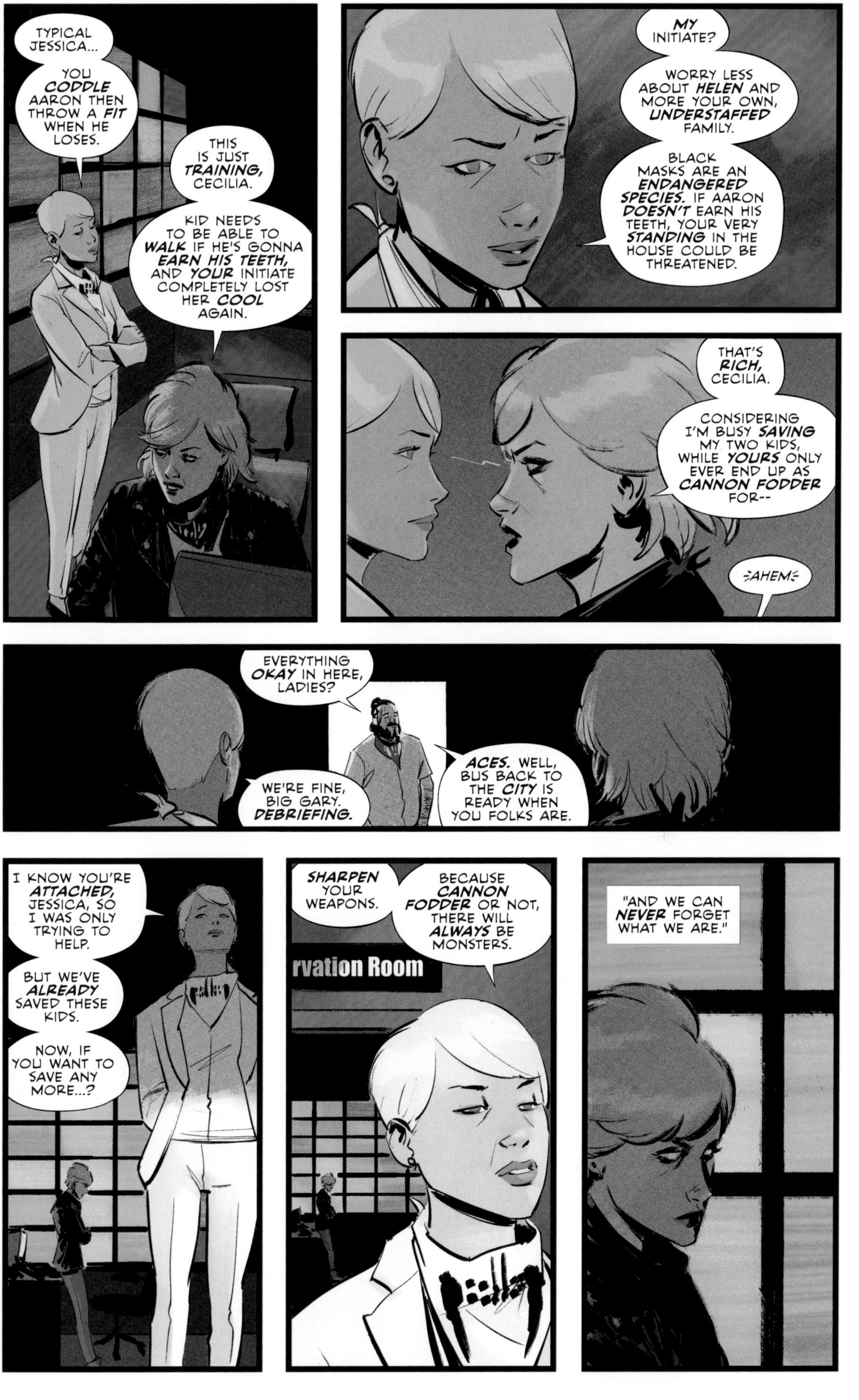
TYPICAL JESSICA...
YOU CODDLE AARON THEN THROW A FIT WHEN HE LOSES.
THIS IS JUST TRAINING, CECILIA.
KID NEEDS TO BE ABLE TO WALK IF HE'S GONNA EARN HIS TEETH, AND YOUR INITIATE COMPLETELY LOST HER COOL AGAIN.
MY INITIATE?
WORRY LESS ABOUT HELEN AND MORE YOUR OWN, UNDERSTAFFED FAMILY.
BLACK MASKS ARE AN ENDANGERED SPECIES. IF AARON DOESN'T EARN HIS TEETH, YOUR VERY STANDING IN THE HOUSE COULD BE THREATENED.
THAT'S RICH, CECILIA.
CONSIDERING I'M BUSY SAVING MY TWO KIDS, WHILE YOURS ONLY EVER END UP AS CANNON FODDER FOR--
AHEM
EVERYTHING OKAY IN HERE, LADIES?
WE'RE FINE, BIG GARY. DEBRIEFING.
ACES. WELL, BUS BACK TO THE CITY IS READY WHEN YOU FOLKS ARE.
I KNOW YOU'RE ATTACHED, JESSICA, SO I WAS ONLY TRYING TO HELP.
BUT WE'VE ALREADY SAVED THESE KIDS.
NOW, IF YOU WANT TO SAVE ANY MORE...?
SHARPEN YOUR WEAPONS.
BECAUSE CANNON FODDER OR NOT, THERE WILL ALWAYS BE MONSTERS.
rvation Room
"AND WE CAN NEVER FORGET WHAT WE ARE."

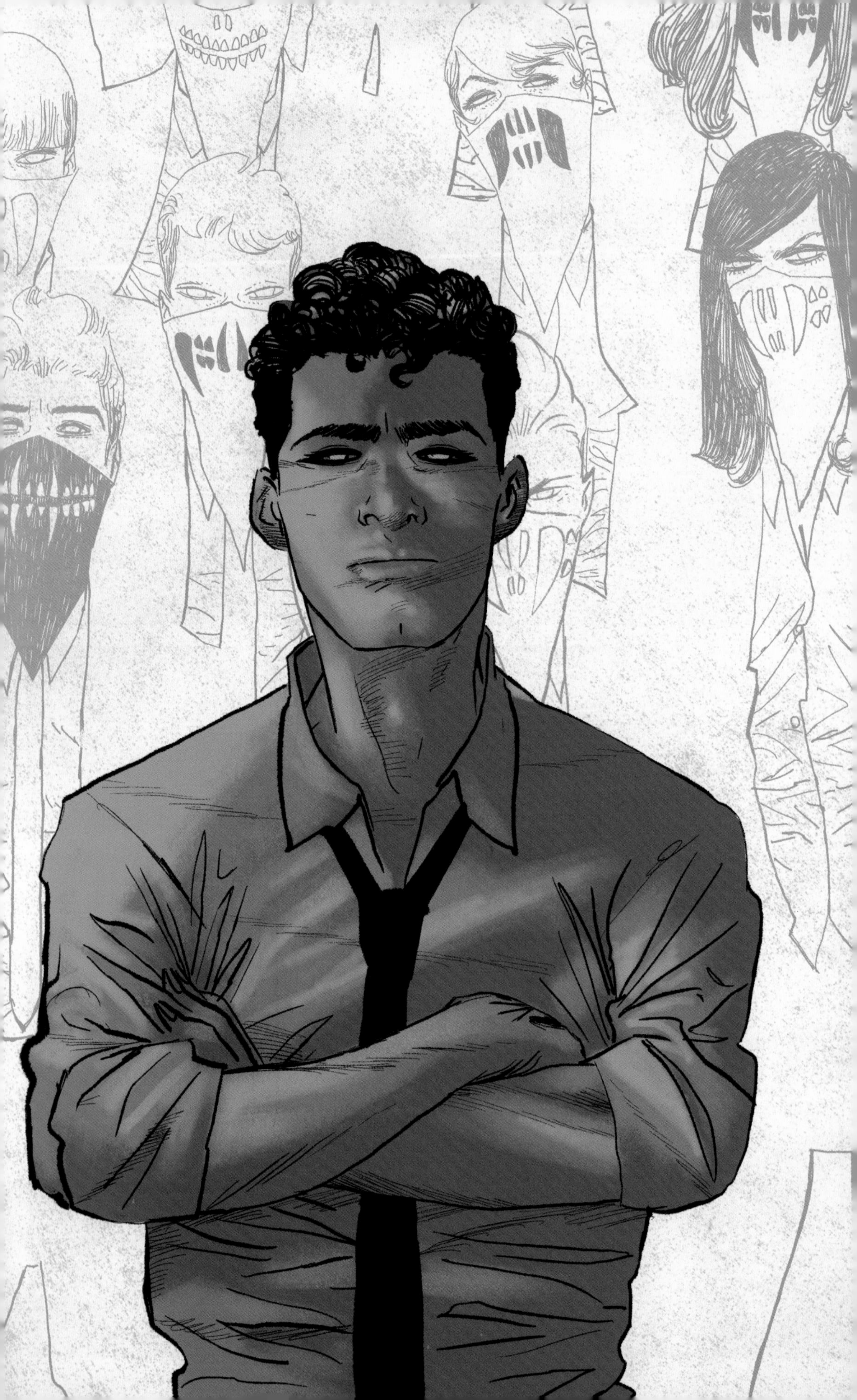

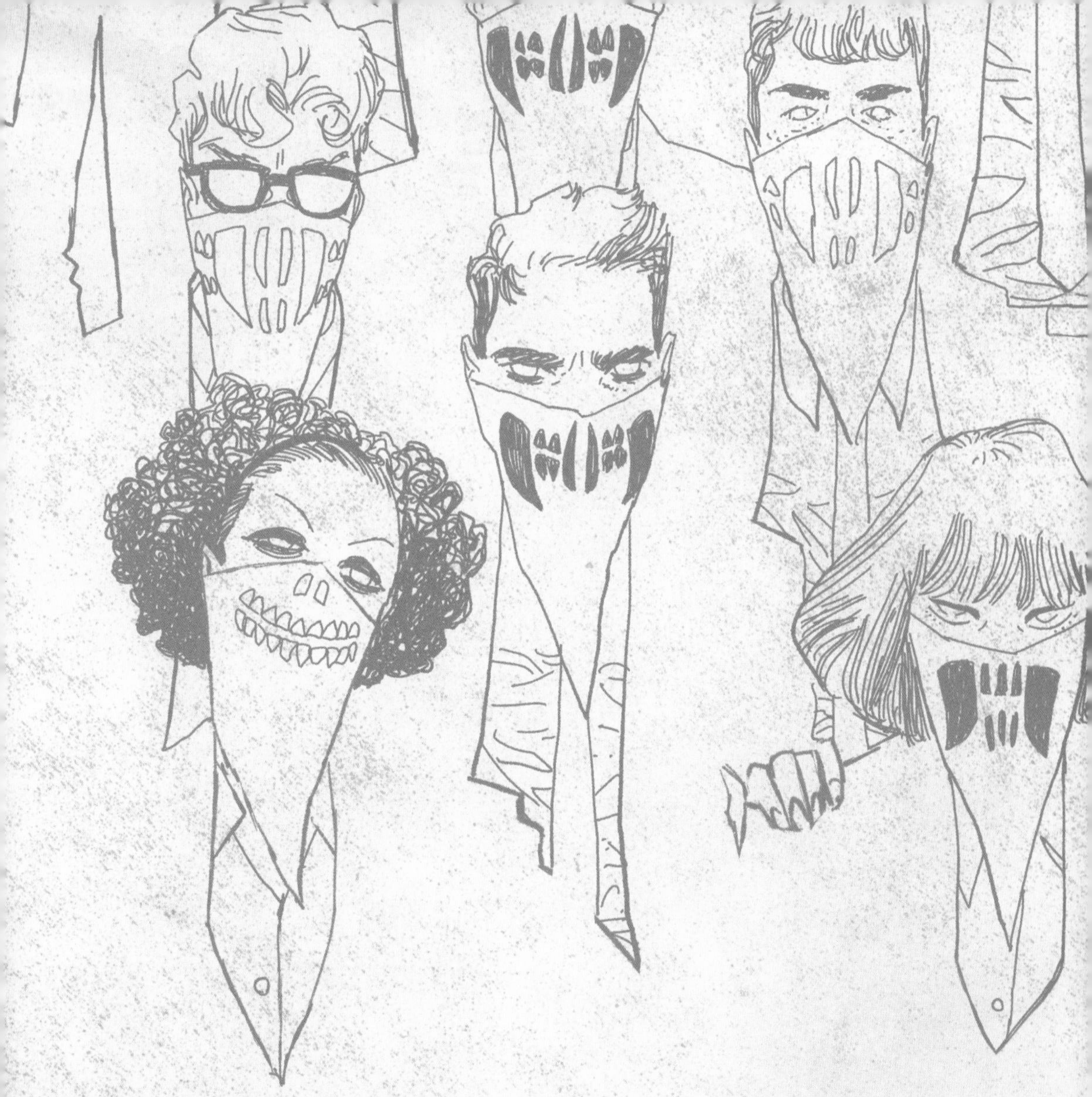

HOUSE OF SLAUGHTER

THE BUTCHER'S MARK

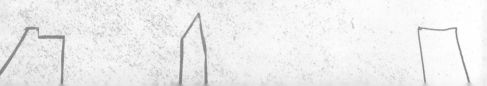

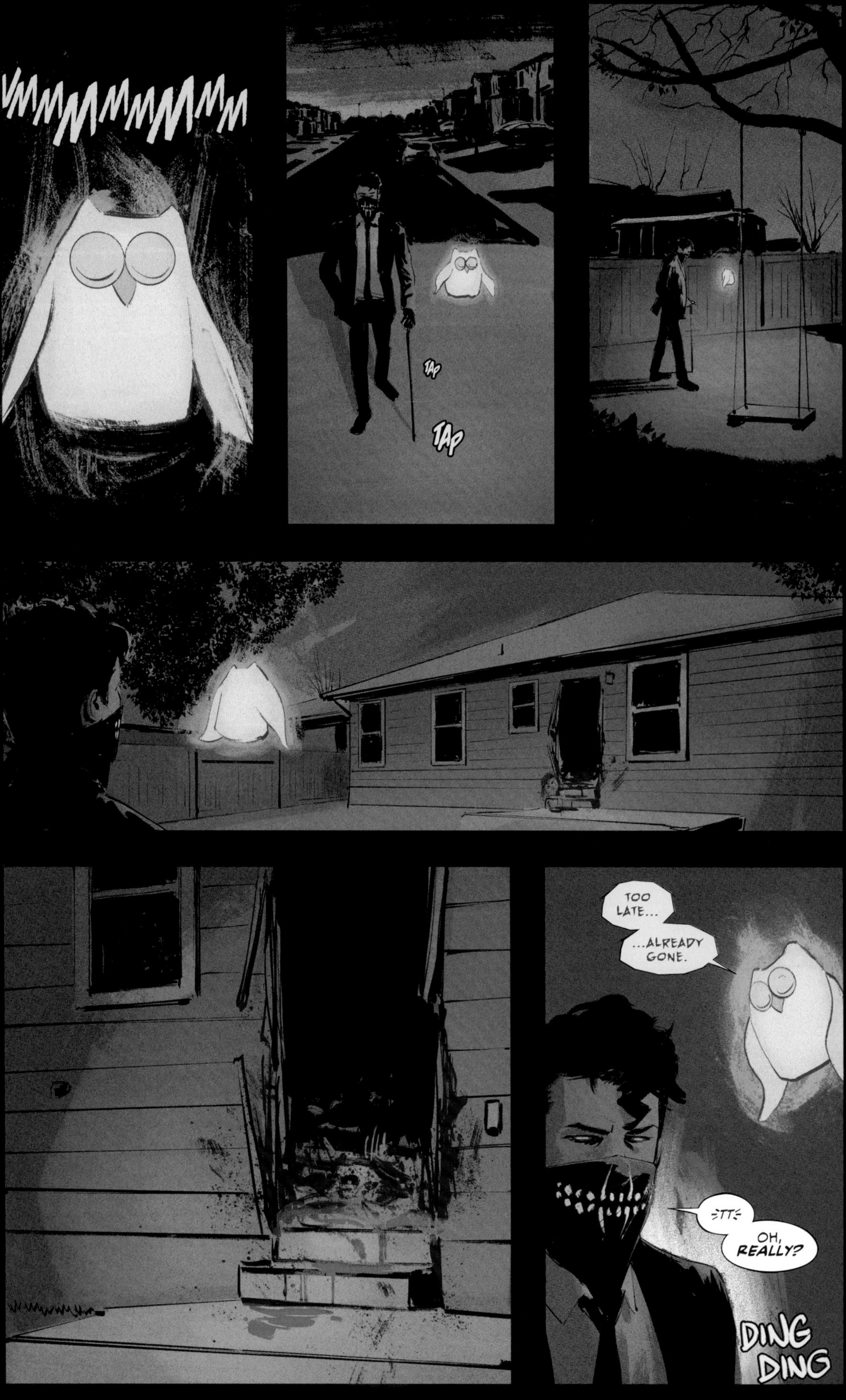
VMMMMMMMMM
TAP
TAP
TOO LATE...
...ALREADY GONE.
=TT=
OH, REALLY?
DING DING

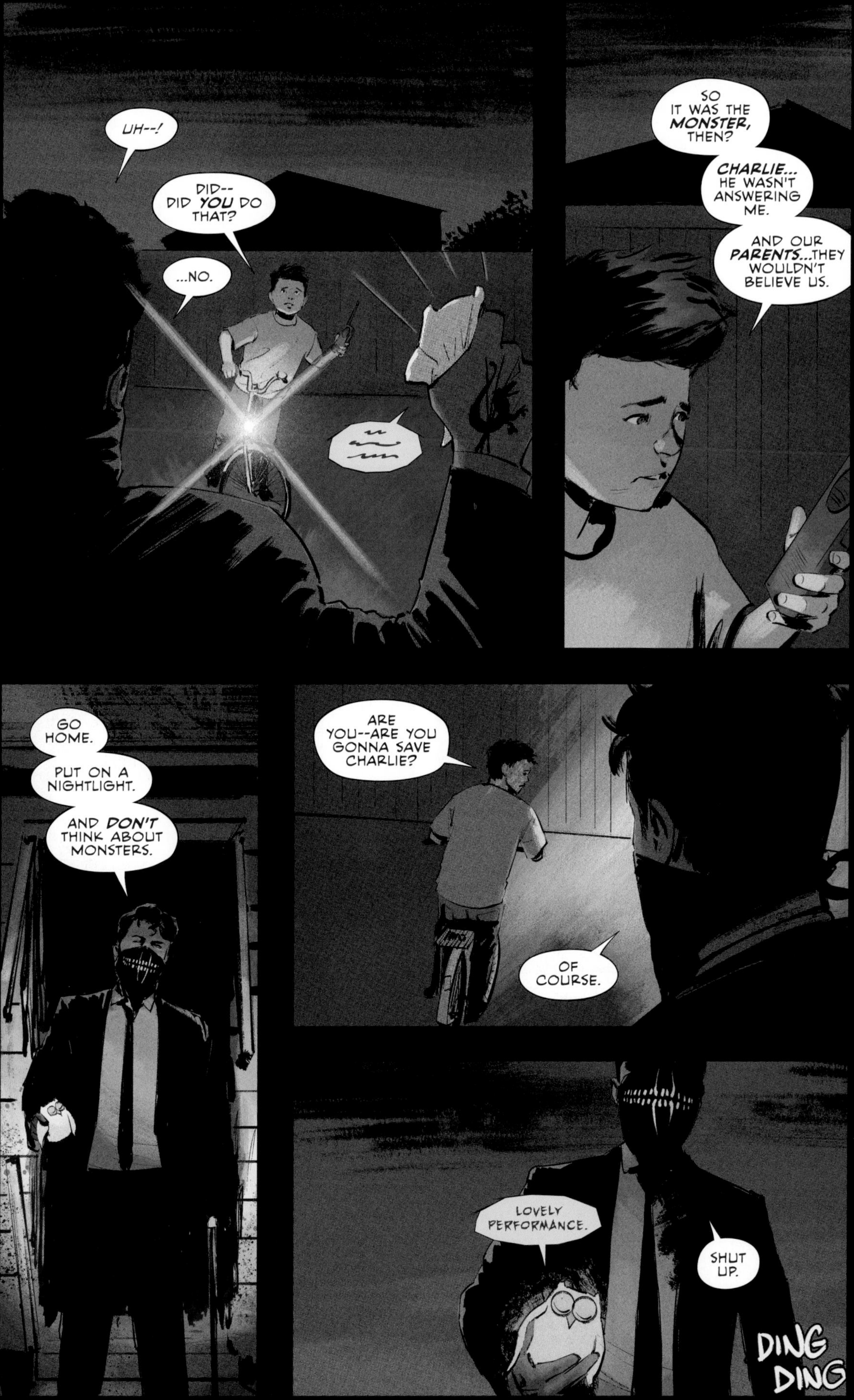
UH--!
DID-- DID YOU DO THAT?
...NO.
SO IT WAS THE MONSTER, THEN?
CHARLIE... HE WASN'T ANSWERING ME.
AND OUR PARENTS...THEY WOULDN'T BELIEVE US.
GO HOME.
PUT ON A NIGHTLIGHT.
AND DON'T THINK ABOUT MONSTERS.
ARE YOU--ARE YOU GONNA SAVE CHARLIE?
OF COURSE.
LOVELY PERFORMANCE.
SHUT UP.
DING DING

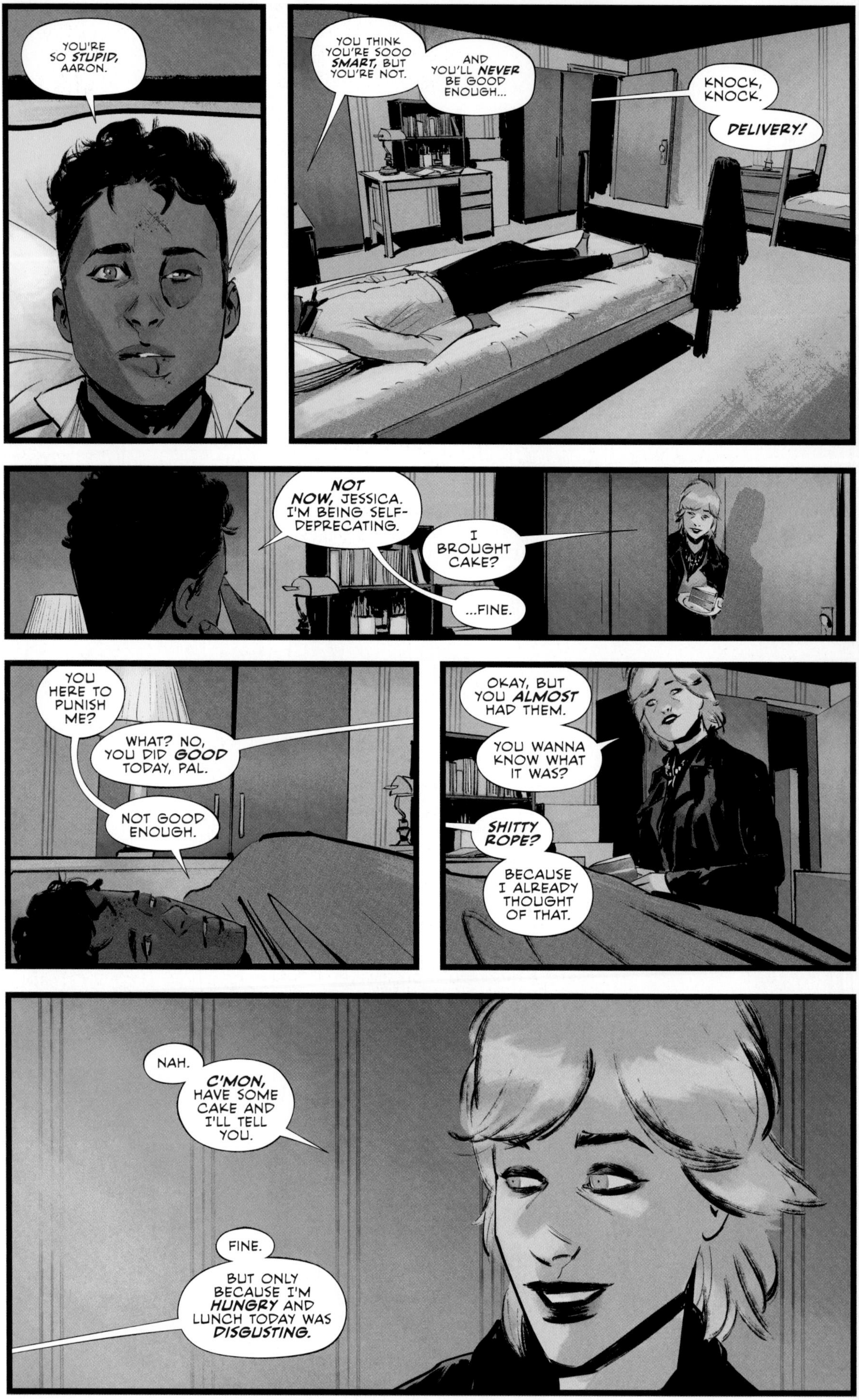
YOU'RE SO STUPID, AARON.
YOU THINK YOU'RE SOOO SMART, BUT YOU'RE NOT.
AND YOU'LL NEVER BE GOOD ENOUGH...
KNOCK, KNOCK.
DELIVERY!
NOT NOW, JESSICA. I'M BEING SELF-DEPRECATING.
I BROUGHT CAKE?
...FINE.
YOU HERE TO PUNISH ME?
WHAT? NO, YOU DID GOOD TODAY, PAL.
NOT GOOD ENOUGH.
OKAY, BUT YOU ALMOST HAD THEM.
YOU WANNA KNOW WHAT IT WAS?
SHITTY ROPE?
BECAUSE I ALREADY THOUGHT OF THAT.
NAH.
C'MON, HAVE SOME CAKE AND I'LL TELL YOU.
FINE.
BUT ONLY BECAUSE I'M HUNGRY AND LUNCH TODAY WAS DISGUSTING.

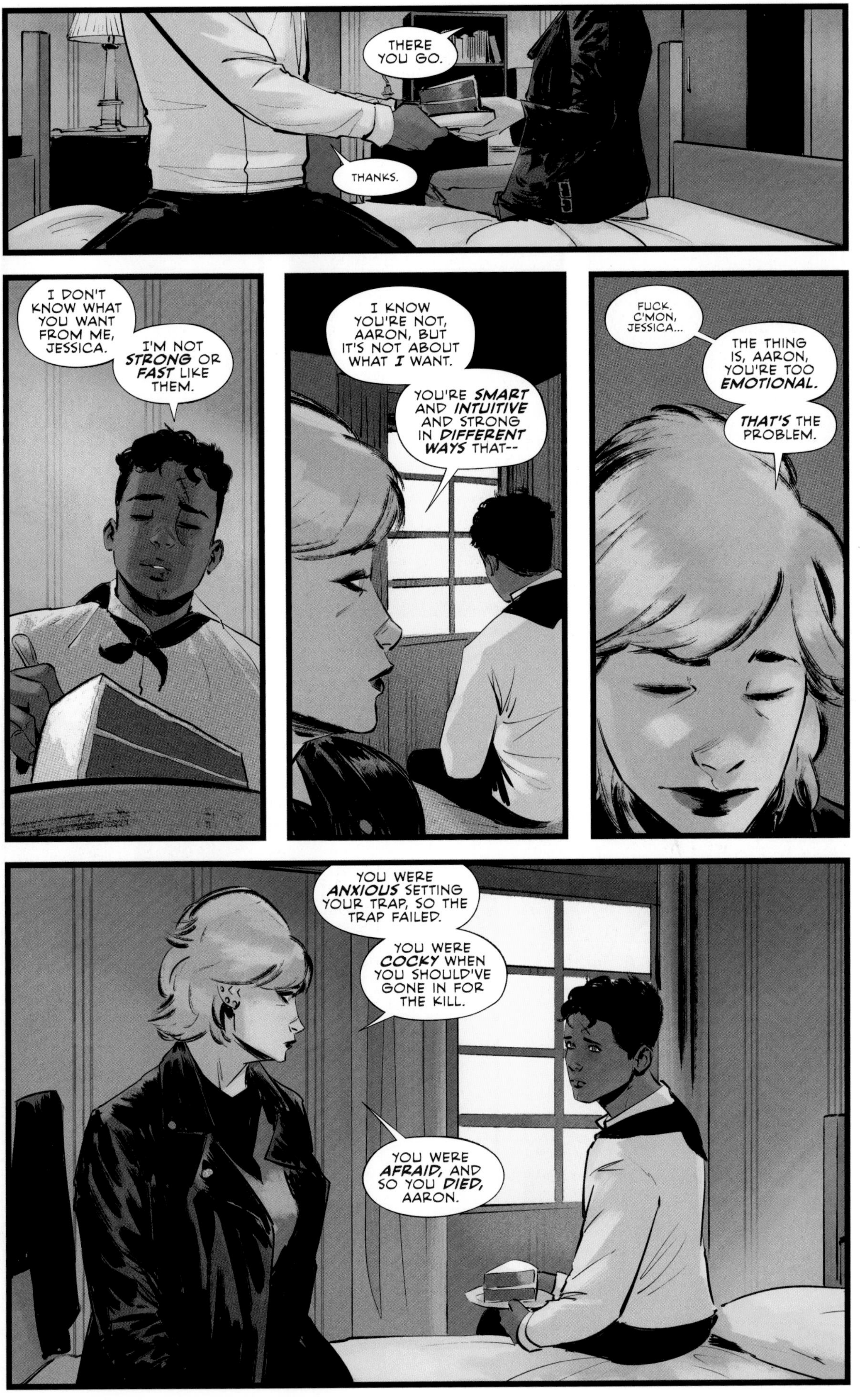
THERE YOU GO.
THANKS.
I DON'T KNOW WHAT YOU WANT FROM ME, JESSICA.
I'M NOT STRONG OR FAST LIKE THEM.
I KNOW YOU'RE NOT, AARON, BUT IT'S NOT ABOUT WHAT I WANT.
YOU'RE SMART AND INTUITIVE AND STRONG IN DIFFERENT WAYS THAT--
FUCK. C'MON, JESSICA...
THE THING IS, AARON, YOU'RE TOO EMOTIONAL.
THAT'S THE PROBLEM.
YOU WERE ANXIOUS SETTING YOUR TRAP, SO THE TRAP FAILED.
YOU WERE COCKY WHEN YOU SHOULD'VE GONE IN FOR THE KILL.
YOU WERE AFRAID, AND SO YOU DIED, AARON.

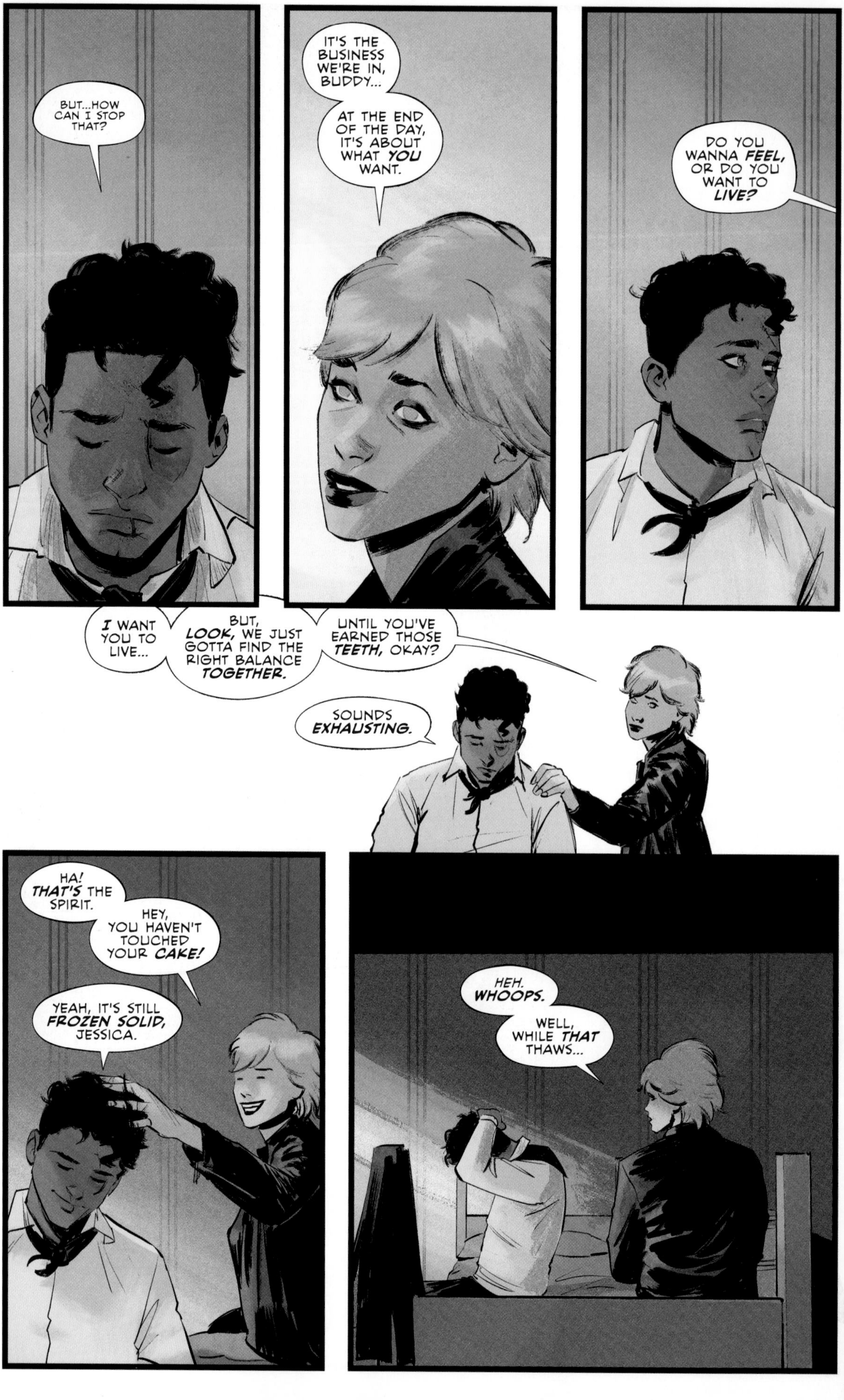
BUT...HOW CAN I STOP THAT?
IT'S THE BUSINESS WE'RE IN, BUDDY...
AT THE END OF THE DAY, IT'S ABOUT WHAT YOU WANT.
DO YOU WANNA FEEL, OR DO YOU WANT TO LIVE?
I WANT YOU TO LIVE...
BUT, LOOK, WE JUST GOTTA FIND THE RIGHT BALANCE TOGETHER.
UNTIL YOU'VE EARNED THOSE TEETH, OKAY?
SOUNDS EXHAUSTING.
HA! THAT'S THE SPIRIT.
HEY, YOU HAVEN'T TOUCHED YOUR CAKE!
YEAH, IT'S STILL FROZEN SOLID, JESSICA.
HEH. WHOOPS.
WELL, WHILE THAT THAWS...

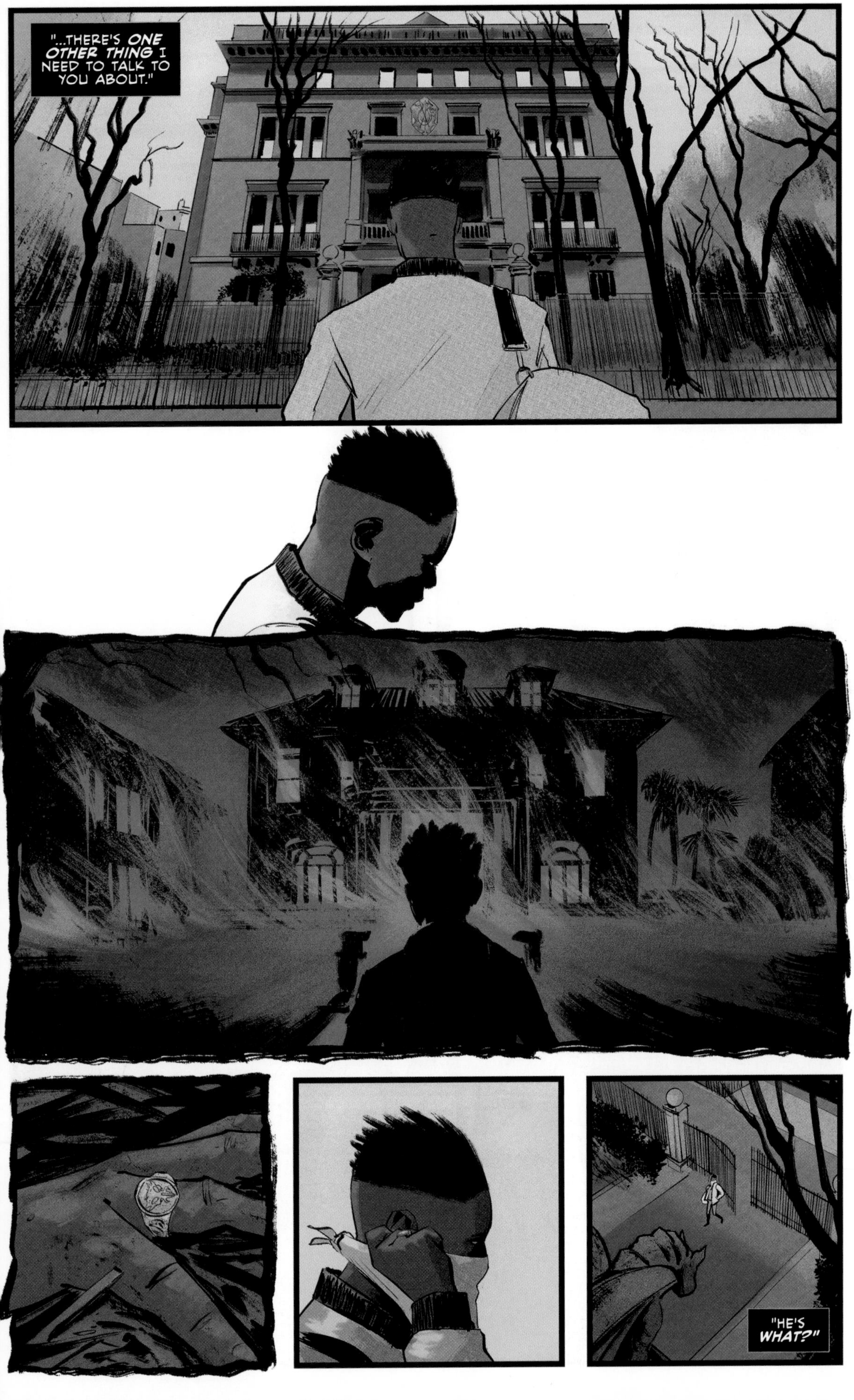
"...THERE'S *ONE OTHER THING* I NEED TO TALK TO YOU ABOUT."
"HE'S *WHAT?*"

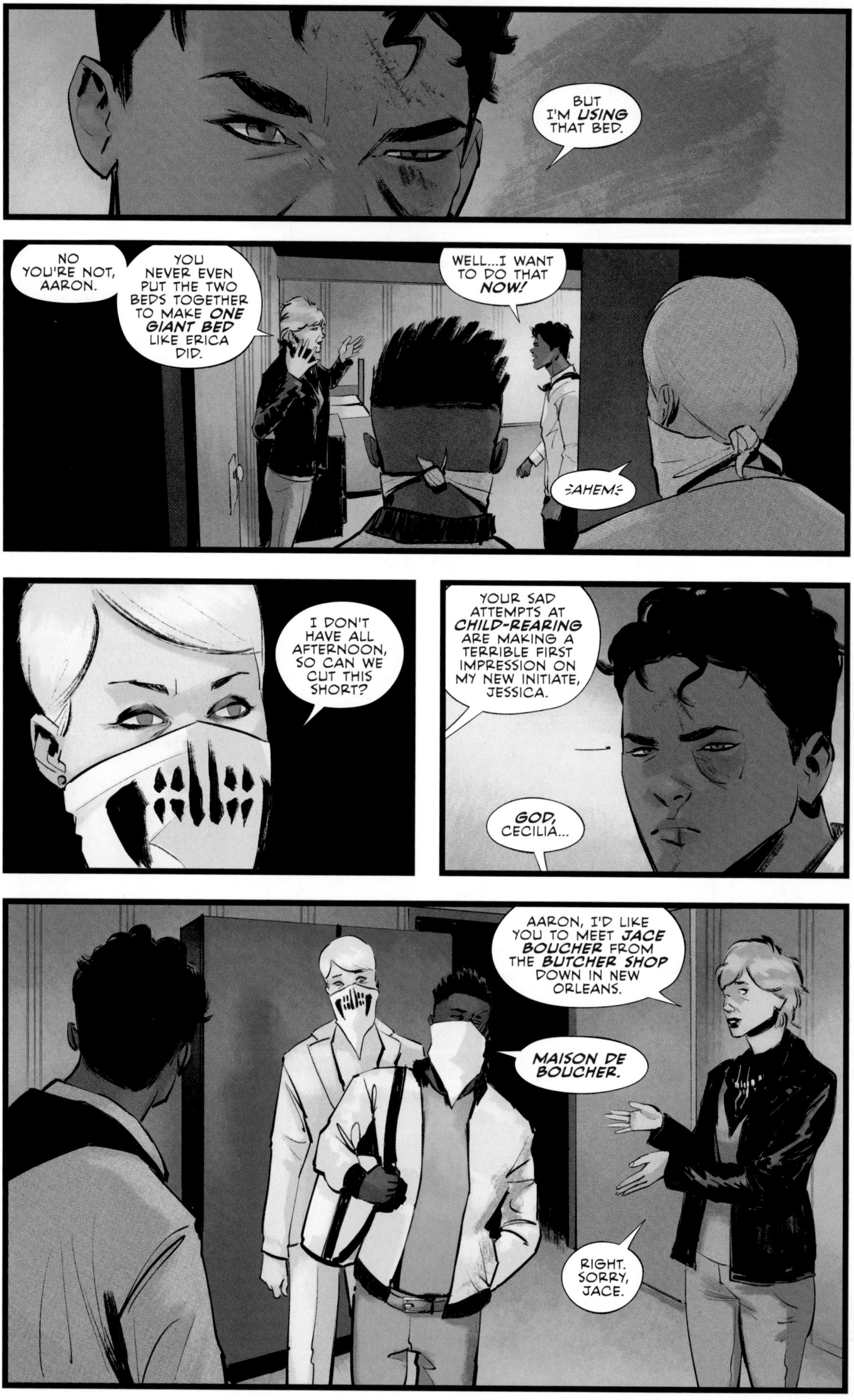
BUT I'M USING THAT BED.
NO YOU'RE NOT, AARON.
YOU NEVER EVEN PUT THE TWO BEDS TOGETHER TO MAKE ONE GIANT BED LIKE ERICA DID.
WELL...I WANT TO DO THAT NOW!
AHEM
I DON'T HAVE ALL AFTERNOON, SO CAN WE CUT THIS SHORT?
YOUR SAD ATTEMPTS AT CHILD-REARING ARE MAKING A TERRIBLE FIRST IMPRESSION ON MY NEW INITIATE, JESSICA.
GOD, CECILIA...
AARON, I'D LIKE YOU TO MEET JACE BOUCHER FROM THE BUTCHER SHOP DOWN IN NEW ORLEANS.
MAISON DE BOUCHER.
RIGHT. SORRY, JACE.

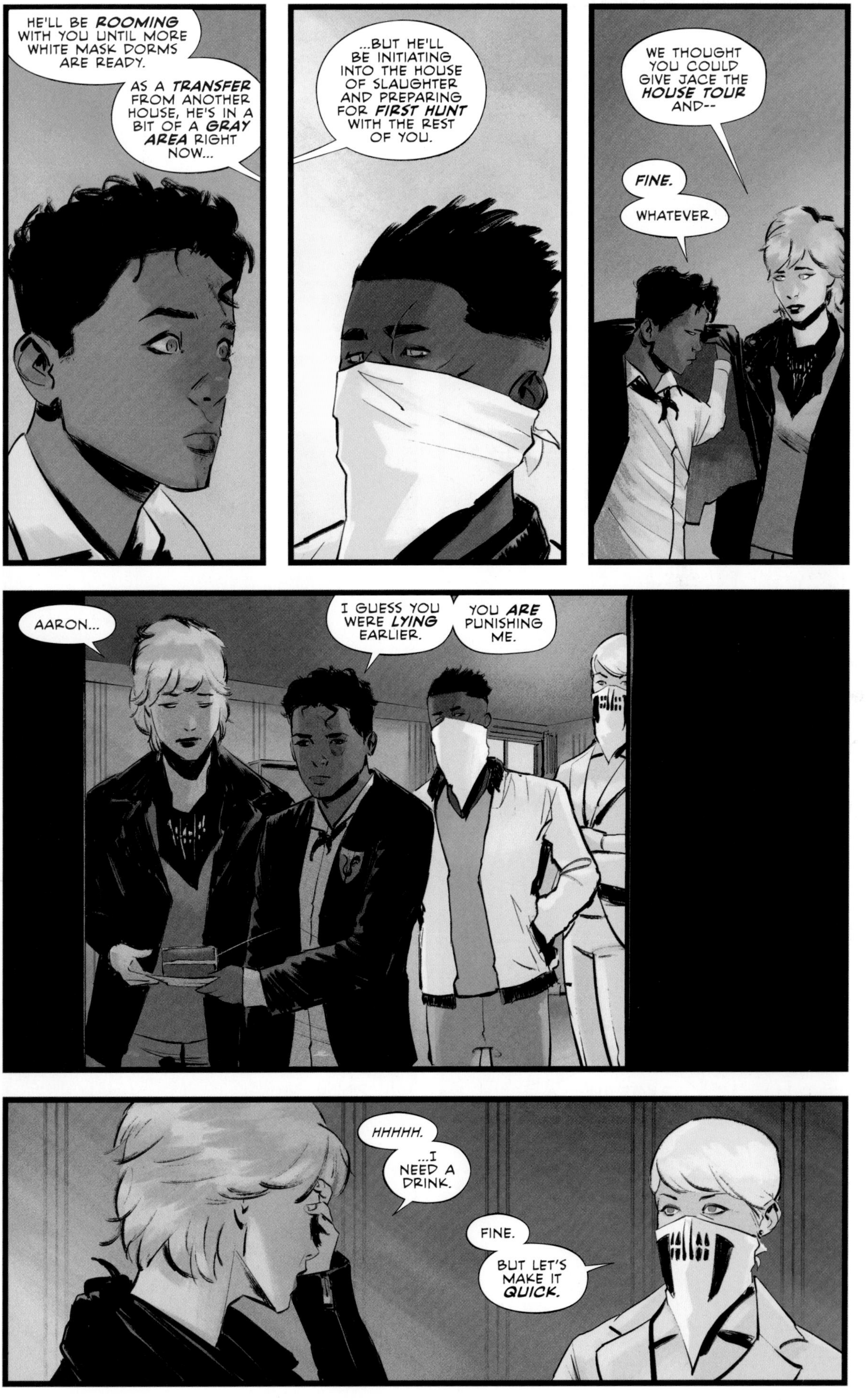
HE'LL BE ROOMING WITH YOU UNTIL MORE WHITE MASK DORMS ARE READY.
AS A TRANSFER FROM ANOTHER HOUSE, HE'S IN A BIT OF A GRAY AREA RIGHT NOW...
...BUT HE'LL BE INITIATING INTO THE HOUSE OF SLAUGHTER AND PREPARING FOR FIRST HUNT WITH THE REST OF YOU.
WE THOUGHT YOU COULD GIVE JACE THE HOUSE TOUR AND--
FINE.
WHATEVER.
AARON...
I GUESS YOU WERE LYING EARLIER.
YOU ARE PUNISHING ME.
HHHHH.
...I NEED A DRINK.
FINE.
BUT LET'S MAKE IT QUICK.

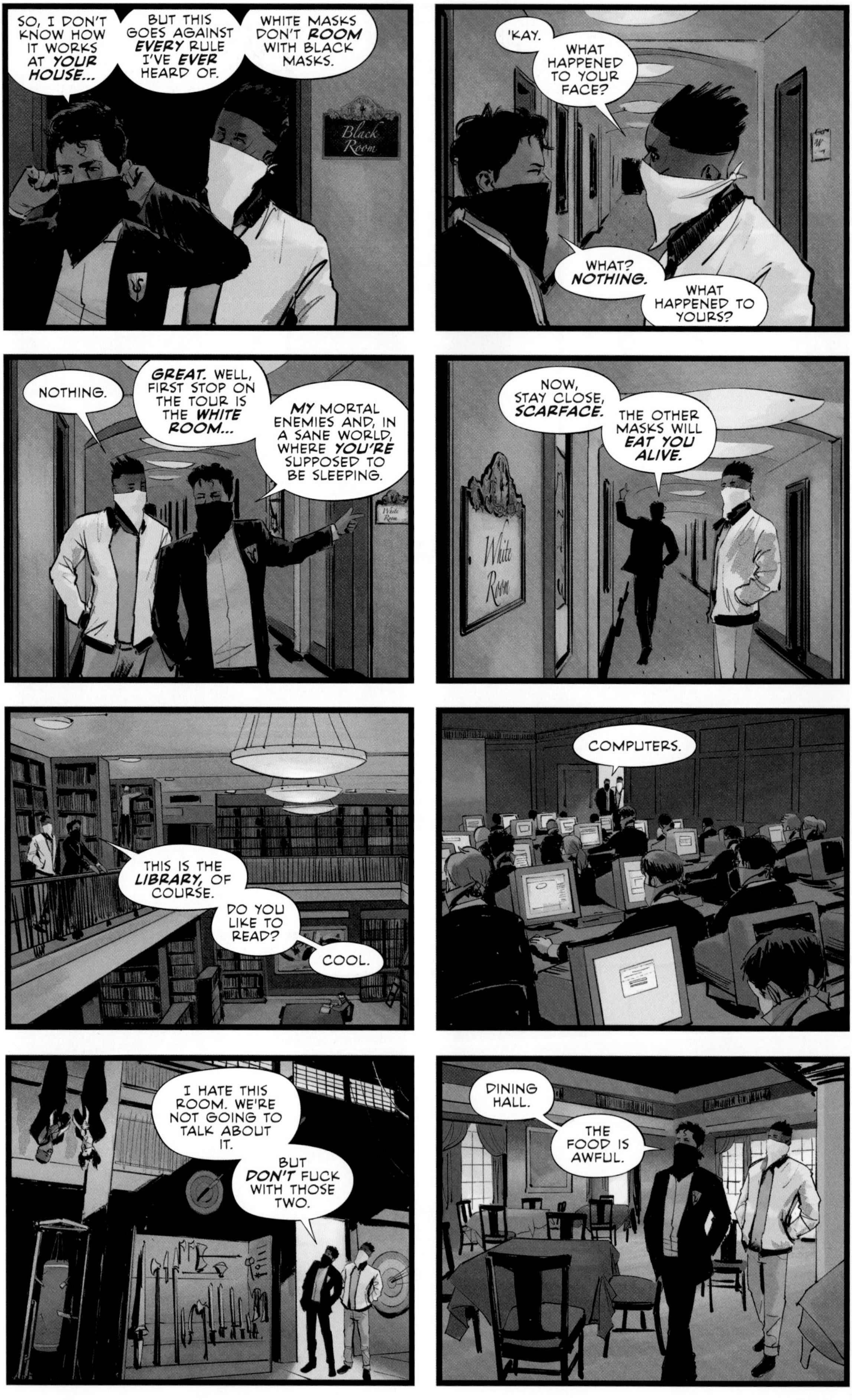
SO, I DON'T KNOW HOW IT WORKS AT YOUR HOUSE...
BUT THIS GOES AGAINST EVERY RULE I'VE EVER HEARD OF.
WHITE MASKS DON'T ROOM WITH BLACK MASKS.
Black Room
'KAY.
WHAT HAPPENED TO YOUR FACE?
WHAT? NOTHING.
WHAT HAPPENED TO YOURS?
NOTHING.
GREAT. WELL, FIRST STOP ON THE TOUR IS THE WHITE ROOM...
MY MORTAL ENEMIES AND, IN A SANE WORLD, WHERE YOU'RE SUPPOSED TO BE SLEEPING.
NOW, STAY CLOSE, SCARFACE.
THE OTHER MASKS WILL EAT YOU ALIVE.
White Room
THIS IS THE LIBRARY, OF COURSE.
DO YOU LIKE TO READ?
COOL.
COMPUTERS.
I HATE THIS ROOM. WE'RE NOT GOING TO TALK ABOUT IT.
BUT DON'T FUCK WITH THOSE TWO.
DINING HALL.
THE FOOD IS AWFUL.

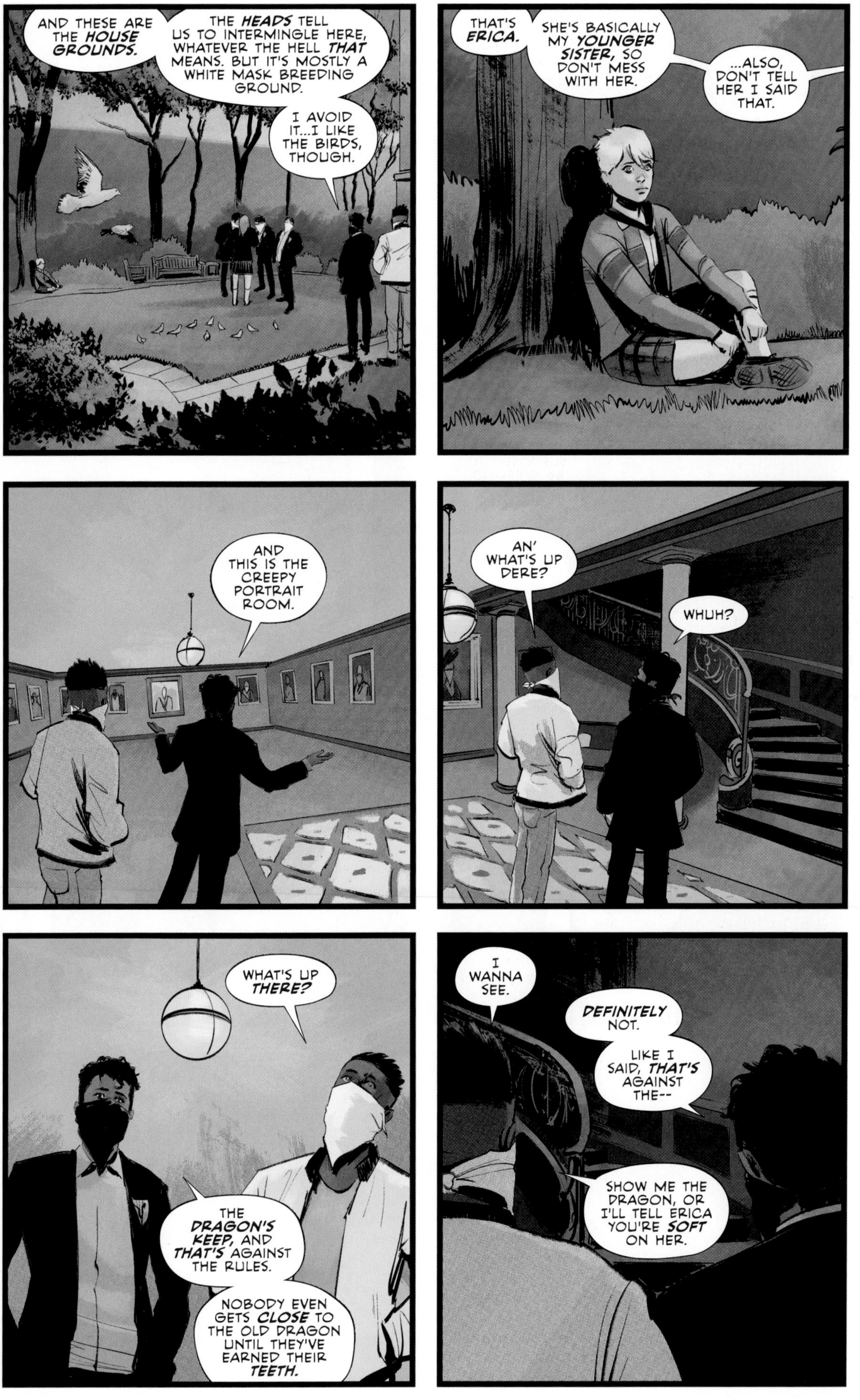
AND THESE ARE THE HOUSE GROUNDS.
THE HEADS TELL US TO INTERMINGLE HERE, WHATEVER THE HELL THAT MEANS. BUT IT'S MOSTLY A WHITE MASK BREEDING GROUND.
I AVOID IT...I LIKE THE BIRDS, THOUGH.
THAT'S ERICA.
SHE'S BASICALLY MY YOUNGER SISTER, SO DON'T MESS WITH HER.
...ALSO, DON'T TELL HER I SAID THAT.
AND THIS IS THE CREEPY PORTRAIT ROOM.
AN' WHAT'S UP DERE?
WHUH?
WHAT'S UP THERE?
THE DRAGON'S KEEP, AND THAT'S AGAINST THE RULES.
NOBODY EVEN GETS CLOSE TO THE OLD DRAGON UNTIL THEY'VE EARNED THEIR TEETH.
I WANNA SEE.
DEFINITELY NOT.
LIKE I SAID, THAT'S AGAINST THE--
SHOW ME THE DRAGON, OR I'LL TELL ERICA YOU'RE SOFT ON HER.

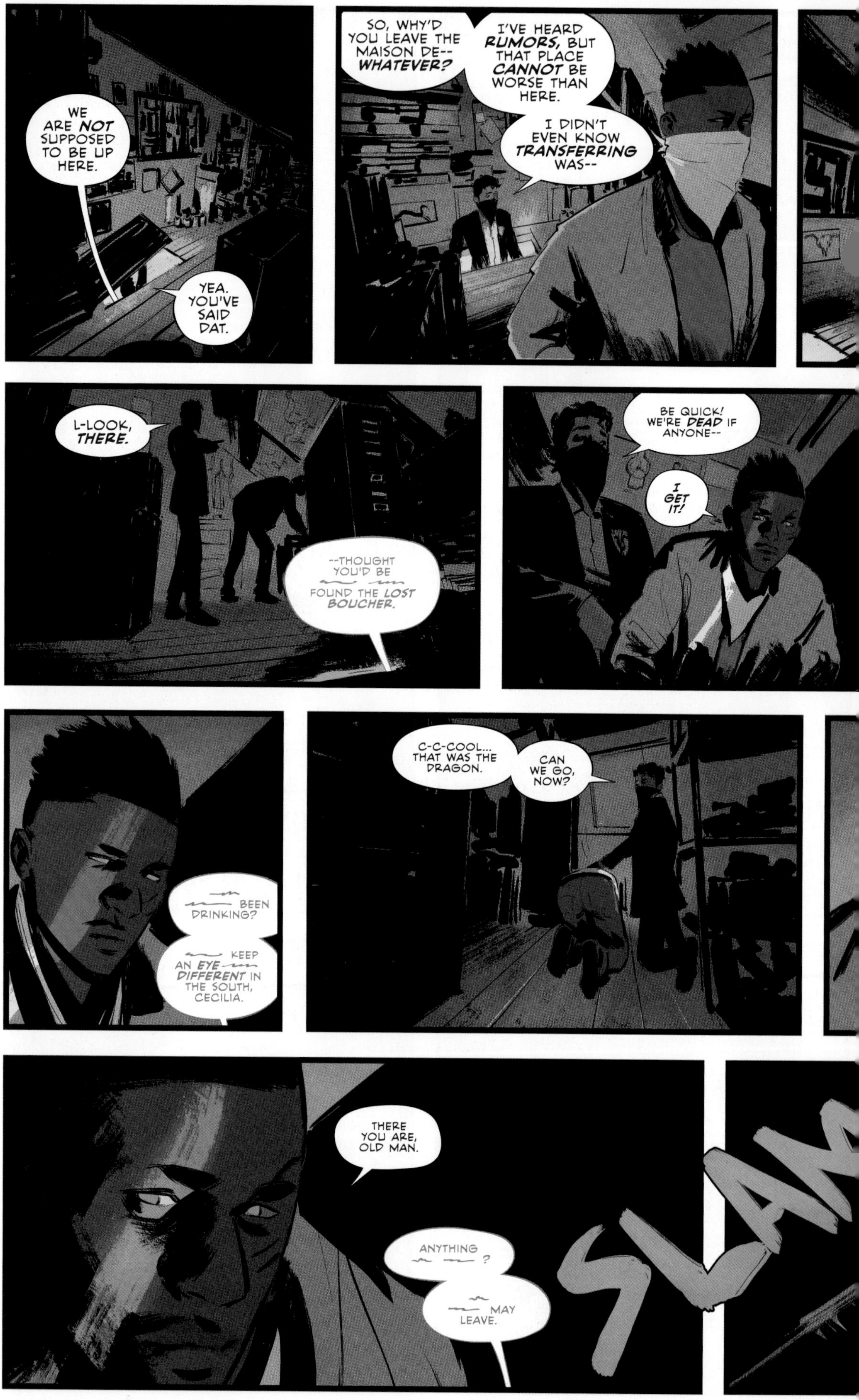
WE ARE NOT SUPPOSED TO BE UP HERE.
YEA. YOU'VE SAID DAT.
SO, WHY'D YOU LEAVE THE MAISON DE-- WHATEVER?
I'VE HEARD RUMORS, BUT THAT PLACE CANNOT BE WORSE THAN HERE.
I DIDN'T EVEN KNOW TRANSFERRING WAS--
L-LOOK, THERE.
--THOUGHT YOU'D BE
FOUND THE LOST BOUCHER.
BE QUICK! WE'RE DEAD IF ANYONE--
I GET IT!
BEEN DRINKING?
KEEP AN EYE
DIFFERENT IN THE SOUTH, CECILIA.
C-C-COOL... THAT WAS THE DRAGON.
CAN WE GO, NOW?
THERE YOU ARE, OLD MAN.
ANYTHING ?
MAY LEAVE.
SLAM

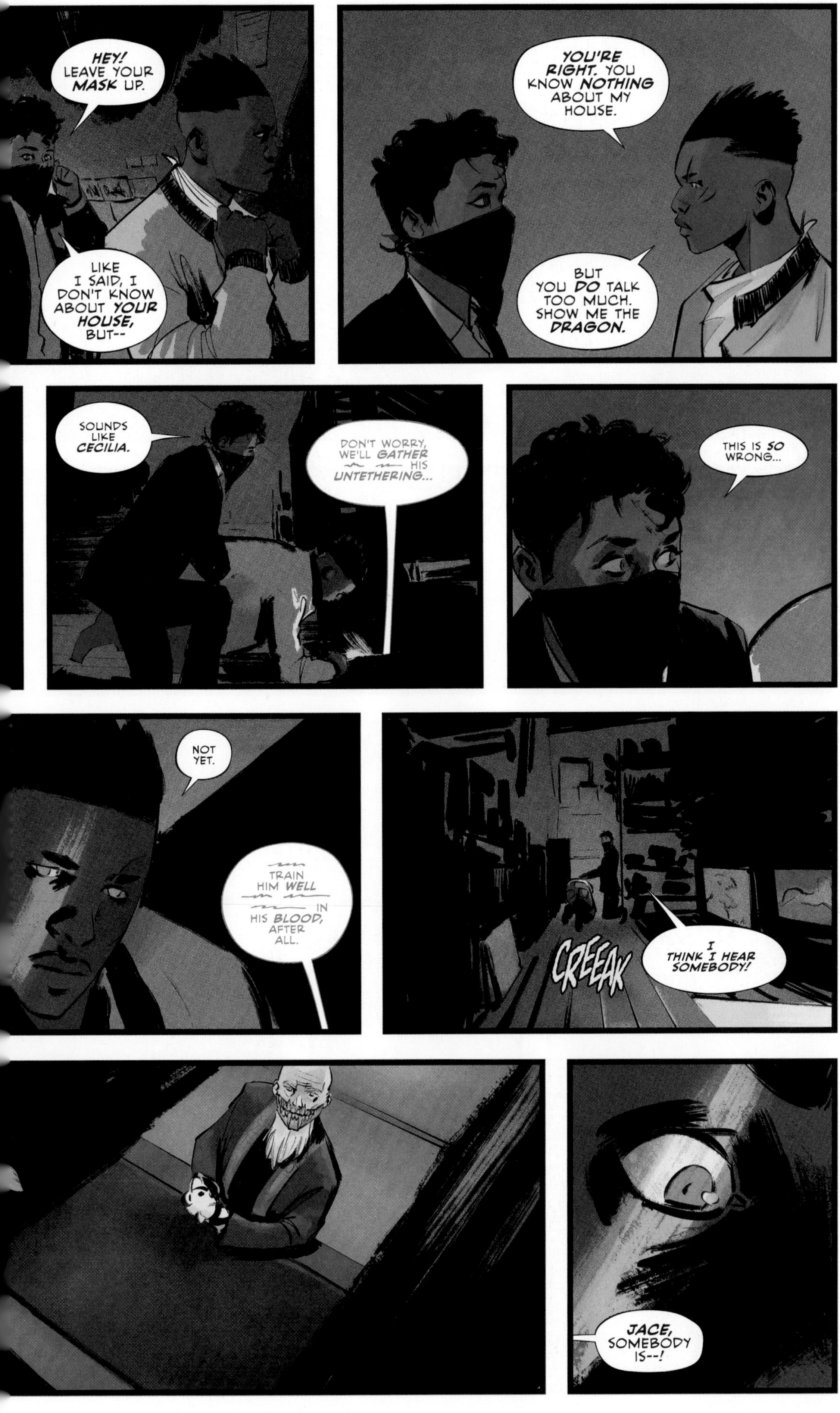
HEY! LEAVE YOUR MASK UP.
LIKE I SAID, I DON'T KNOW ABOUT YOUR HOUSE, BUT--
YOU'RE RIGHT. YOU KNOW NOTHING ABOUT MY HOUSE.
BUT YOU DO TALK TOO MUCH. SHOW ME THE DRAGON.
SOUNDS LIKE CECILIA.
DON'T WORRY, WE'LL GATHER HIS UNTETHERING...
THIS IS SO WRONG...
NOT YET.
TRAIN HIM WELL IN HIS BLOOD, AFTER ALL.
CREEAK
I THINK I HEAR SOMEBODY!
JACE, SOMEBODY IS--!

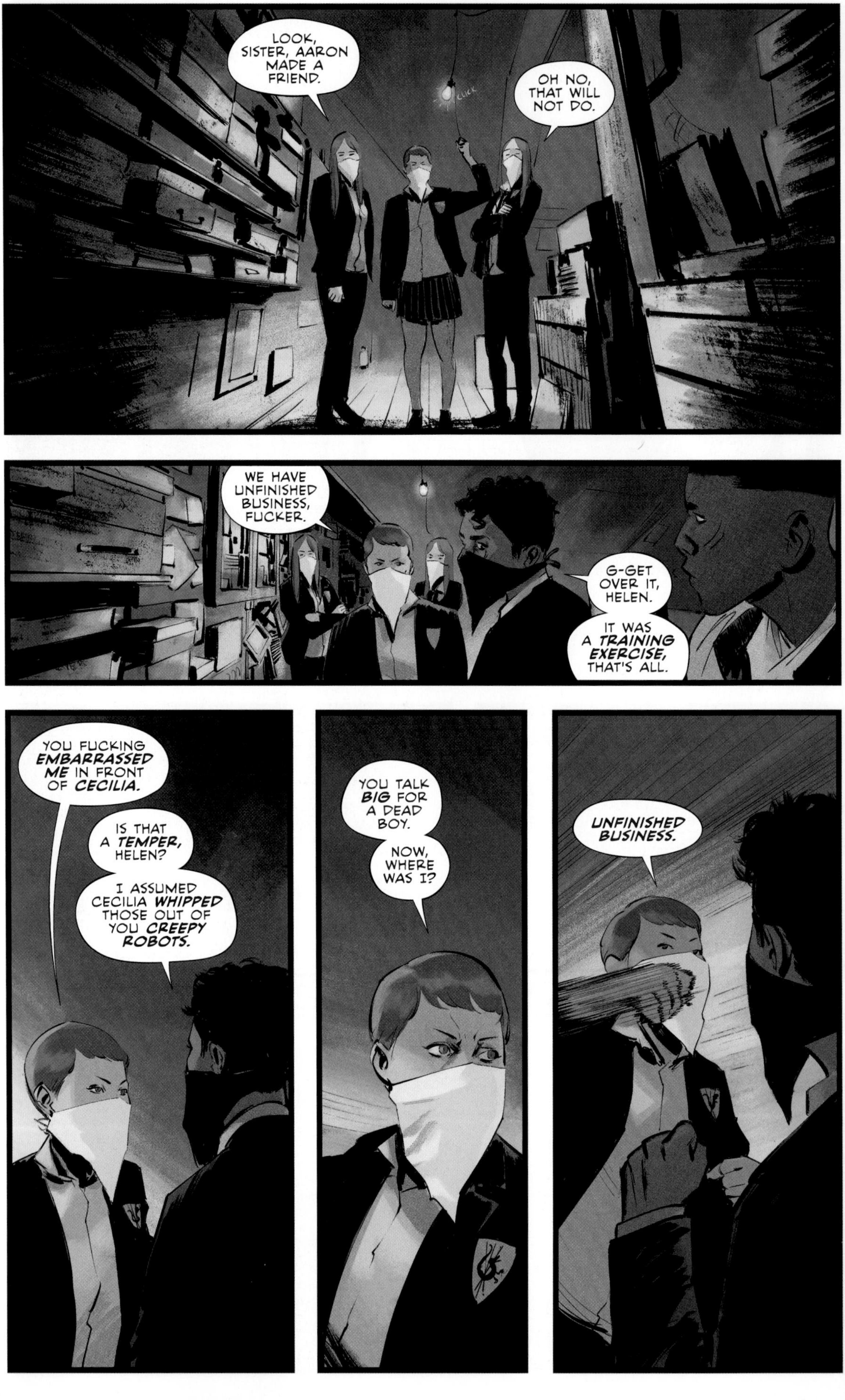
LOOK, SISTER, AARON MADE A FRIEND.
CLICK
OH NO, THAT WILL NOT DO.
WE HAVE UNFINISHED BUSINESS, FUCKER.
G-GET OVER IT, HELEN.
IT WAS A *TRAINING EXERCISE,* THAT'S ALL.
YOU FUCKING *EMBARRASSED ME* IN FRONT OF *CECILIA.*
IS THAT A *TEMPER,* HELEN?
I ASSUMED CECILIA *WHIPPED* THOSE OUT OF YOU *CREEPY ROBOTS.*
YOU TALK *BIG* FOR A DEAD BOY.
NOW, WHERE WAS I?
UNFINISHED BUSINESS.

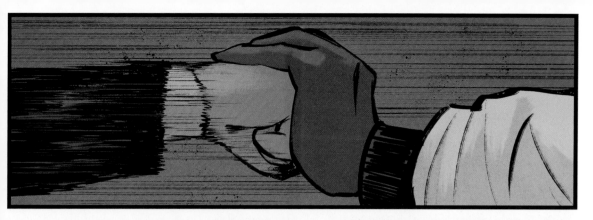

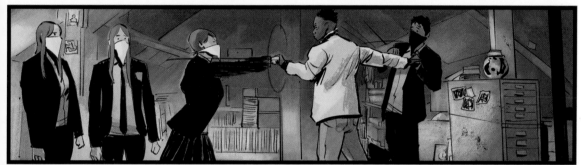

THAT'S MY ROOMMATE.

SO, DON'T MESS WITH HIM.

As I said, this won't be some shorthand account.

I have all the details. I might even draw you pictures...

Because I'm not Erica.

FUCK.

Because the House of Slaughter sent me on this Hunt for a reason--

--and I have something to prove.

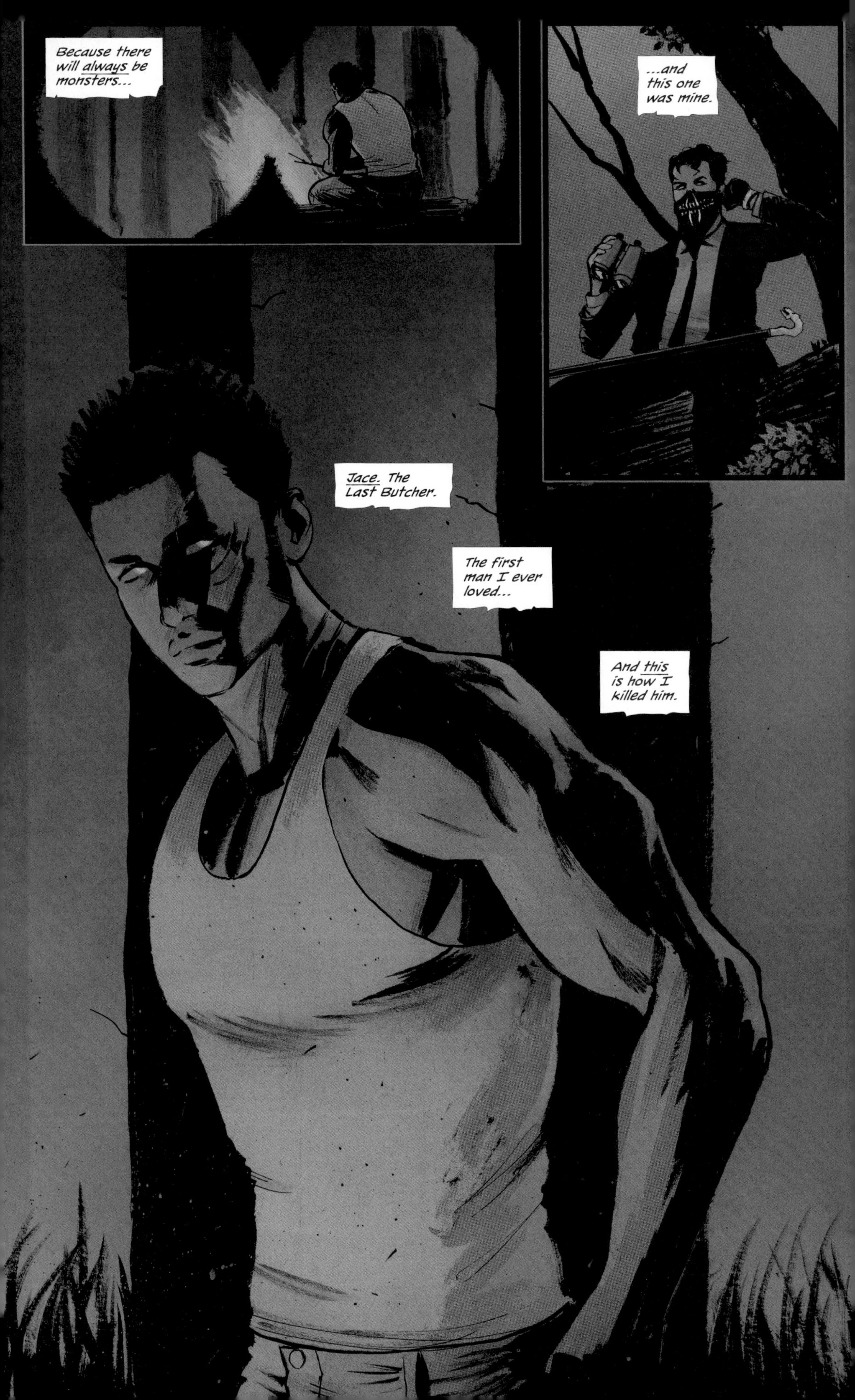
Because there will always be monsters...
...and this one was mine.
Jace. The Last Butcher.
The first man I ever loved...
And this is how I killed him.

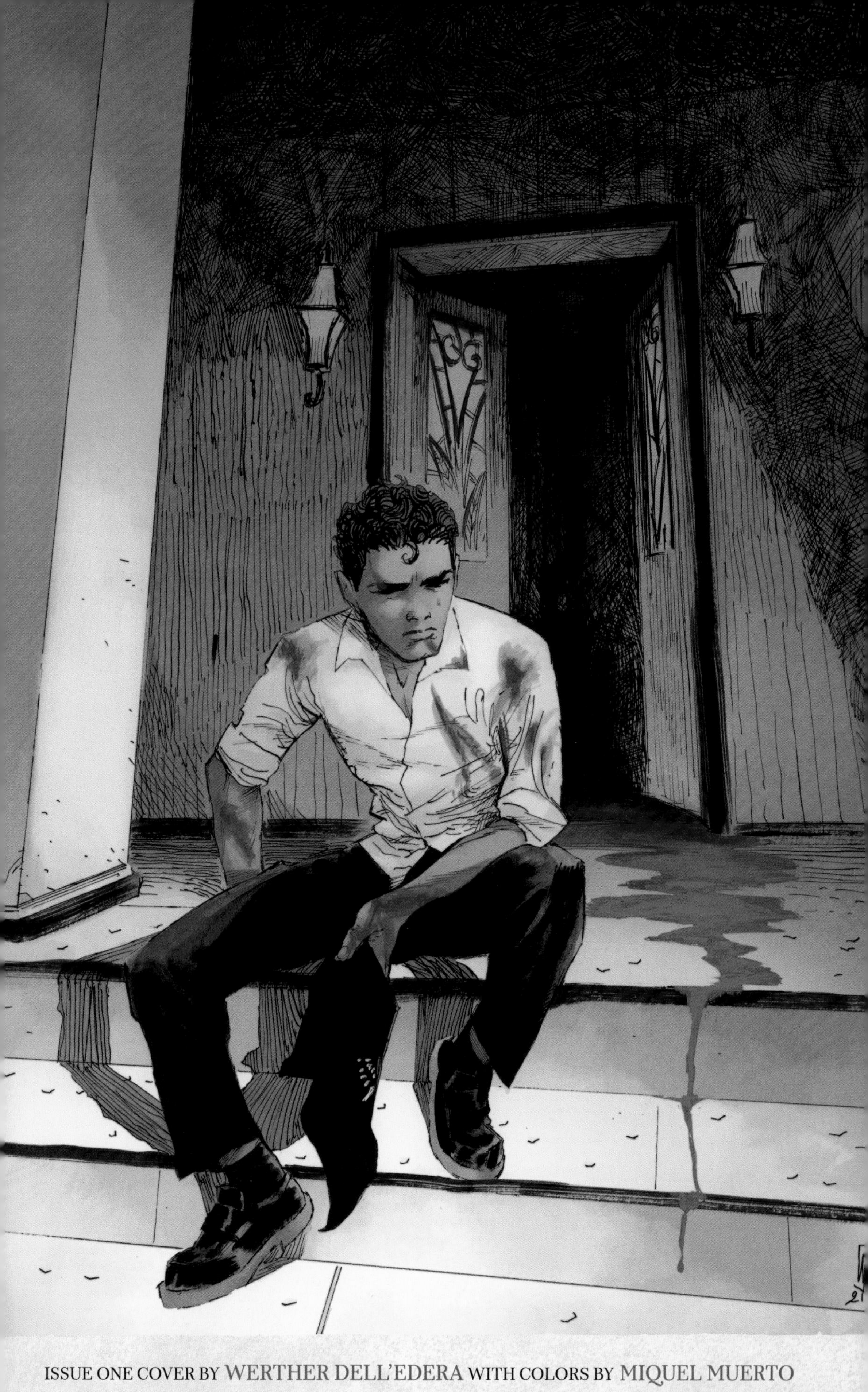

ISSUE ONE COVER BY WERTHER DELL'EDERA WITH COLORS BY MIQUEL MUERTO

PART TWO

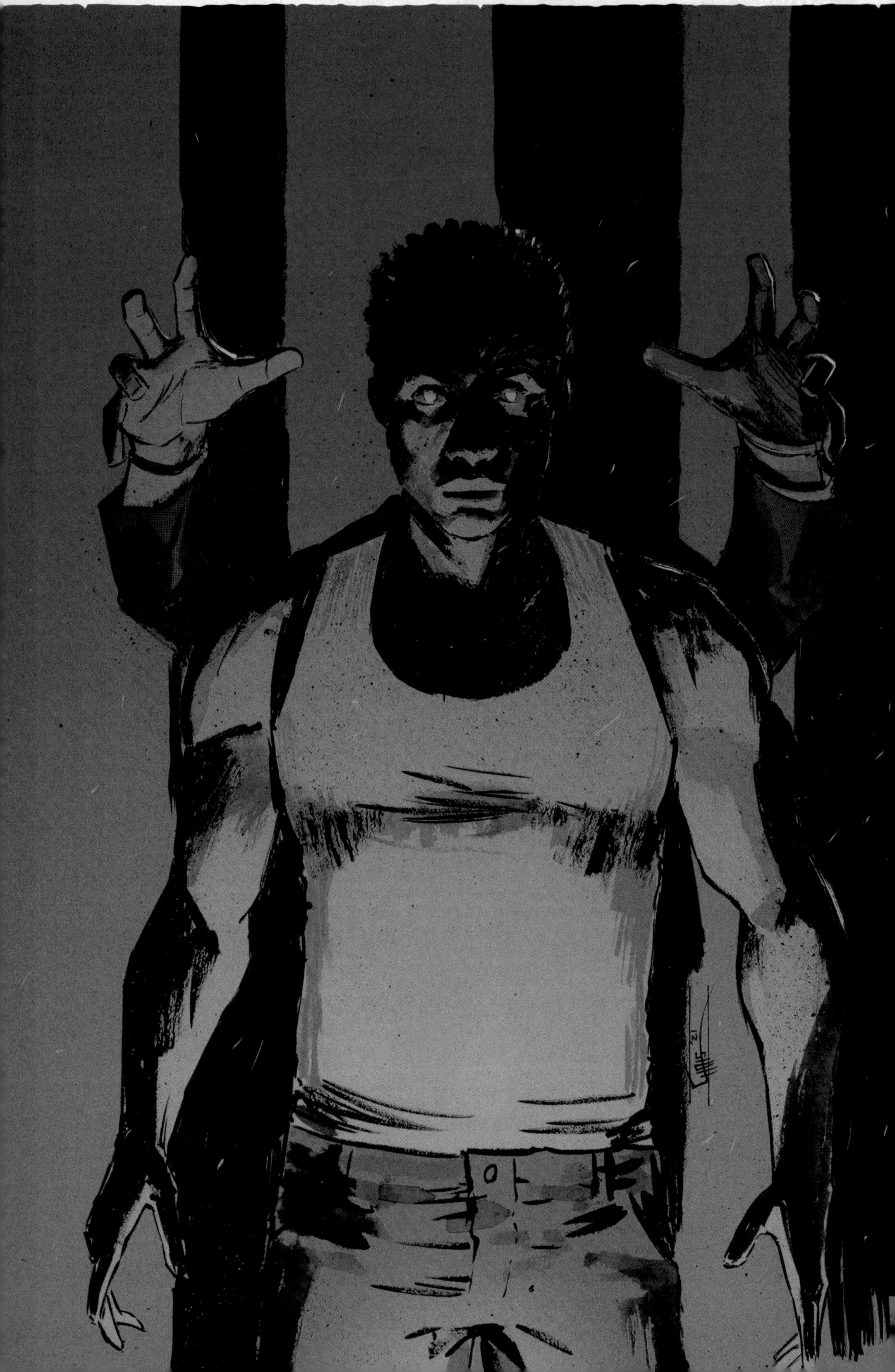

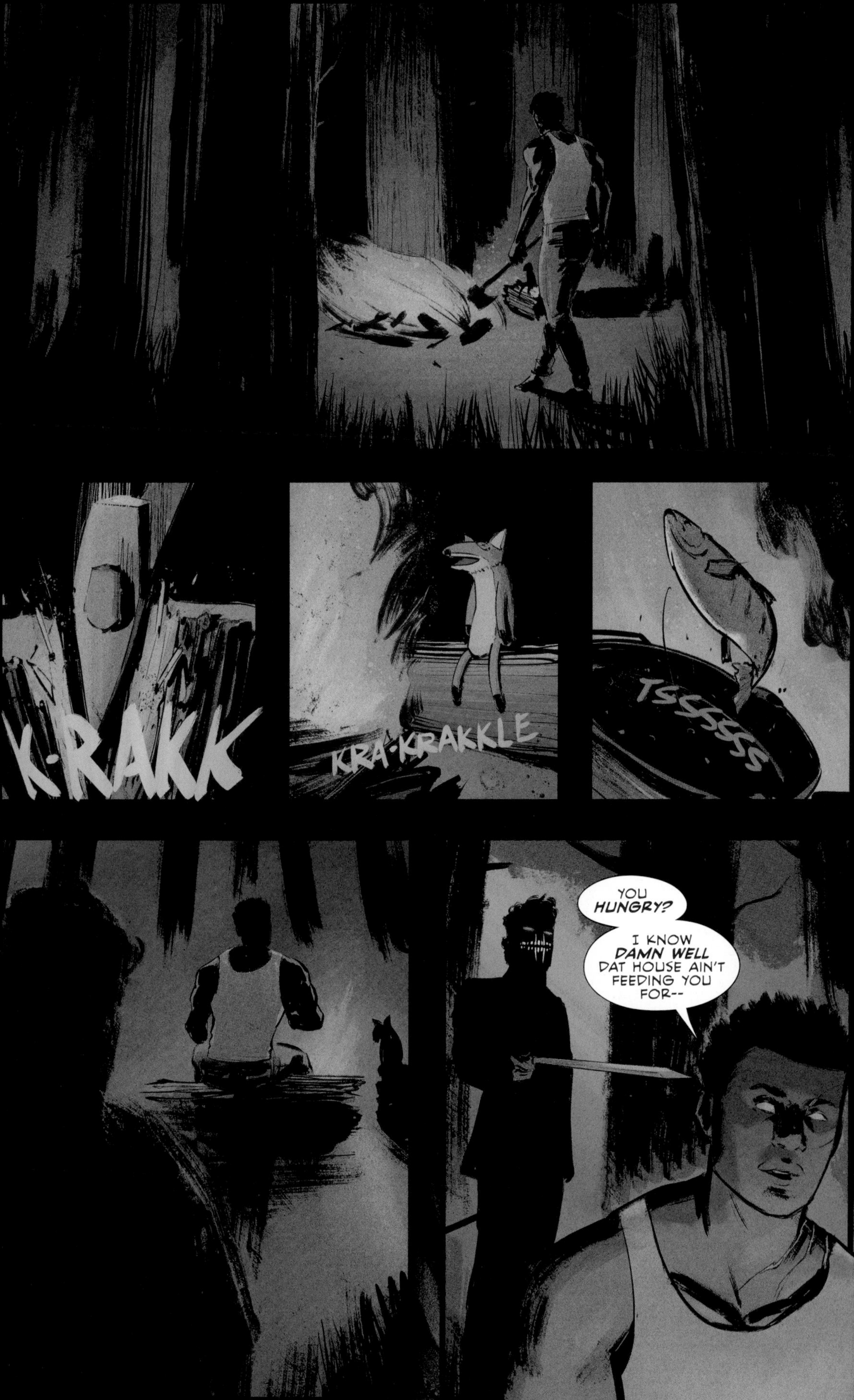
K-RAKK
KRA-KRAKKLE
TSSSSSSS
YOU HUNGRY?
I KNOW DAMN WELL DAT HOUSE AIN'T FEEDING YOU FOR--

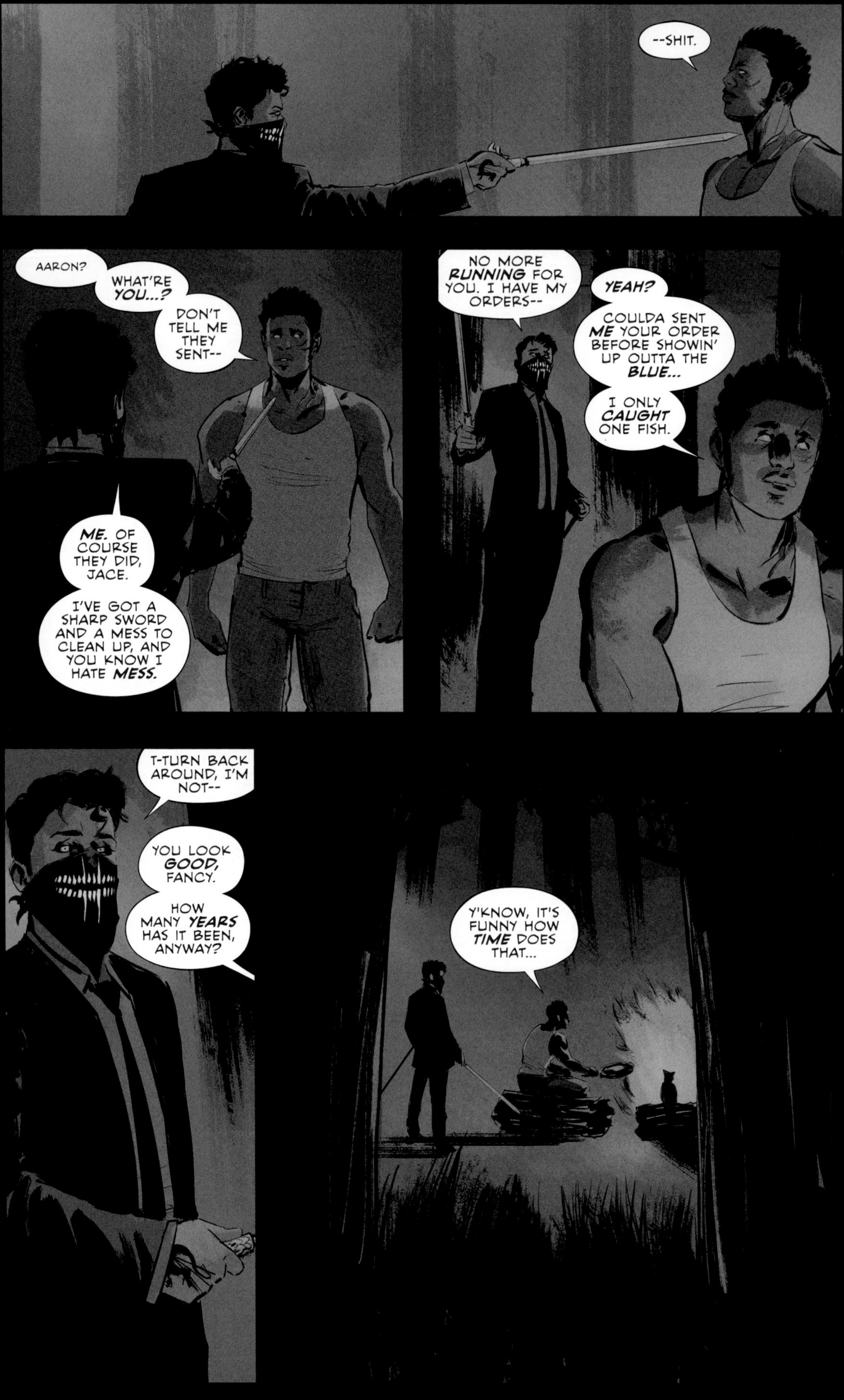
--SHIT.
AARON?
WHAT'RE YOU...?
DON'T TELL ME THEY SENT--
ME. OF COURSE THEY DID, JACE.
I'VE GOT A SHARP SWORD AND A MESS TO CLEAN UP, AND YOU KNOW I HATE MESS.
NO MORE RUNNING FOR YOU. I HAVE MY ORDERS--
YEAH?
COULDA SENT ME YOUR ORDER BEFORE SHOWIN' UP OUTTA THE BLUE...
I ONLY CAUGHT ONE FISH.
T-TURN BACK AROUND, I'M NOT--
YOU LOOK GOOD, FANCY.
HOW MANY YEARS HAS IT BEEN, ANYWAY?
Y'KNOW, IT'S FUNNY HOW TIME DOES THAT...

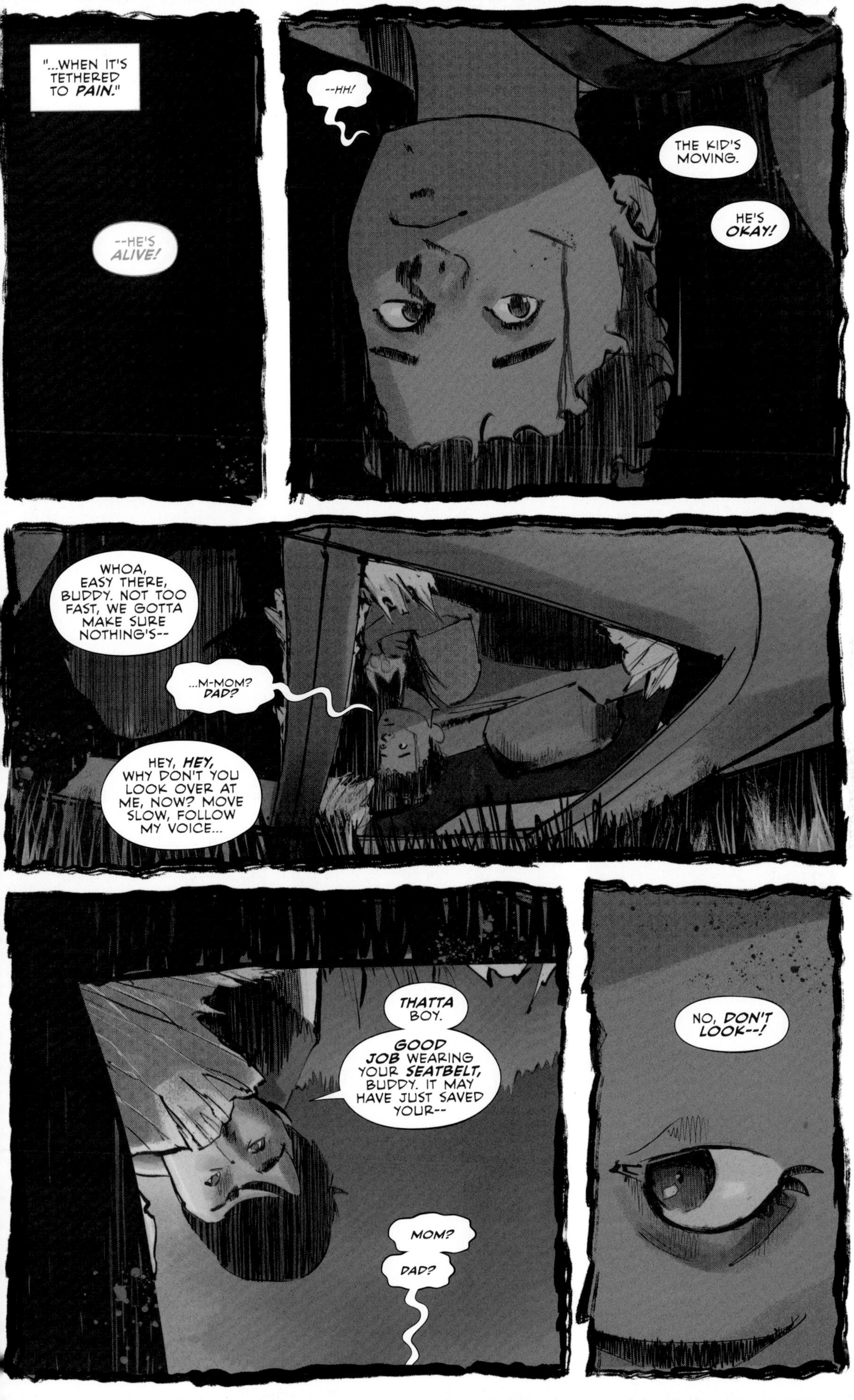
"...WHEN IT'S TETHERED TO PAIN."
--HE'S ALIVE!
--HH!
THE KID'S MOVING.
HE'S OKAY!
WHOA, EASY THERE, BUDDY. NOT TOO FAST, WE GOTTA MAKE SURE NOTHING'S--
...M-MOM? DAD?
HEY, HEY, WHY DON'T YOU LOOK OVER AT ME, NOW? MOVE SLOW, FOLLOW MY VOICE...
THATTA BOY.
GOOD JOB WEARING YOUR SEATBELT, BUDDY. IT MAY HAVE JUST SAVED YOUR--
MOM?
DAD?
NO, DON'T LOOK--!

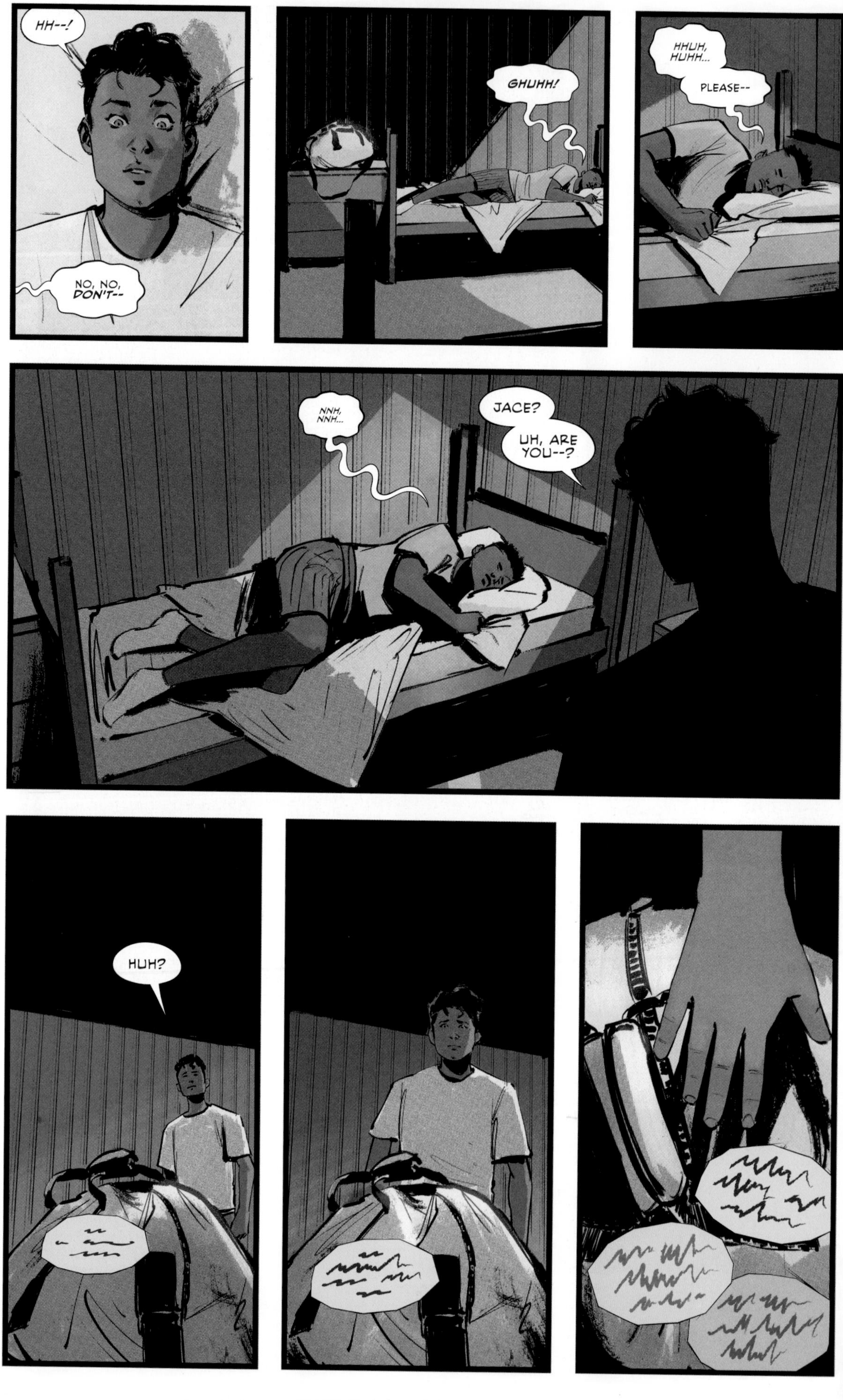
HH--!
NO, NO, DON'T--
GHUHH!
HHUH, HUHH...
PLEASE--
NNH, NNH...
JACE?
UH, ARE YOU--?
HUH?

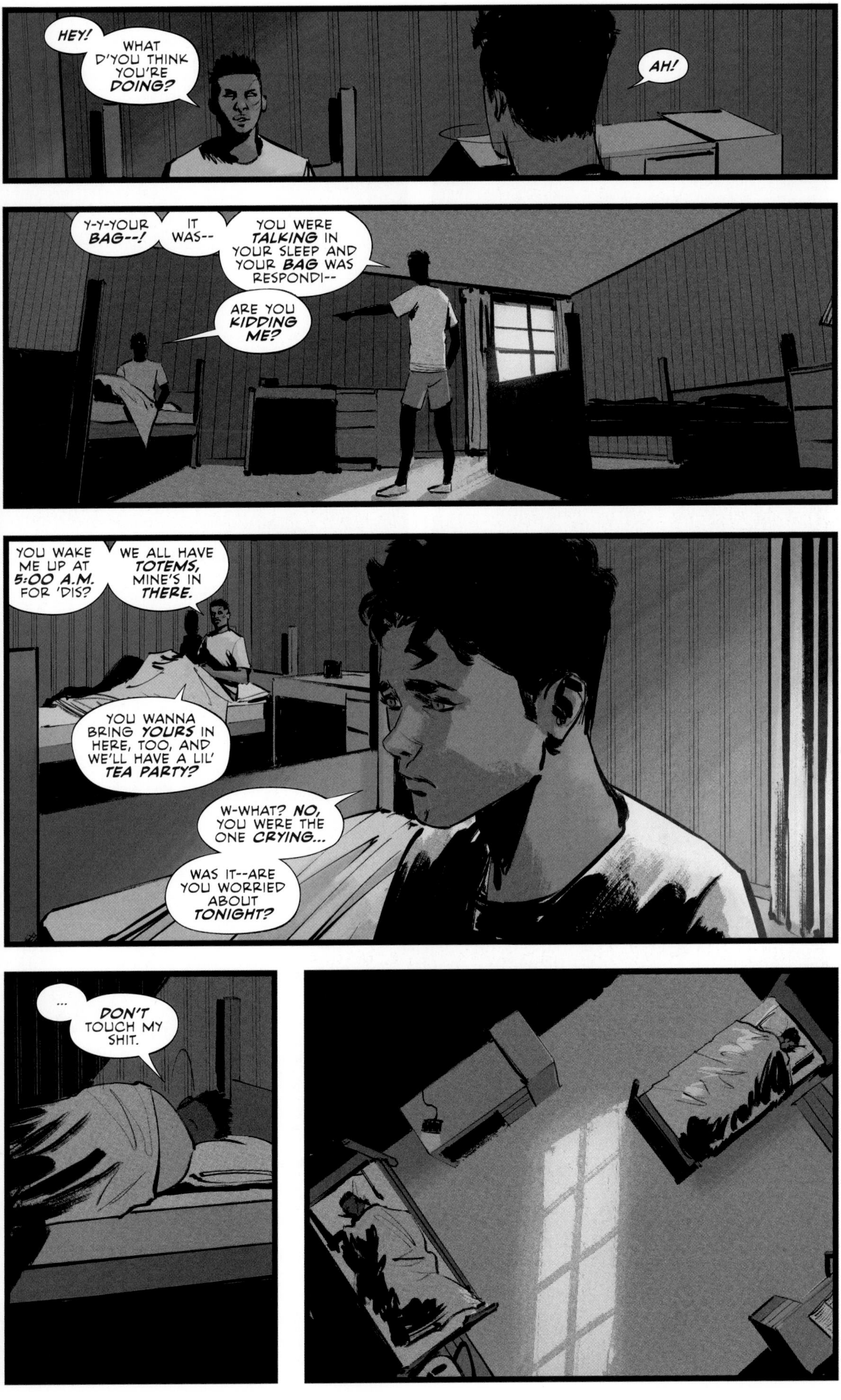
HEY!
WHAT D'YOU THINK YOU'RE DOING?
AH!
Y-Y-YOUR BAG--!
IT WAS--
YOU WERE TALKING IN YOUR SLEEP AND YOUR BAG WAS RESPONDI--
ARE YOU KIDDING ME?
YOU WAKE ME UP AT 5:00 A.M. FOR 'DIS?
WE ALL HAVE TOTEMS, MINE'S IN THERE.
YOU WANNA BRING YOURS IN HERE, TOO, AND WE'LL HAVE A LIL' TEA PARTY?
W-WHAT? NO, YOU WERE THE ONE CRYING...
WAS IT--ARE YOU WORRIED ABOUT TONIGHT?
...
DON'T TOUCH MY SHIT.

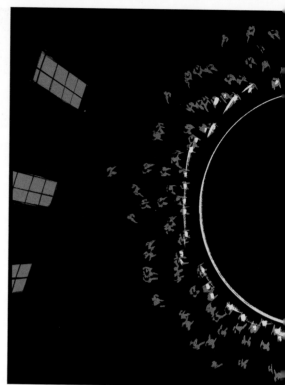

WELCOME, ALL, TO OUR *GATHERING OF A THOUSAND EYES...*

CENTURIES MAY HAVE PASSED, BUT OUR *MISSION* REMAINS THE SAME.

THERE WILL *ALWAYS* BE MONSTERS, AND SO THERE MUST ALWAYS BE THOSE WHO *HUNT.*

IT IS OUR SACRED *OATH* THAT BINDS US TO THIS MISSION, TO THIS HOUSE, TO THIS ORDER...

...*SIGNIFIED* BY THE UNHOLY BOND BETWEEN A HUNTER AND THEIR TOTEM.

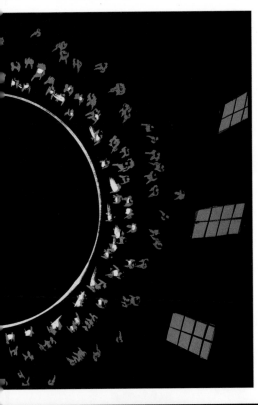

WHEN OUR **FOREBEARS** FIRST ARRIVED IN AMERICA, THEY SOUGHT TO **UPHOLD** THE SACRED MISSION OF THE **ORDER OF ST. GEORGE** IN A NEW LAND.

WHAT THEY **DISCOVERED** WAS A NEW WORLD **RAVAGED** BY NEW MONSTERS...

AND IT WAS IN THEIR **SLAUGHTER** THAT OUR **HOUSE** WAS FORMED.

THESE **TOTEMS**, ONCE PROTECTORS OF OUR INFANCY, NOW HARBOR OUR **GREATEST MONSTERS.**

SWORN TO PROTECT.

SWORN TO SERVE.

BUT NOT **ALL OATHS** ARE LEGITIMATE IN OUR HOUSE, IN OUR **EYES.**

NO...

...NOT WHEN THERE'S A **STRANGER** AMONG US.

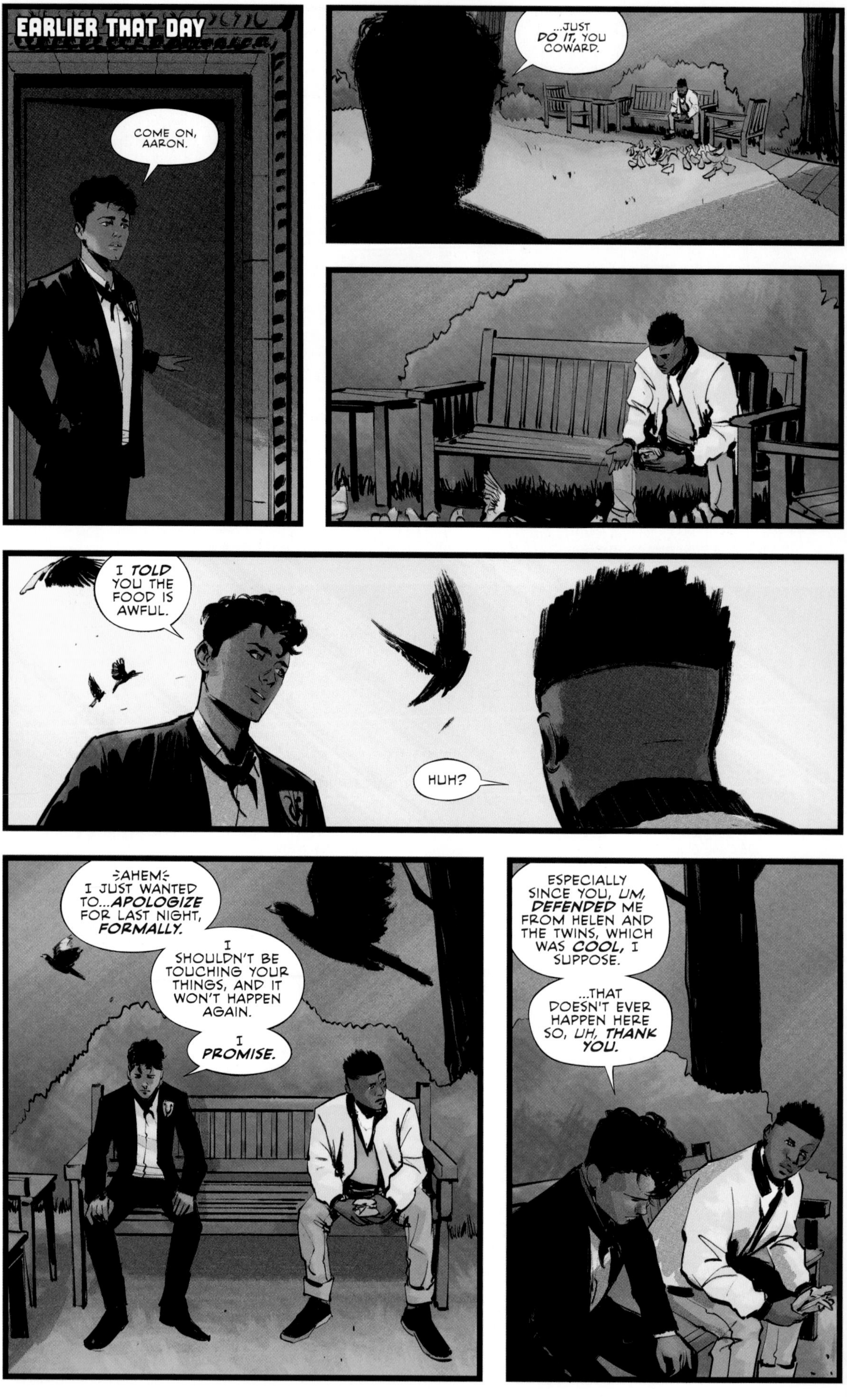
EARLIER THAT DAY
COME ON, AARON.
...JUST DO IT, YOU COWARD.
I TOLD YOU THE FOOD IS AWFUL.
HUH?
-AHEM- I JUST WANTED TO...APOLOGIZE FOR LAST NIGHT, FORMALLY.
I SHOULDN'T BE TOUCHING YOUR THINGS, AND IT WON'T HAPPEN AGAIN.
I PROMISE.
ESPECIALLY SINCE YOU, UM, DEFENDED ME FROM HELEN AND THE TWINS, WHICH WAS COOL, I SUPPOSE.
...THAT DOESN'T EVER HAPPEN HERE SO, UH, THANK YOU.

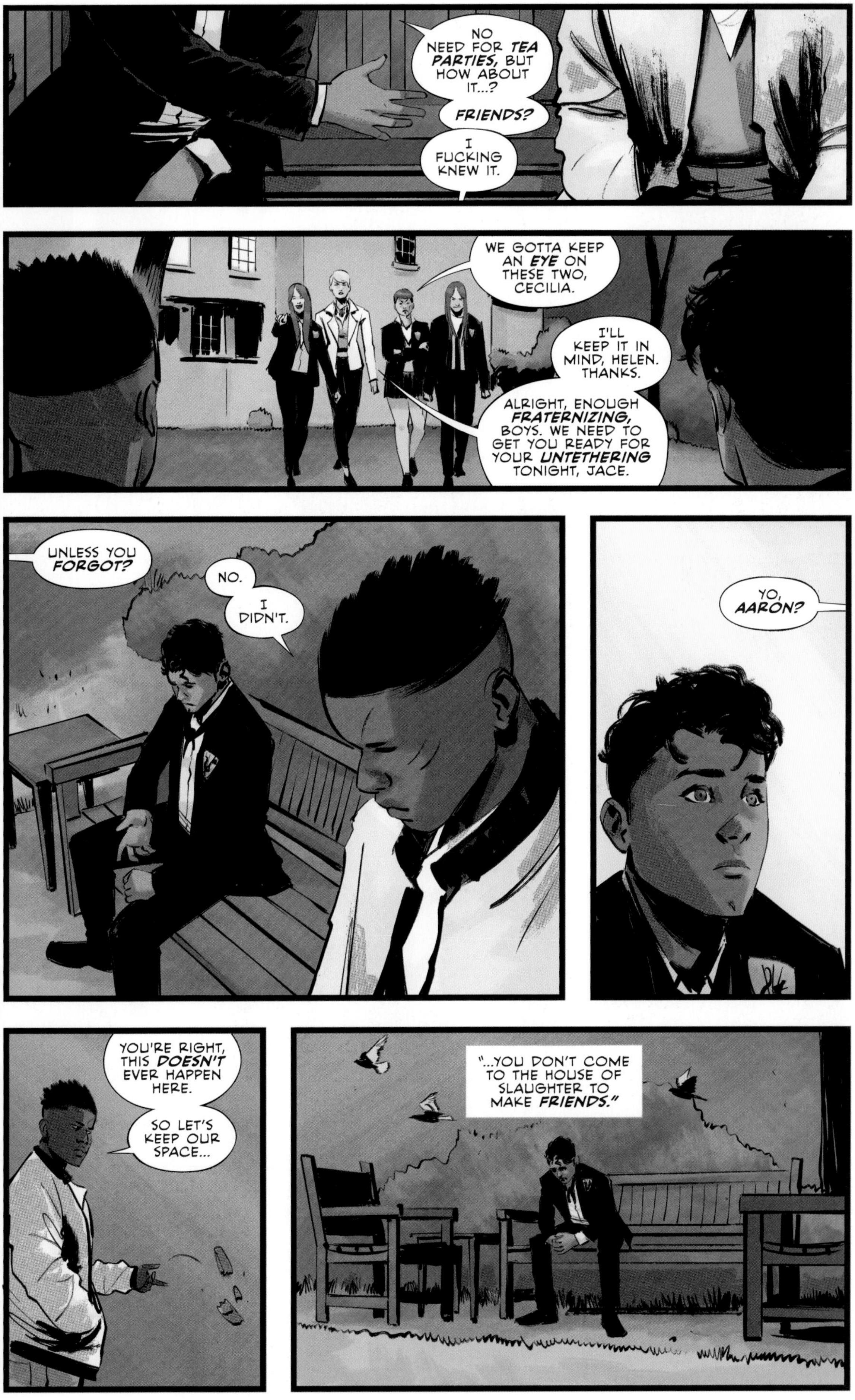
NO NEED FOR TEA PARTIES, BUT HOW ABOUT IT...?
FRIENDS?
I FUCKING KNEW IT.
WE GOTTA KEEP AN EYE ON THESE TWO, CECILIA.
I'LL KEEP IT IN MIND, HELEN. THANKS.
ALRIGHT, ENOUGH FRATERNIZING, BOYS. WE NEED TO GET YOU READY FOR YOUR UNTETHERING TONIGHT, JACE.
UNLESS YOU FORGOT?
NO.
I DIDN'T.
YO, AARON?
YOU'RE RIGHT, THIS DOESN'T EVER HAPPEN HERE.
SO LET'S KEEP OUR SPACE...
"...YOU DON'T COME TO THE HOUSE OF SLAUGHTER TO MAKE FRIENDS."

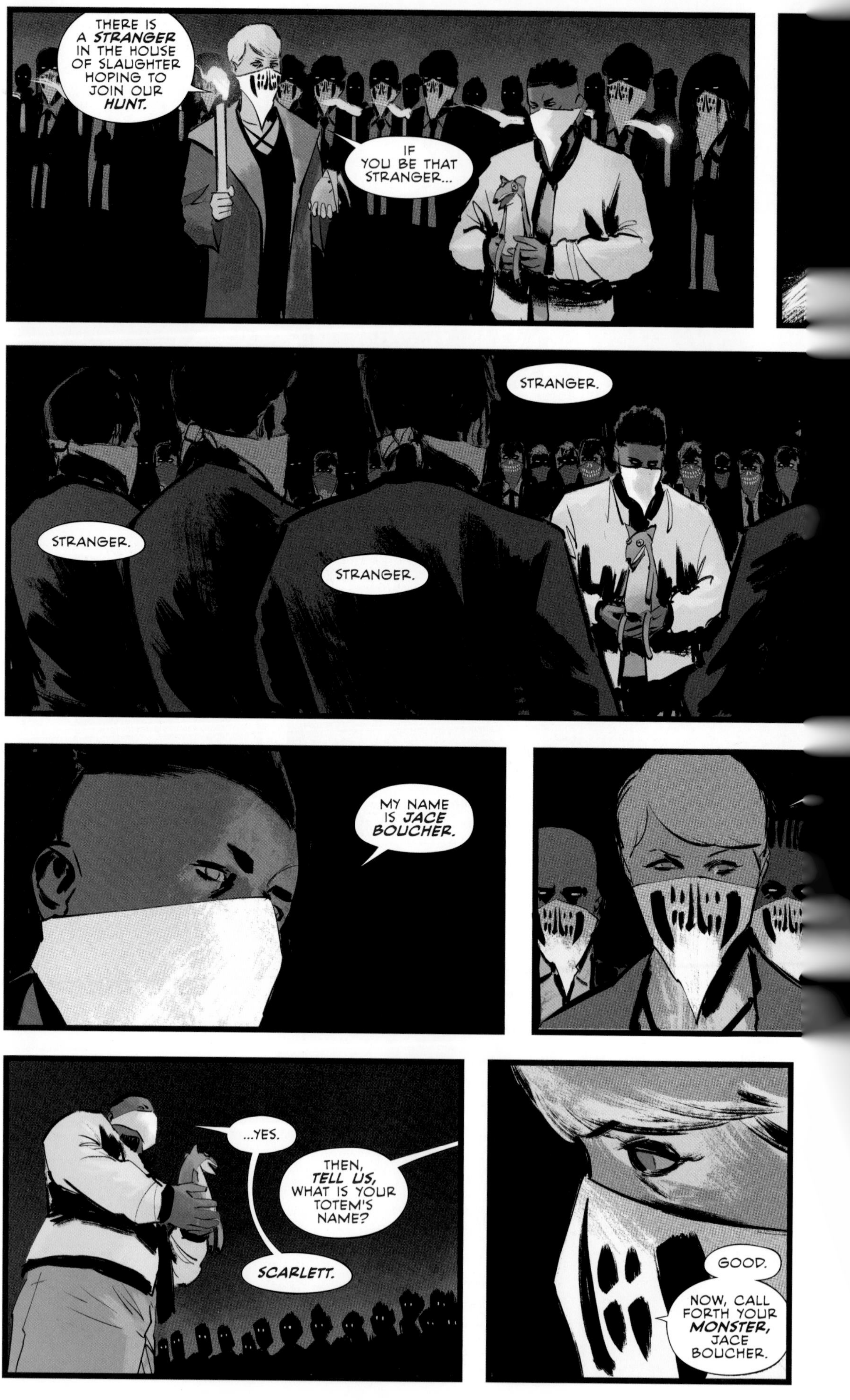
THERE IS A STRANGER IN THE HOUSE OF SLAUGHTER HOPING TO JOIN OUR HUNT.
IF YOU BE THAT STRANGER...
STRANGER.
STRANGER.
STRANGER.
MY NAME IS JACE BOUCHER.
...YES.
THEN, TELL US, WHAT IS YOUR TOTEM'S NAME?
SCARLETT.
GOOD.
NOW, CALL FORTH YOUR MONSTER, JACE BOUCHER.

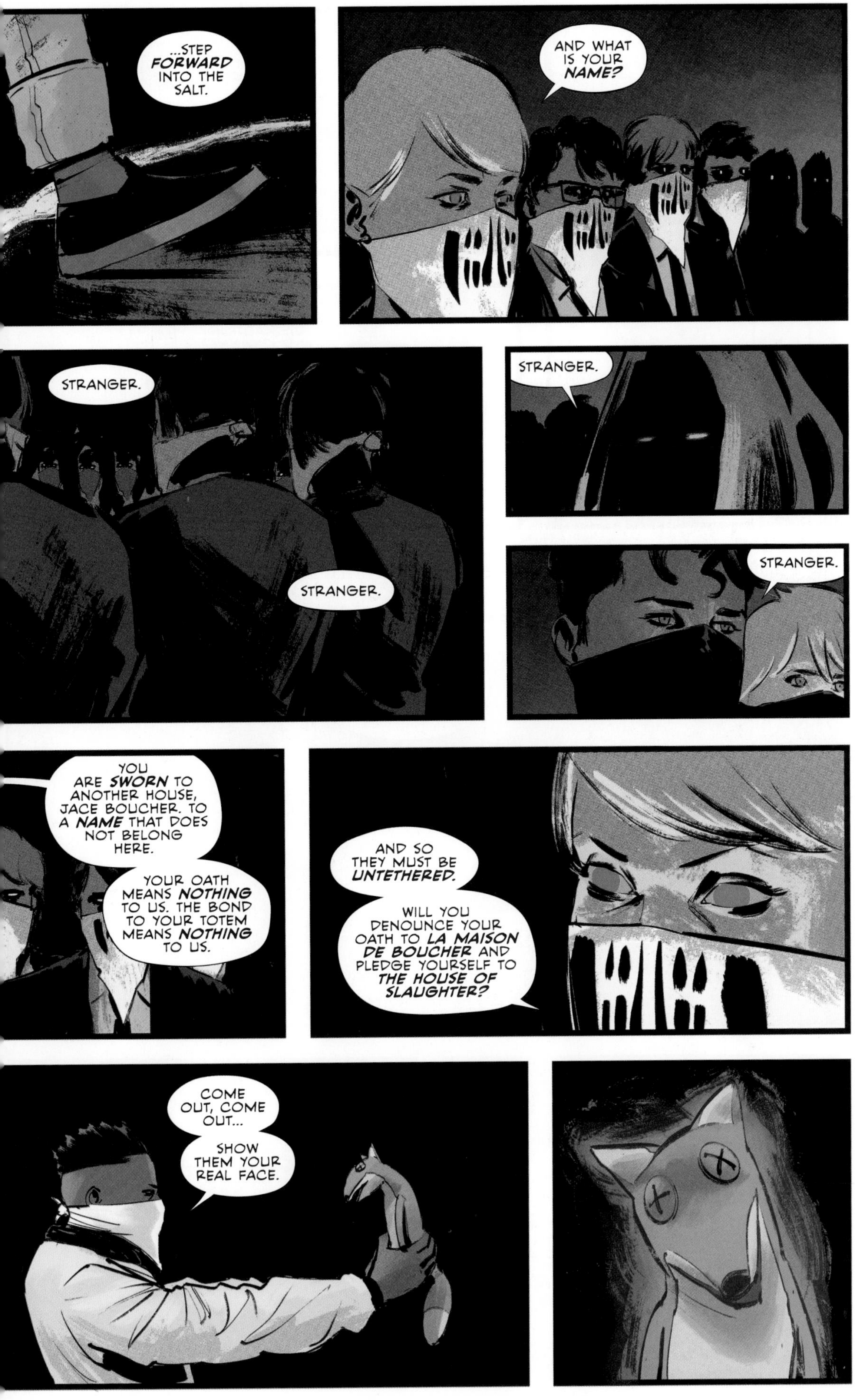
...STEP FORWARD INTO THE SALT.
AND WHAT IS YOUR NAME?
STRANGER.
STRANGER.
STRANGER.
STRANGER.
YOU ARE SWORN TO ANOTHER HOUSE, JACE BOUCHER. TO A NAME THAT DOES NOT BELONG HERE.
YOUR OATH MEANS NOTHING TO US. THE BOND TO YOUR TOTEM MEANS NOTHING TO US.
AND SO THEY MUST BE UNTETHERED.
WILL YOU DENOUNCE YOUR OATH TO LA MAISON DE BOUCHER AND PLEDGE YOURSELF TO THE HOUSE OF SLAUGHTER?
COME OUT, COME OUT...
SHOW THEM YOUR REAL FACE.

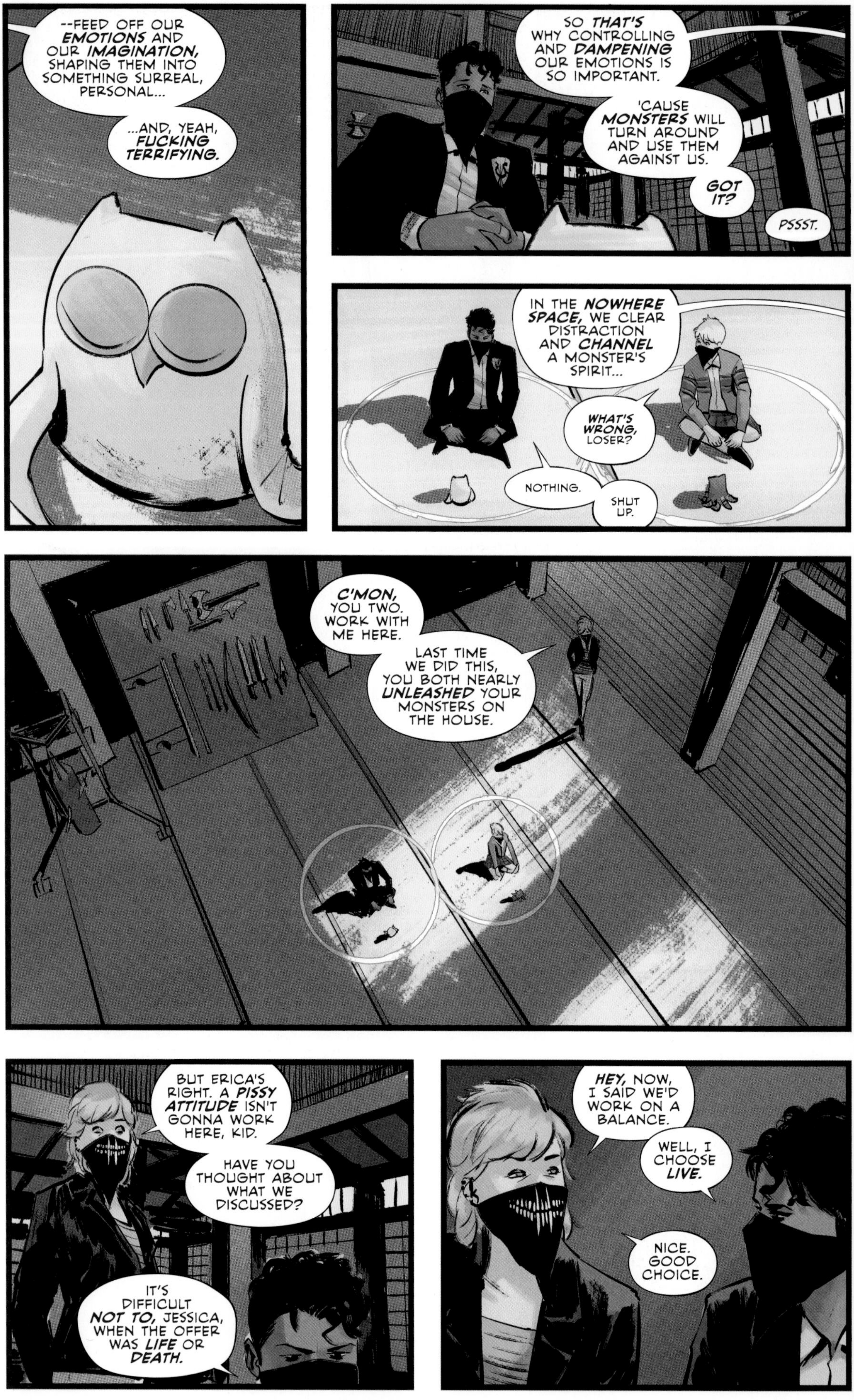
--FEED OFF OUR EMOTIONS AND OUR IMAGINATION, SHAPING THEM INTO SOMETHING SURREAL, PERSONAL...
...AND, YEAH, FUCKING TERRIFYING.
SO THAT'S WHY CONTROLLING AND DAMPENING OUR EMOTIONS IS SO IMPORTANT.
'CAUSE MONSTERS WILL TURN AROUND AND USE THEM AGAINST US.
GOT IT?
PSSST.
IN THE NOWHERE SPACE, WE CLEAR DISTRACTION AND CHANNEL A MONSTER'S SPIRIT...
WHAT'S WRONG, LOSER?
NOTHING.
SHUT UP.
C'MON, YOU TWO. WORK WITH ME HERE.
LAST TIME WE DID THIS, YOU BOTH NEARLY UNLEASHED YOUR MONSTERS ON THE HOUSE.
BUT ERICA'S RIGHT. A PISSY ATTITUDE ISN'T GONNA WORK HERE, KID.
HAVE YOU THOUGHT ABOUT WHAT WE DISCUSSED?
IT'S DIFFICULT NOT TO, JESSICA, WHEN THE OFFER WAS LIFE OR DEATH.
HEY, NOW, I SAID WE'D WORK ON A BALANCE.
WELL, I CHOOSE LIVE.
NICE. GOOD CHOICE.

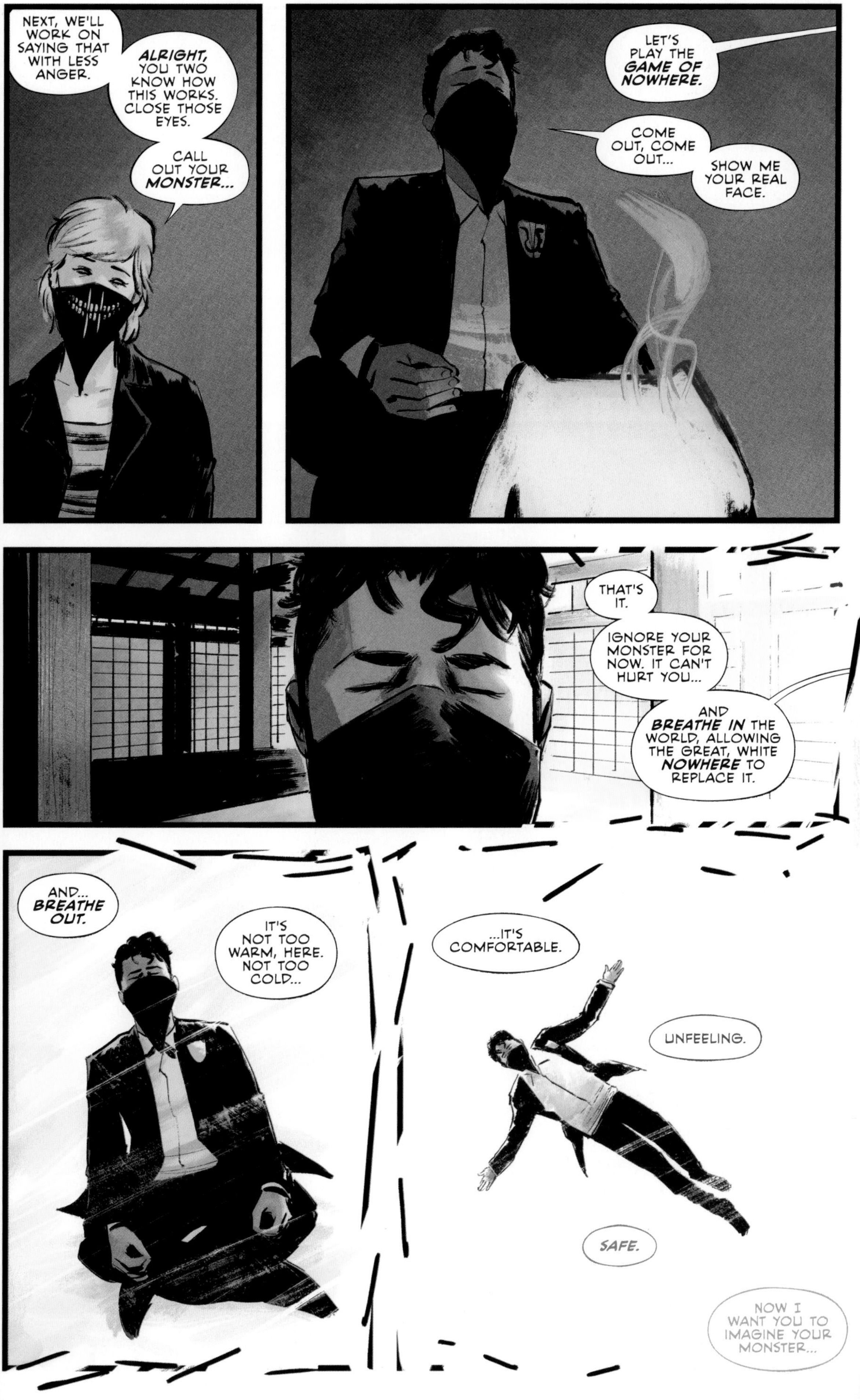
NEXT, WE'LL WORK ON SAYING THAT WITH LESS ANGER.
ALRIGHT, YOU TWO KNOW HOW THIS WORKS. CLOSE THOSE EYES.
CALL OUT YOUR MONSTER...
LET'S PLAY THE GAME OF NOWHERE.
COME OUT, COME OUT...
SHOW ME YOUR REAL FACE.
THAT'S IT.
IGNORE YOUR MONSTER FOR NOW. IT CAN'T HURT YOU...
AND BREATHE IN THE WORLD, ALLOWING THE GREAT, WHITE NOWHERE TO REPLACE IT.
AND... BREATHE OUT.
IT'S NOT TOO WARM, HERE. NOT TOO COLD...
...IT'S COMFORTABLE.
UNFEELING.
SAFE.
NOW I WANT YOU TO IMAGINE YOUR MONSTER...

UNTETHER YOUR MONSTER, JACE BOUCHER.

AND IF YOU SURVIVE, **REFORGE** YOUR BOND ANEW.

UNTETHERED.

SNIP

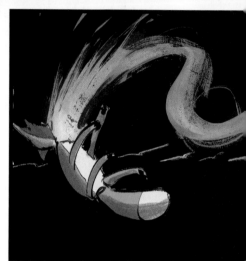

UNWISE... BOY.

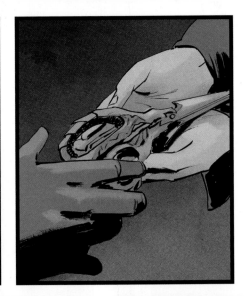

BY THIS INCISION, I **FREE** YOU, MONSTER.

OUR BOND, **BROKEN,** I COMMAND YOU...

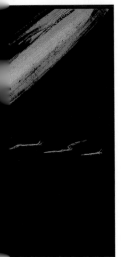

RRRRREAARGH

YOU BOUND ME, **WEAK.** NOW, I AM **FREE.**

I **SURVIVED** YOU, BOY. **TASTED** YOUR **FEARRRS. CHEWED** ON YOUR T-T-TRAUMAS. NO LONGER...THE MONSTER YOU **ONCE** FACED.

NOOO, FORSAKEN PRINCE... **LAST** OF THE **LEGACY BUTCHERS,** YOUR **ASHEN TRUTHSSS** ARE MY TRUTHS...

AND I **KNOW** THEM **ALL.**

'KAY.

JUST DON'T CALL ME **BOY.**

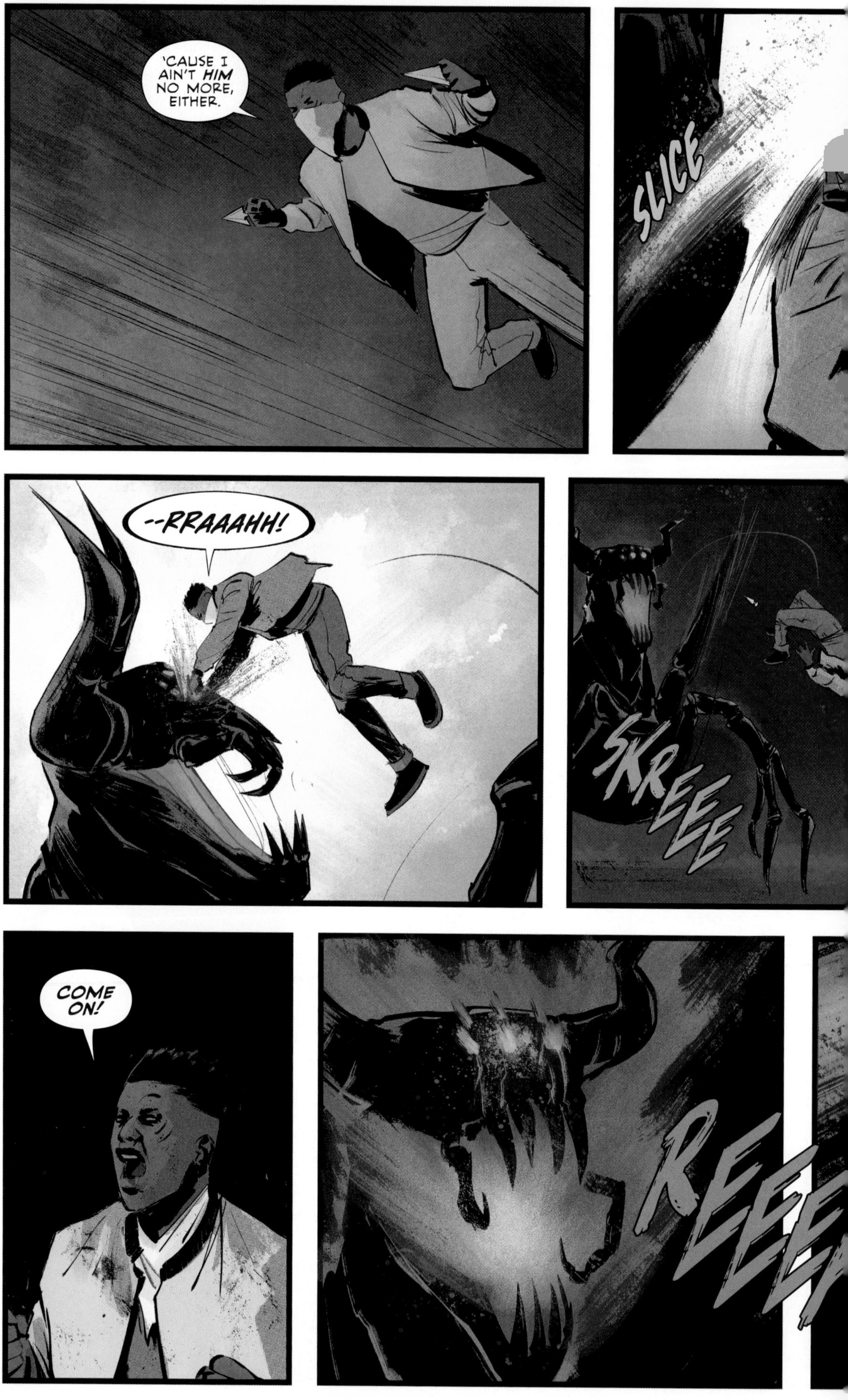
'CAUSE I AIN'T HIM NO MORE, EITHER.
SLICE
--RRAAAHH!
SKREEE
COME ON!
REEE

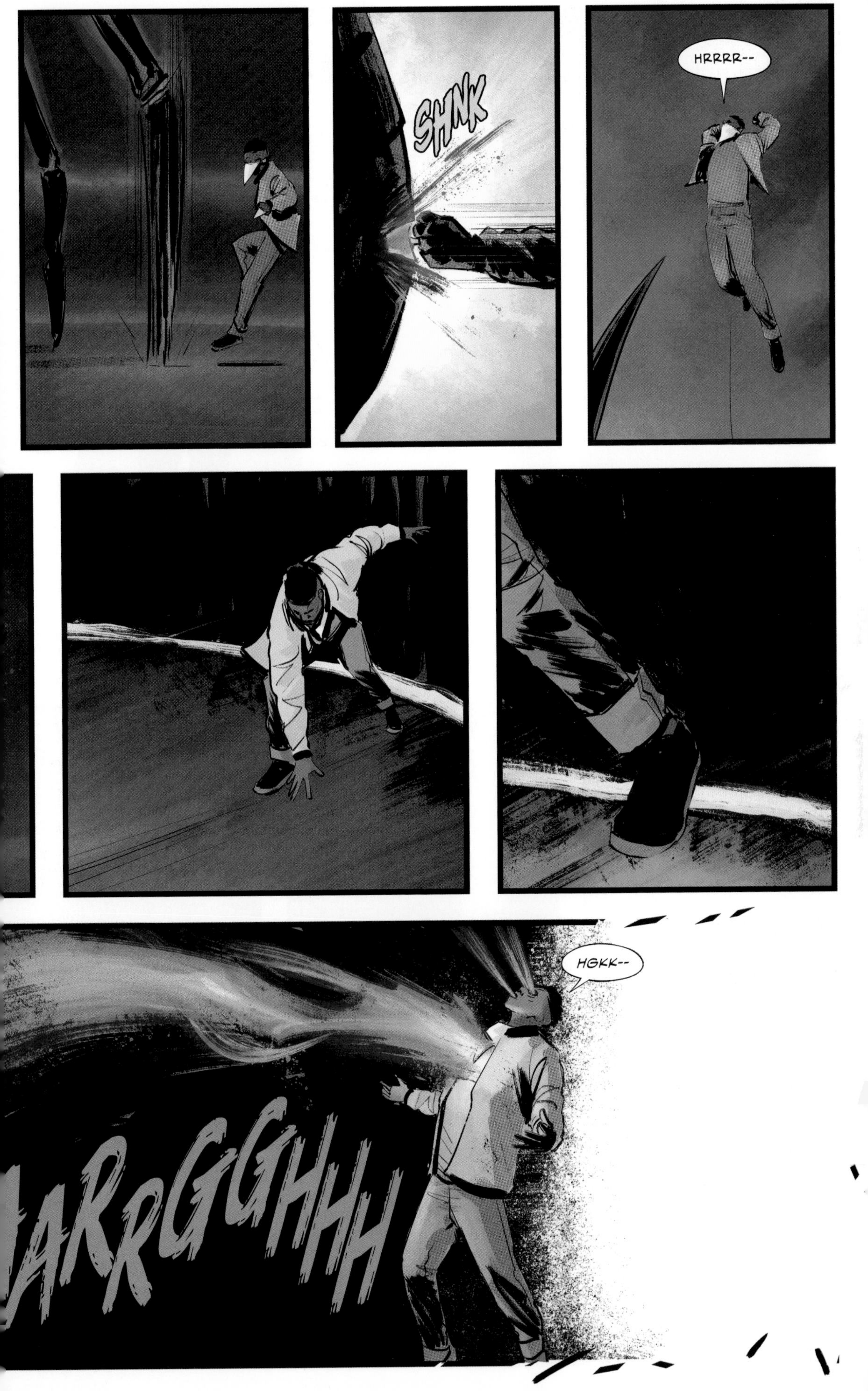
SHNK
HRRRR--
HGKK--
ARRGGHHH

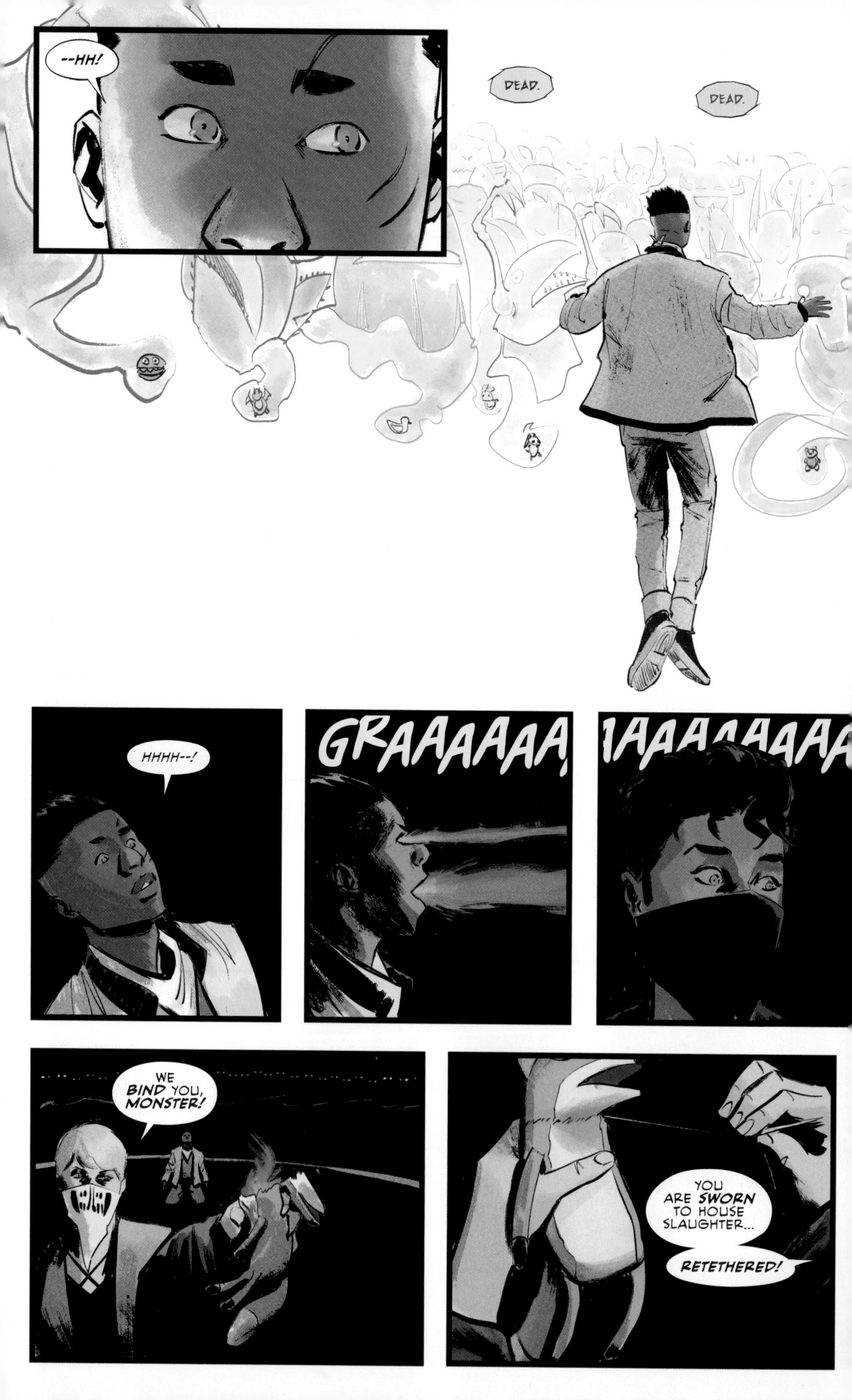
--HH!
DEAD.
DEAD.
HHHH--!
GRAAAAAAAAAAAAAAAA
WE BIND YOU, MONSTER!
YOU ARE SWORN TO HOUSE SLAUGHTER...
RETETHERED!

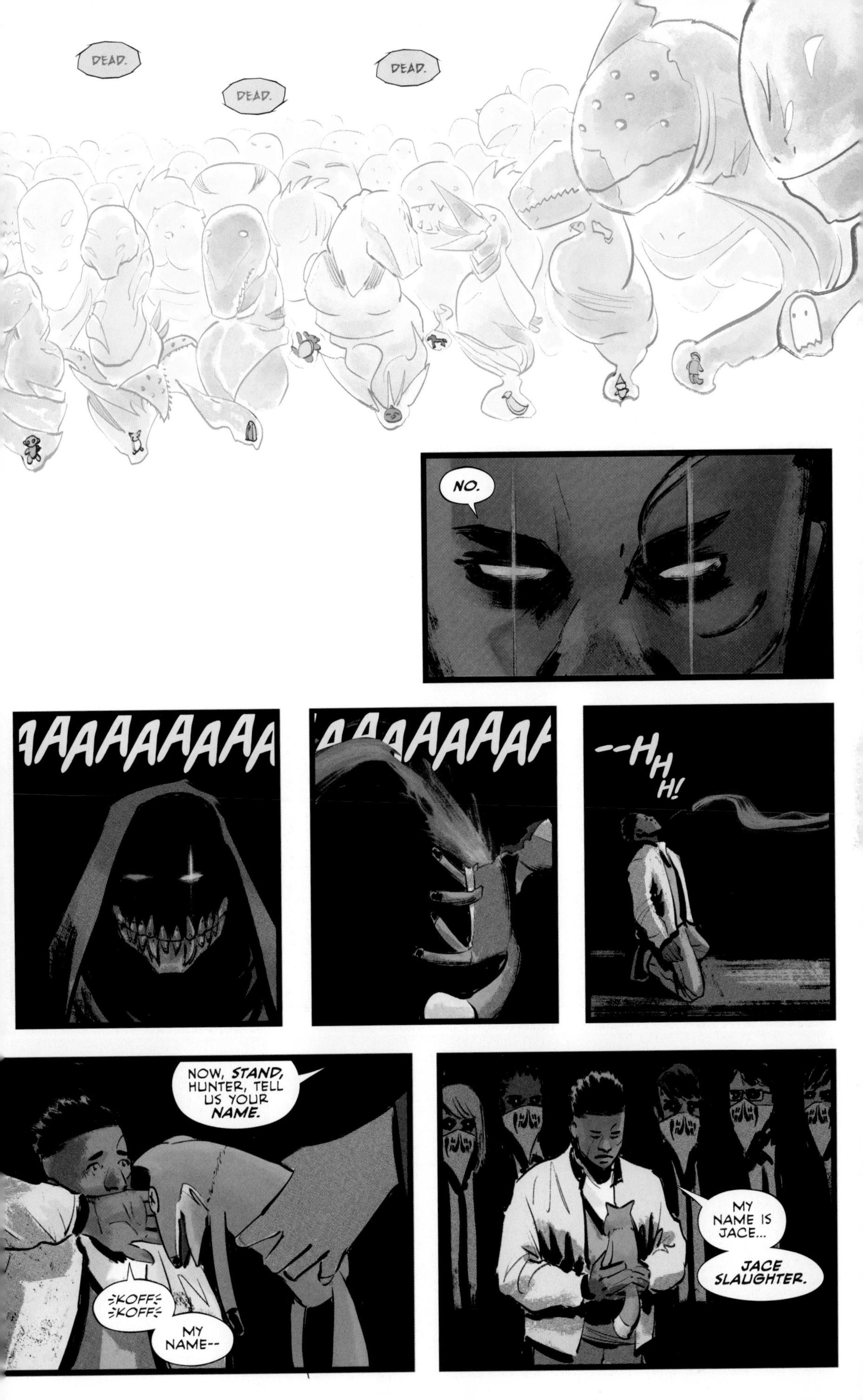
DEAD.
DEAD.
DEAD.
NO.
AAAAAAAAA
AAAAAAAAA
--HHH!
NOW, STAND, HUNTER, TELL US YOUR NAME.
KOFF KOFF
MY NAME--
MY NAME IS JACE...
JACE SLAUGHTER.

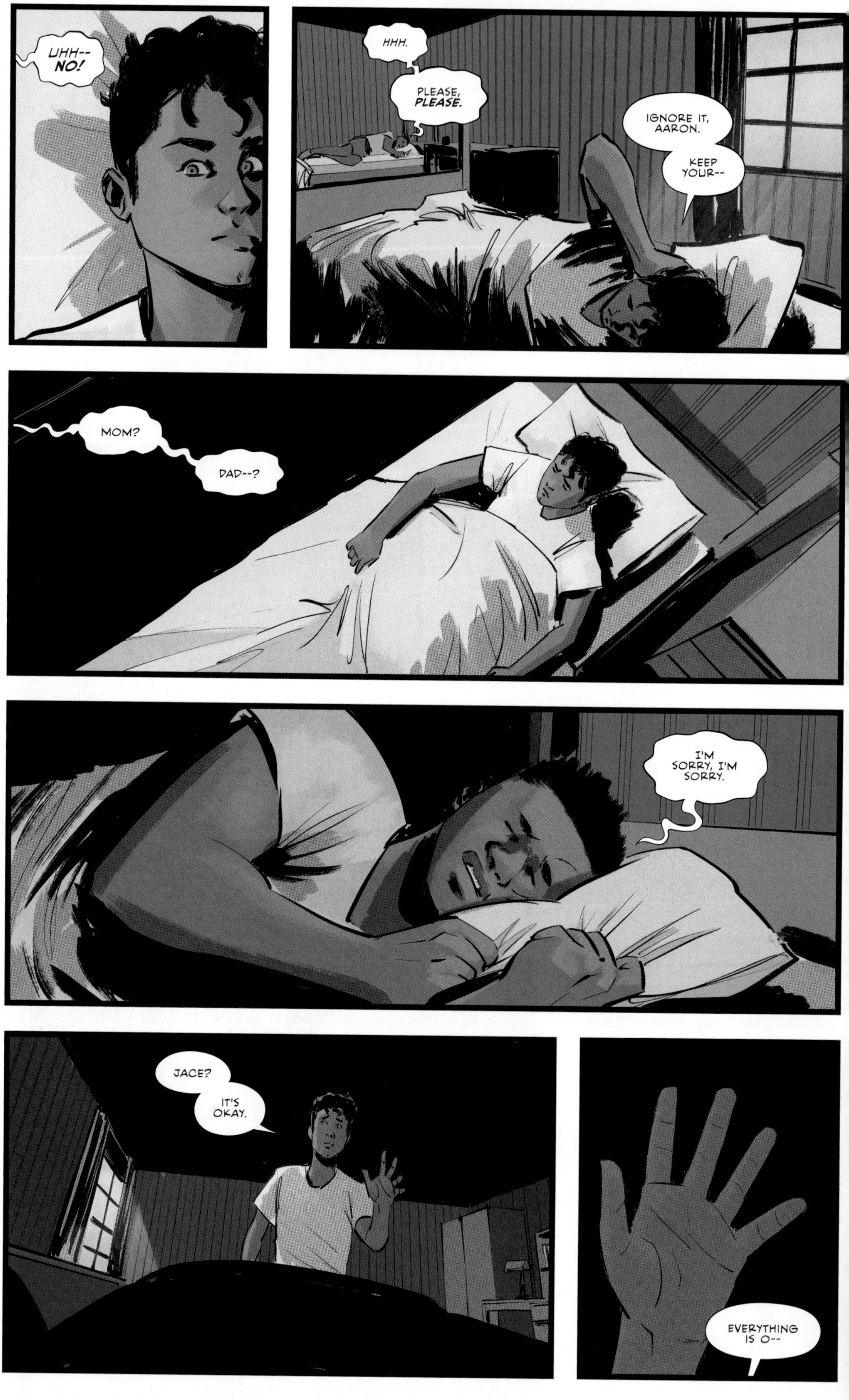
UHH--
NO!
HHH.
PLEASE,
PLEASE.
IGNORE IT, AARON.
KEEP YOUR--
MOM?
DAD--?
I'M SORRY, I'M SORRY.
JACE?
IT'S OKAY.
EVERYTHING IS O--

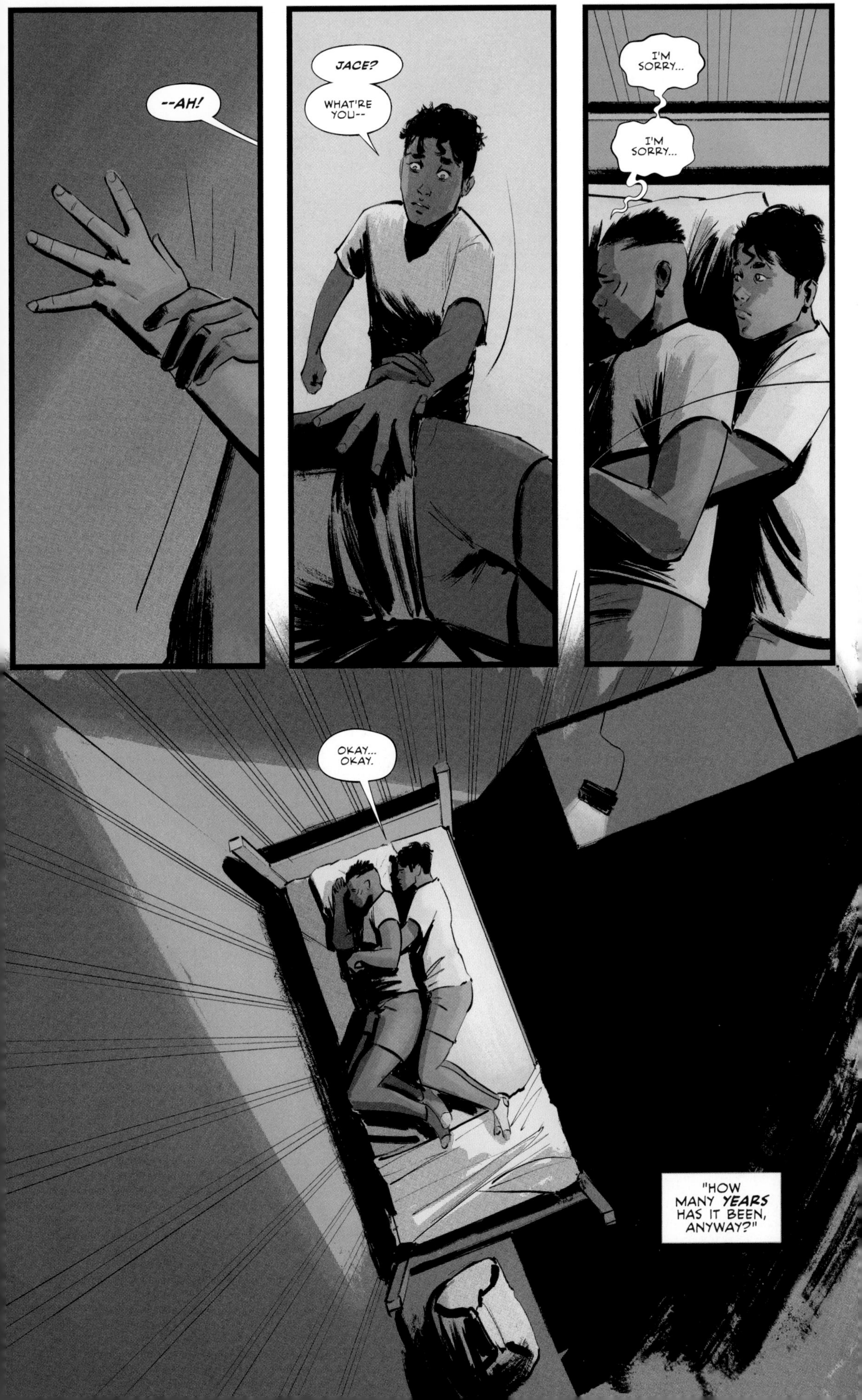
--AH!
JACE?
WHAT'RE YOU--
I'M SORRY...
I'M SORRY...
OKAY... OKAY.
"HOW MANY YEARS HAS IT BEEN, ANYWAY?"

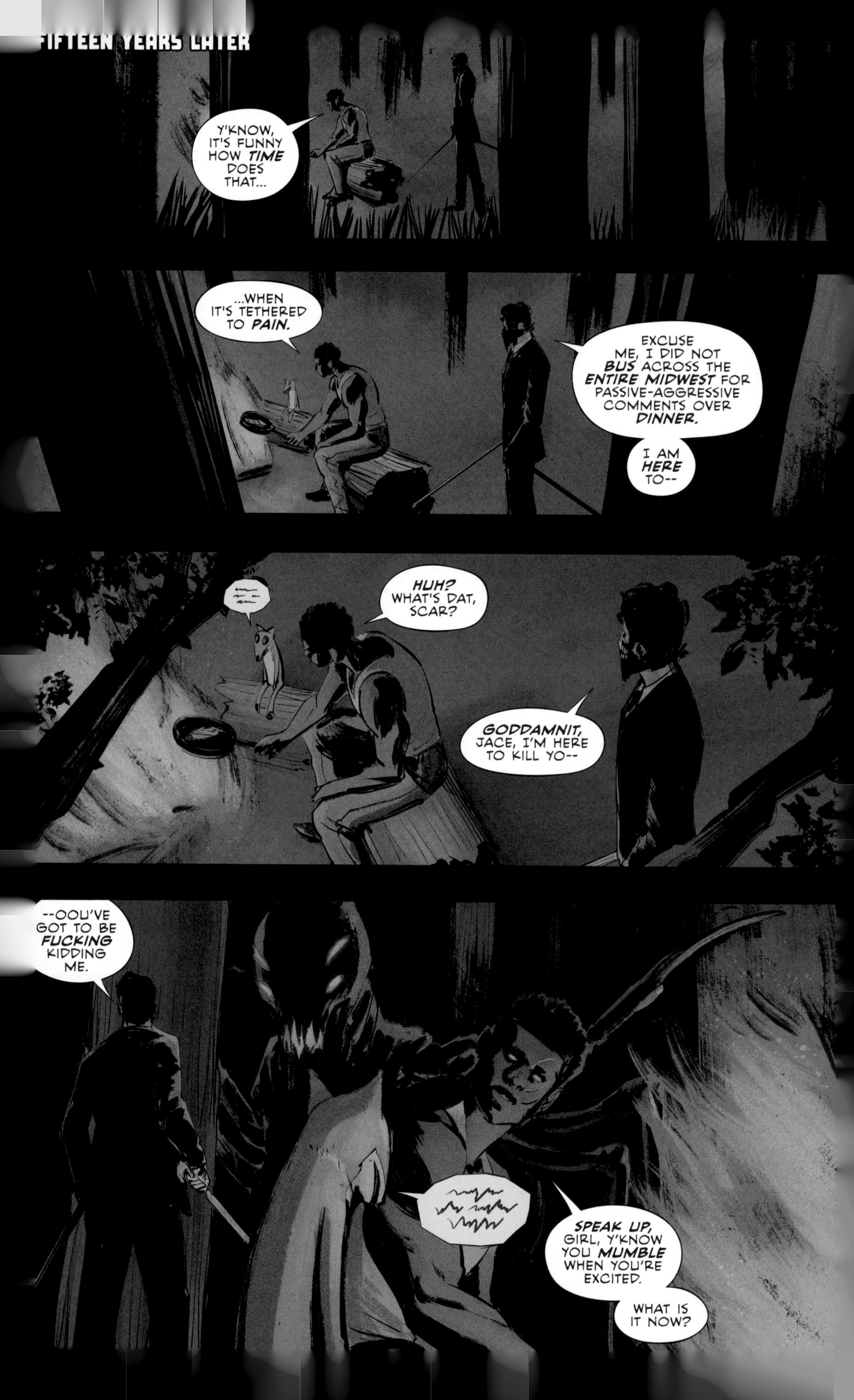
FIFTEEN YEARS LATER
Y'KNOW, IT'S FUNNY HOW TIME DOES THAT...
...WHEN IT'S TETHERED TO PAIN.
EXCUSE ME, I DID NOT BUS ACROSS THE ENTIRE MIDWEST FOR PASSIVE-AGGRESSIVE COMMENTS OVER DINNER.
I AM HERE TO--
HUH? WHAT'S DAT, SCAR?
GODDAMNIT, JACE, I'M HERE TO KILL YO--
--OOU'VE GOT TO BE FUCKING KIDDING ME.
SPEAK UP, GIRL, Y'KNOW YOU MUMBLE WHEN YOU'RE EXCITED.
WHAT IS IT NOW?

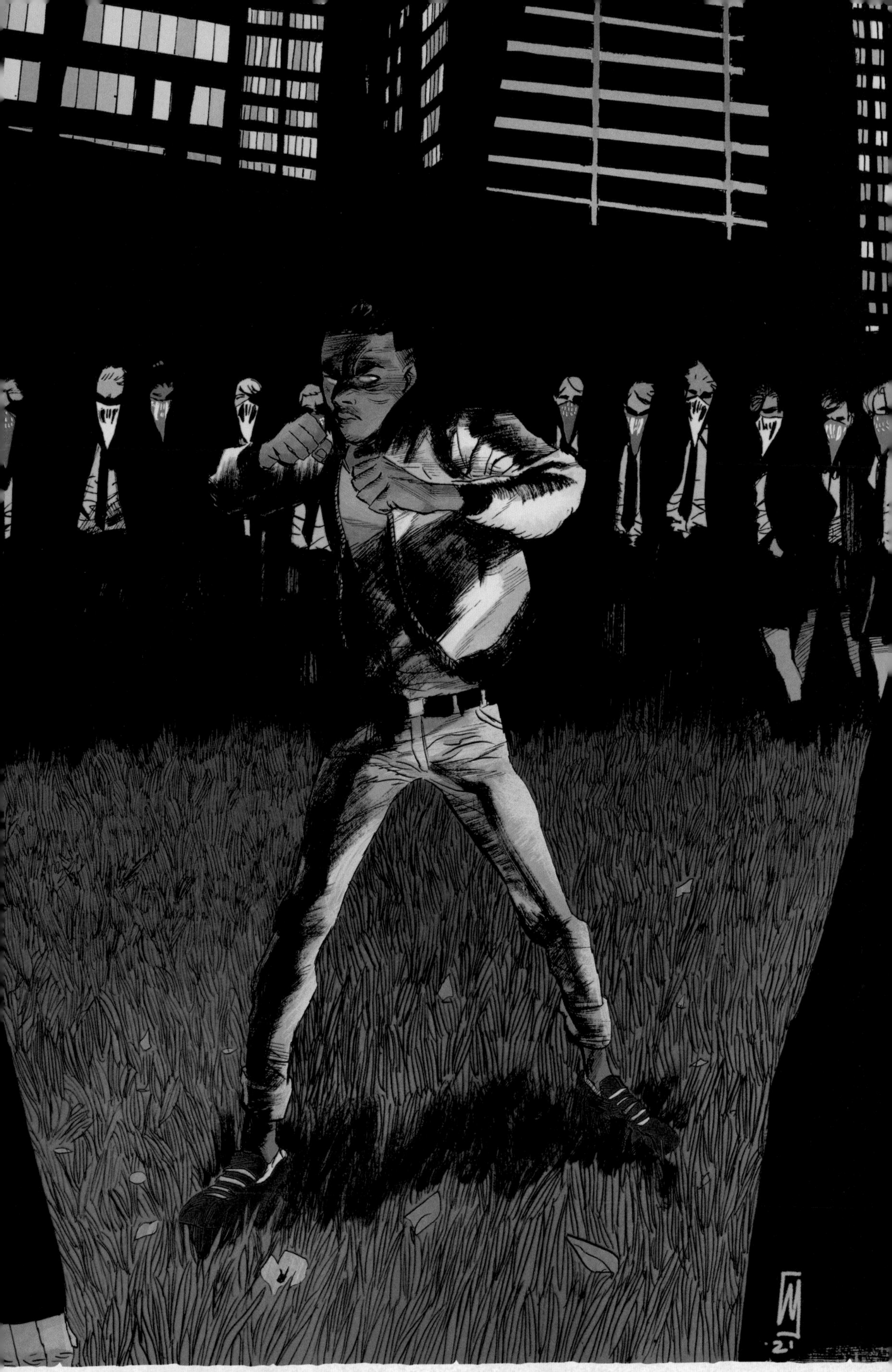

ISSUE TWO COVER BY WERTHER DELL'EDERA WITH COLORS BY MIQUEL MUERTO

PART THREE

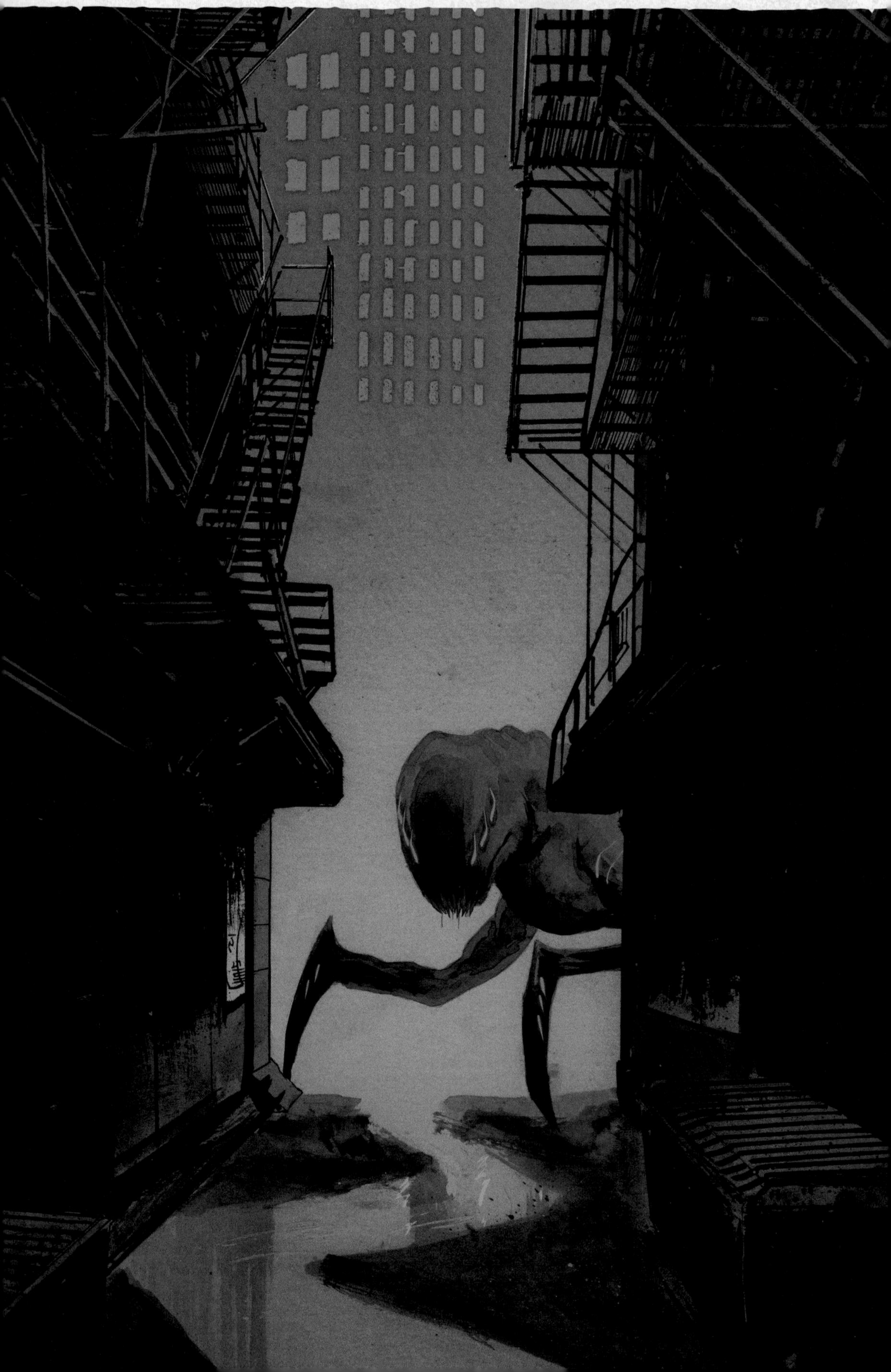

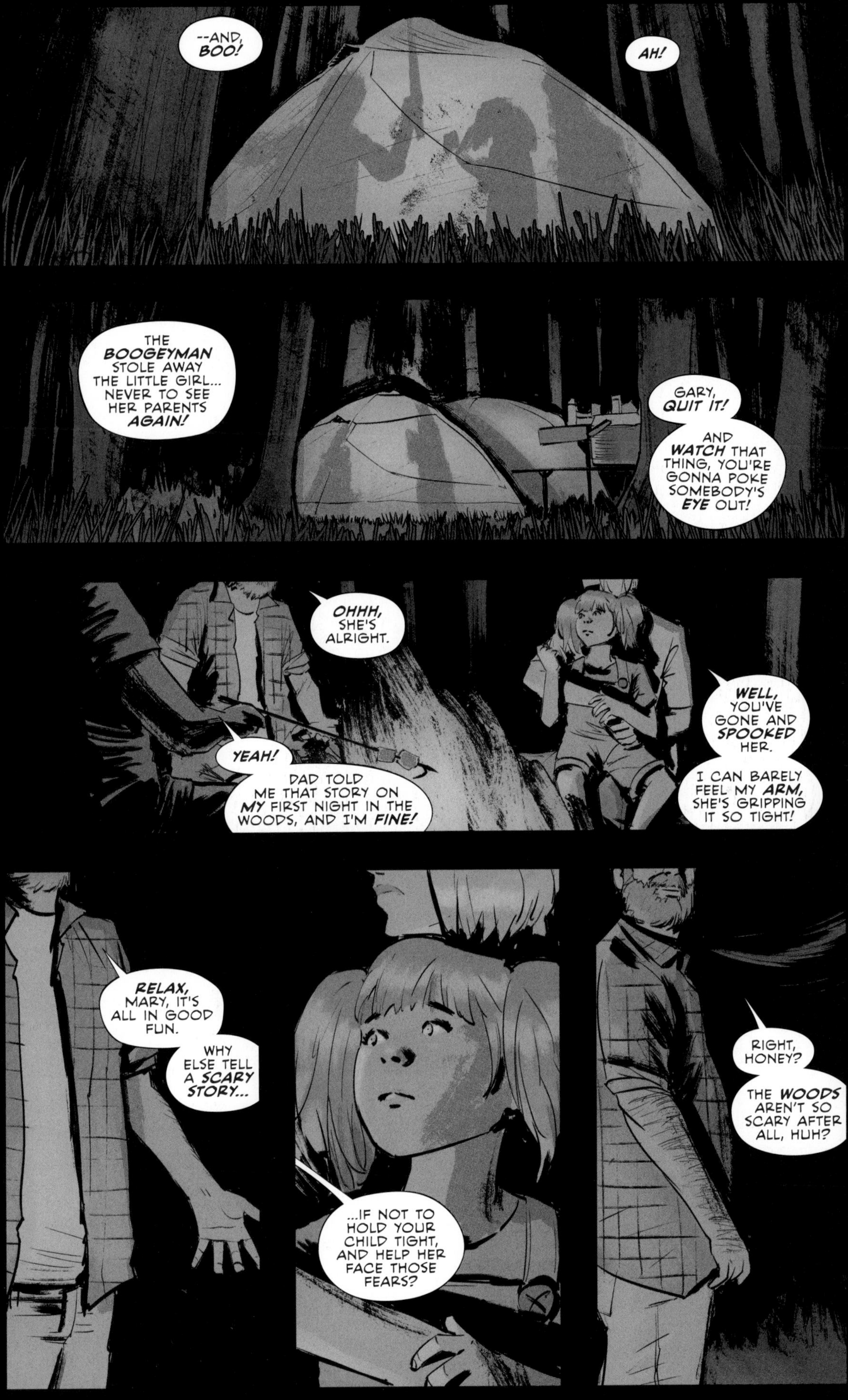
--AND, BOO!
AH!
THE BOOGEYMAN STOLE AWAY THE LITTLE GIRL... NEVER TO SEE HER PARENTS AGAIN!
GARY, QUIT IT!
AND WATCH THAT THING, YOU'RE GONNA POKE SOMEBODY'S EYE OUT!
OHHH, SHE'S ALRIGHT.
YEAH!
DAD TOLD ME THAT STORY ON MY FIRST NIGHT IN THE WOODS, AND I'M FINE!
WELL, YOU'VE GONE AND SPOOKED HER.
I CAN BARELY FEEL MY ARM, SHE'S GRIPPING IT SO TIGHT!
RELAX, MARY, IT'S ALL IN GOOD FUN.
WHY ELSE TELL A SCARY STORY...
...IF NOT TO HOLD YOUR CHILD TIGHT, AND HELP HER FACE THOSE FEARS?
RIGHT, HONEY?
THE WOODS AREN'T SO SCARY AFTER ALL, HUH?

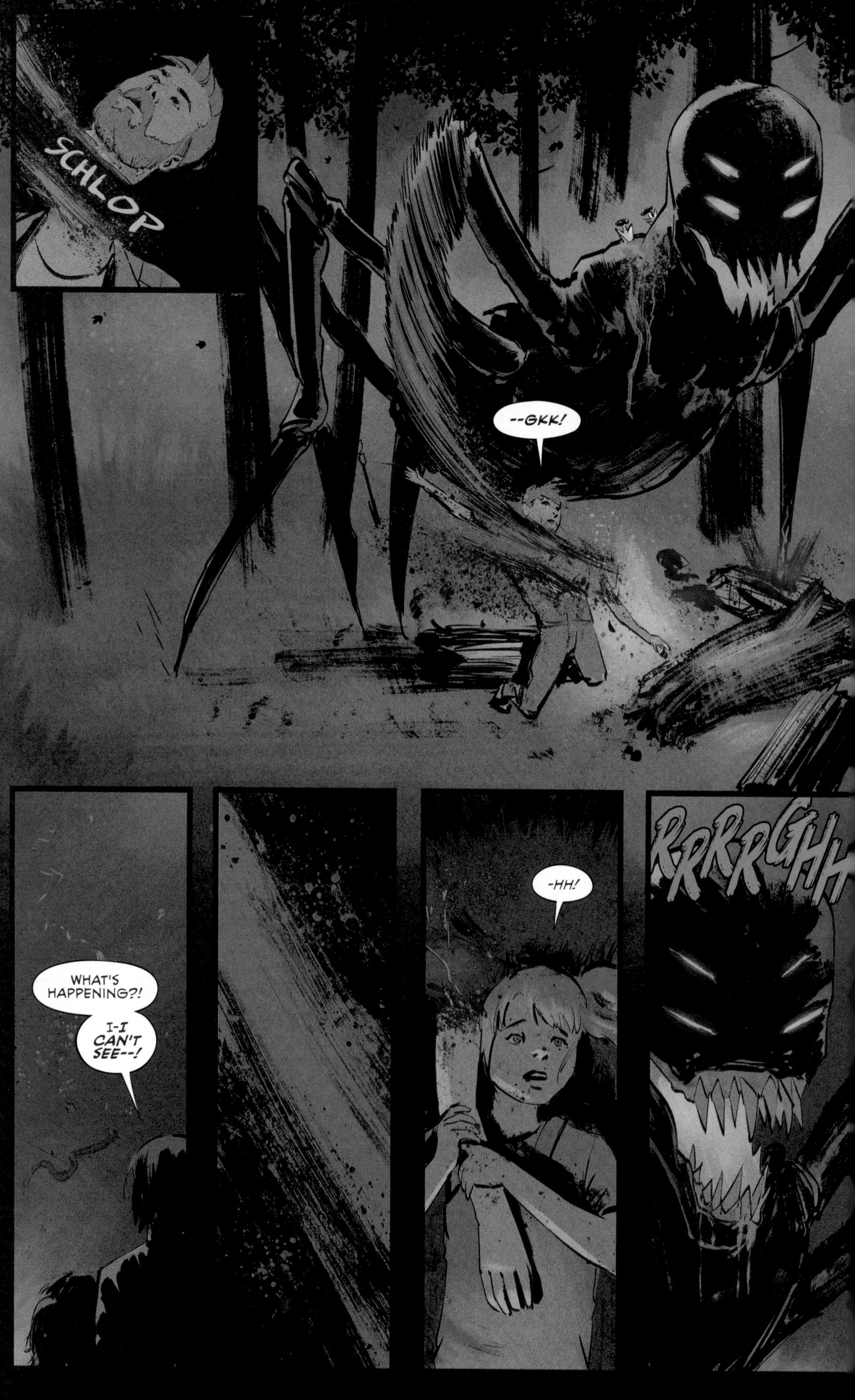
SCHLOP
--GKK!
WHAT'S HAPPENING?!
I-I CAN'T SEE--!
-HH!
RRRRGHH

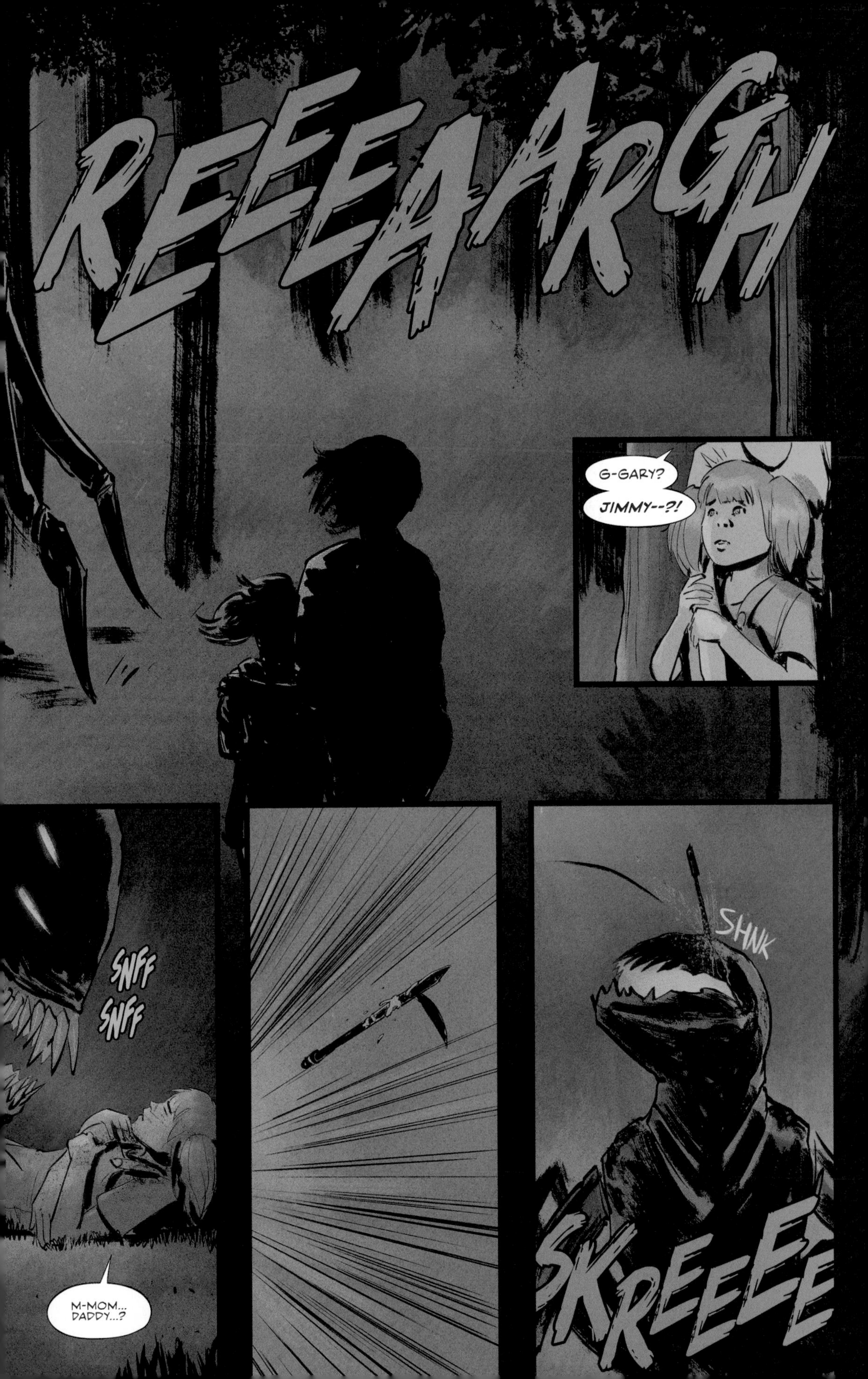
REEEAARGH
G-GARY?
JIMMY--?!
SNFF
SNFF
M-MOM... DADDY...?
SHNK
SKREEEE

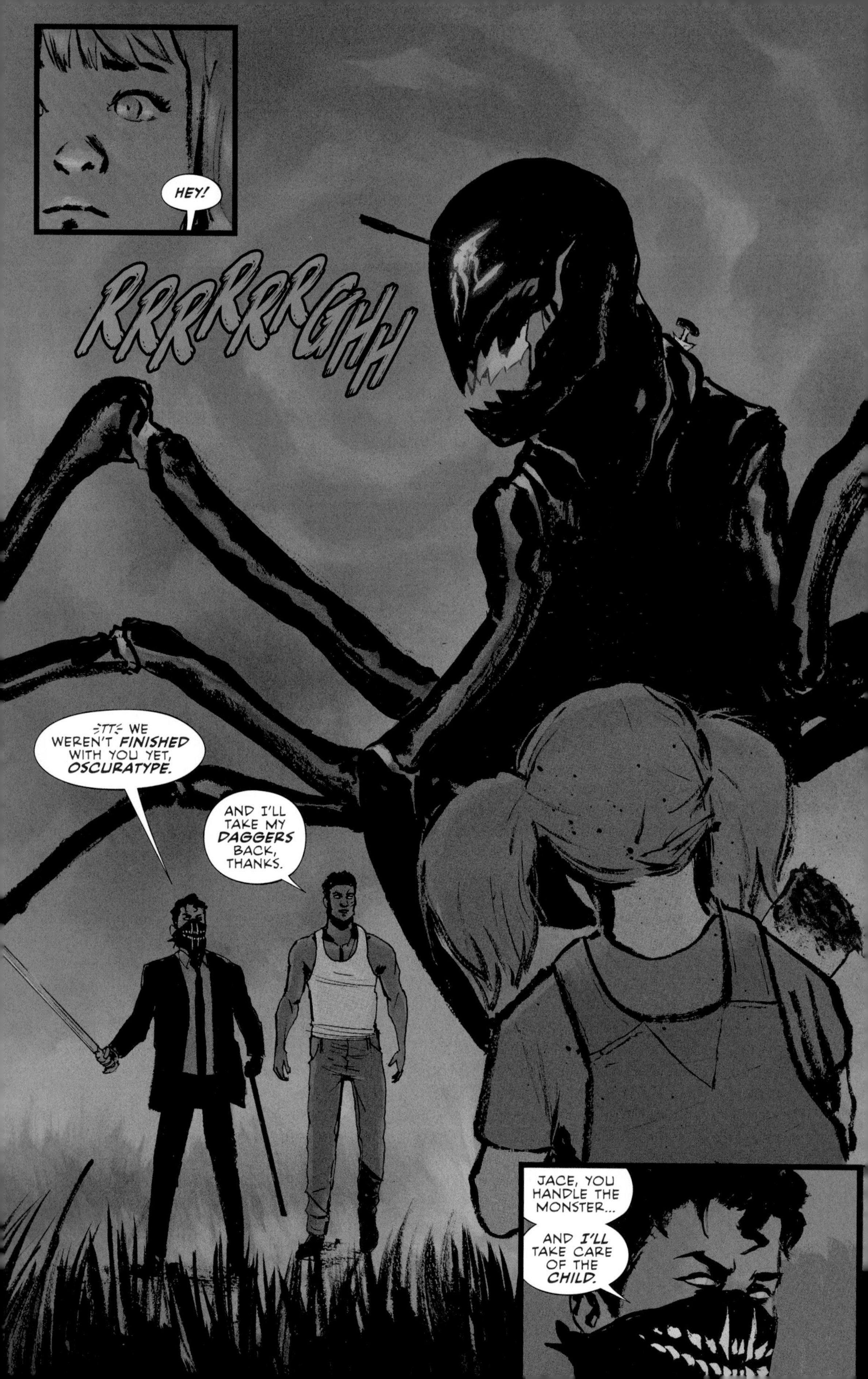
HEY!
RRRRRRGHH
TT WE WEREN'T FINISHED WITH YOU YET, OSCURATYPE.
AND I'LL TAKE MY DAGGERS BACK, THANKS.
JACE, YOU HANDLE THE MONSTER...
AND I'LL TAKE CARE OF THE CHILD.

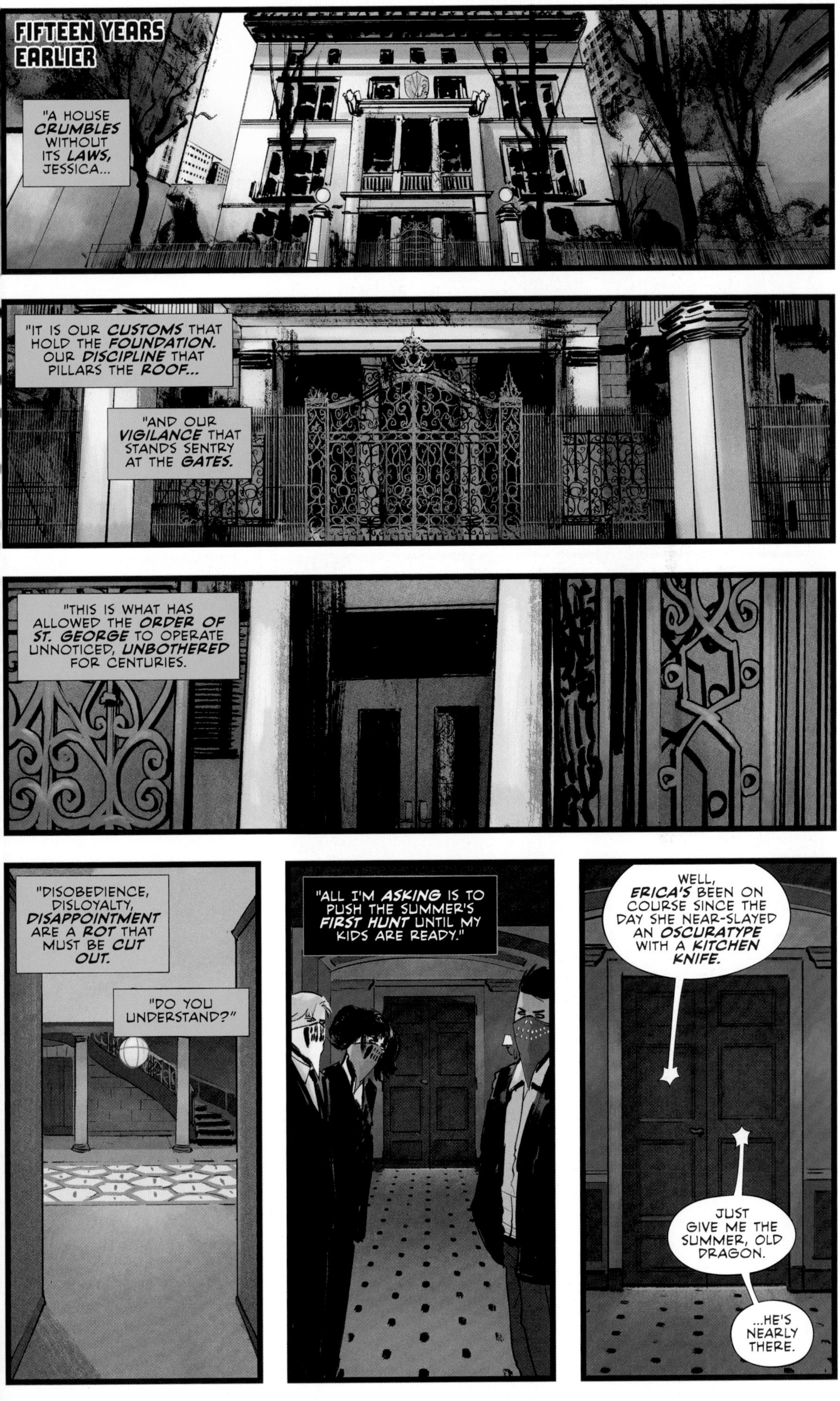
FIFTEEN YEARS EARLIER
"A HOUSE CRUMBLES WITHOUT ITS LAWS, JESSICA...
"IT IS OUR CUSTOMS THAT HOLD THE FOUNDATION. OUR DISCIPLINE THAT PILLARS THE ROOF...
"AND OUR VIGILANCE THAT STANDS SENTRY AT THE GATES.
"THIS IS WHAT HAS ALLOWED THE ORDER OF ST. GEORGE TO OPERATE UNNOTICED, UNBOTHERED FOR CENTURIES.
"DISOBEDIENCE, DISLOYALTY, DISAPPOINTMENT ARE A ROT THAT MUST BE CUT OUT.
"DO YOU UNDERSTAND?"
"ALL I'M ASKING IS TO PUSH THE SUMMER'S FIRST HUNT UNTIL MY KIDS ARE READY."
WELL, ERICA'S BEEN ON COURSE SINCE THE DAY SHE NEAR-SLAYED AN OSCURATYPE WITH A KITCHEN KNIFE.
JUST GIVE ME THE SUMMER, OLD DRAGON.
...HE'S NEARLY THERE.

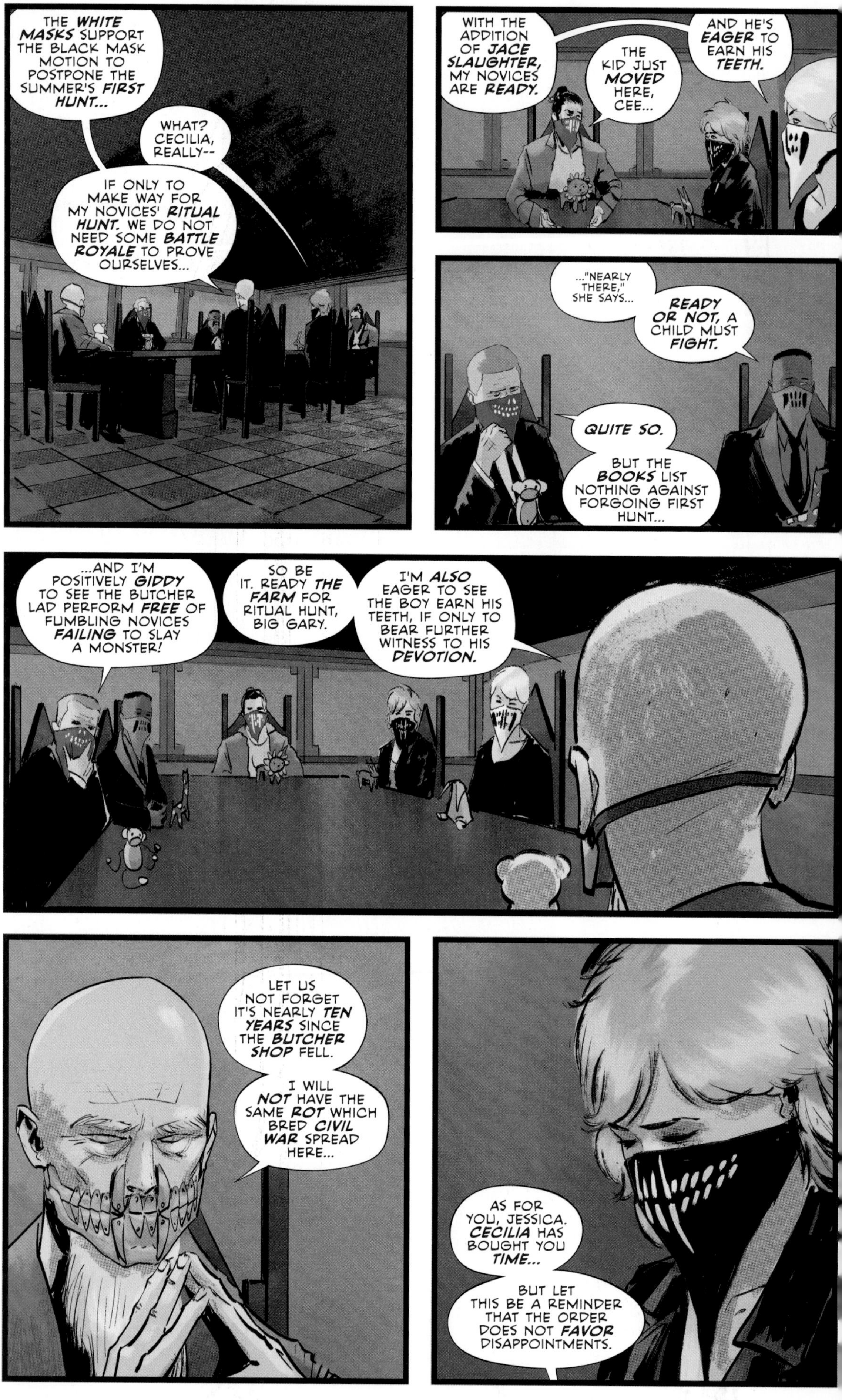
THE WHITE MASKS SUPPORT THE BLACK MASK MOTION TO POSTPONE THE SUMMER'S FIRST HUNT...
WHAT? CECILIA, REALLY--
IF ONLY TO MAKE WAY FOR MY NOVICES' RITUAL HUNT. WE DO NOT NEED SOME BATTLE ROYALE TO PROVE OURSELVES...
WITH THE ADDITION OF JACE SLAUGHTER, MY NOVICES ARE READY.
THE KID JUST MOVED HERE, CEE...
AND HE'S EAGER TO EARN HIS TEETH.
..."NEARLY THERE," SHE SAYS...
READY OR NOT, A CHILD MUST FIGHT.
QUITE SO.
BUT THE BOOKS LIST NOTHING AGAINST FORGOING FIRST HUNT...
...AND I'M POSITIVELY GIDDY TO SEE THE BUTCHER LAD PERFORM FREE OF FUMBLING NOVICES FAILING TO SLAY A MONSTER!
SO BE IT. READY THE FARM FOR RITUAL HUNT, BIG GARY.
I'M ALSO EAGER TO SEE THE BOY EARN HIS TEETH, IF ONLY TO BEAR FURTHER WITNESS TO HIS DEVOTION.
LET US NOT FORGET IT'S NEARLY TEN YEARS SINCE THE BUTCHER SHOP FELL.
I WILL NOT HAVE THE SAME ROT WHICH BRED CIVIL WAR SPREAD HERE...
AS FOR YOU, JESSICA. CECILIA HAS BOUGHT YOU TIME...
BUT LET THIS BE A REMINDER THAT THE ORDER DOES NOT FAVOR DISAPPOINTMENTS.

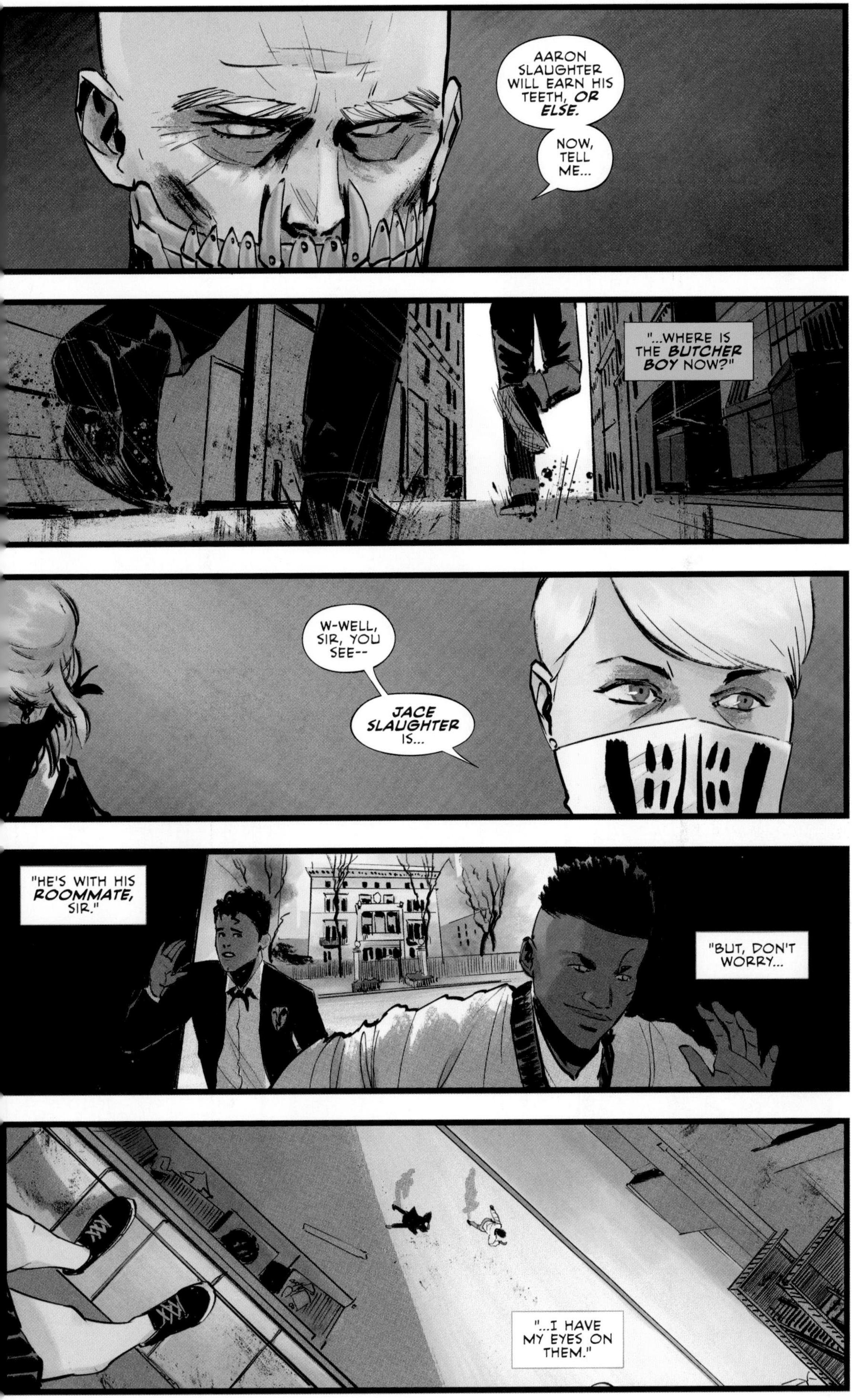
AARON SLAUGHTER WILL EARN HIS TEETH, OR ELSE.
NOW, TELL ME...
"...WHERE IS THE BUTCHER BOY NOW?"
W-WELL, SIR, YOU SEE--
JACE SLAUGHTER IS...
"HE'S WITH HIS ROOMMATE, SIR."
"BUT, DON'T WORRY...
"...I HAVE MY EYES ON THEM."

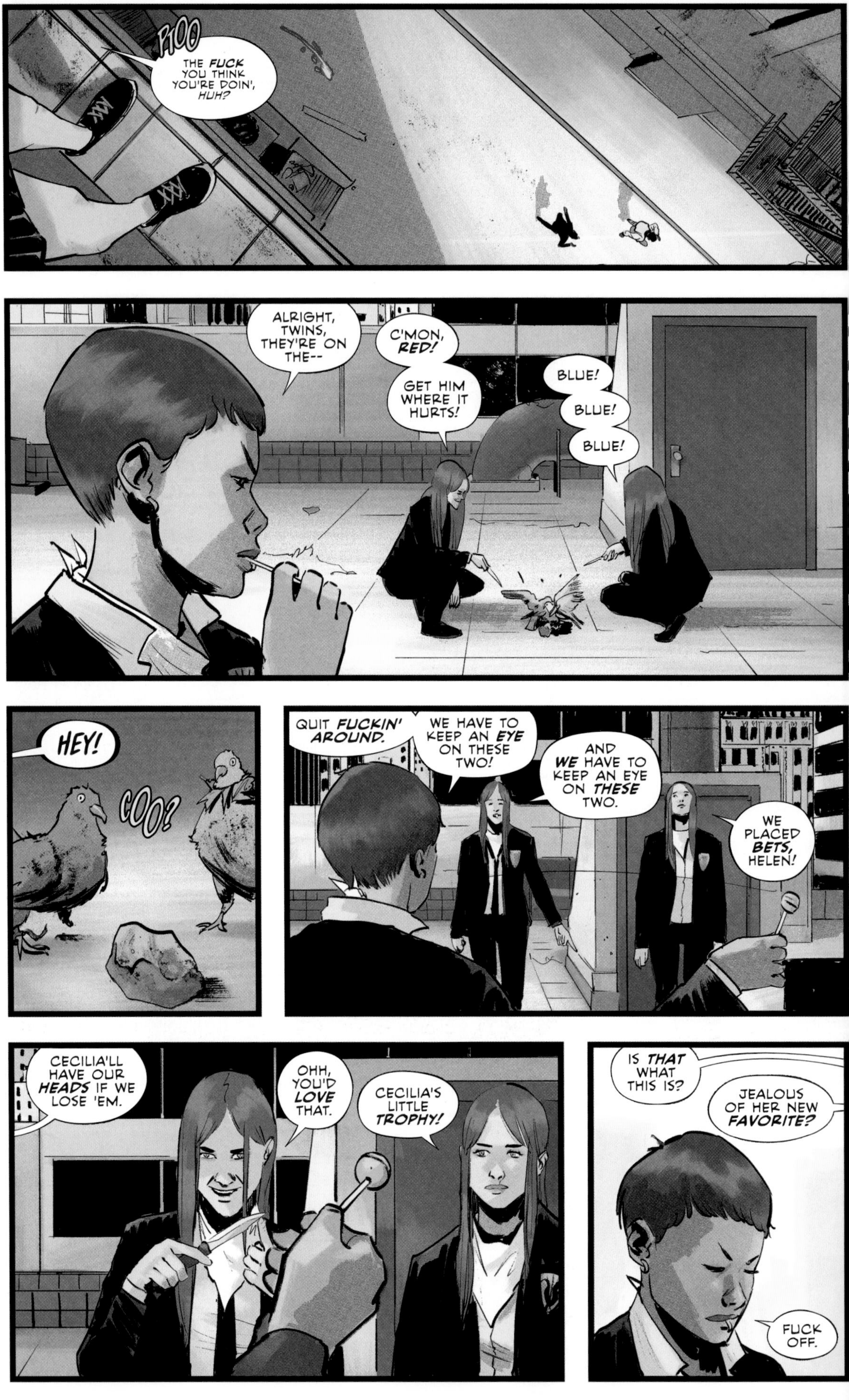
PTOO
THE FUCK YOU THINK YOU'RE DOIN', HUH?
ALRIGHT, TWINS, THEY'RE ON THE--
C'MON, RED!
GET HIM WHERE IT HURTS!
BLUE!
BLUE!
BLUE!
HEY!
COO?
QUIT FUCKIN' AROUND.
WE HAVE TO KEEP AN EYE ON THESE TWO!
AND WE HAVE TO KEEP AN EYE ON THESE TWO.
WE PLACED BETS, HELEN!
CECILIA'LL HAVE OUR HEADS IF WE LOSE 'EM.
OHH, YOU'D LOVE THAT.
CECILIA'S LITTLE TROPHY!
IS THAT WHAT THIS IS?
JEALOUS OF HER NEW FAVORITE?
FUCK OFF.

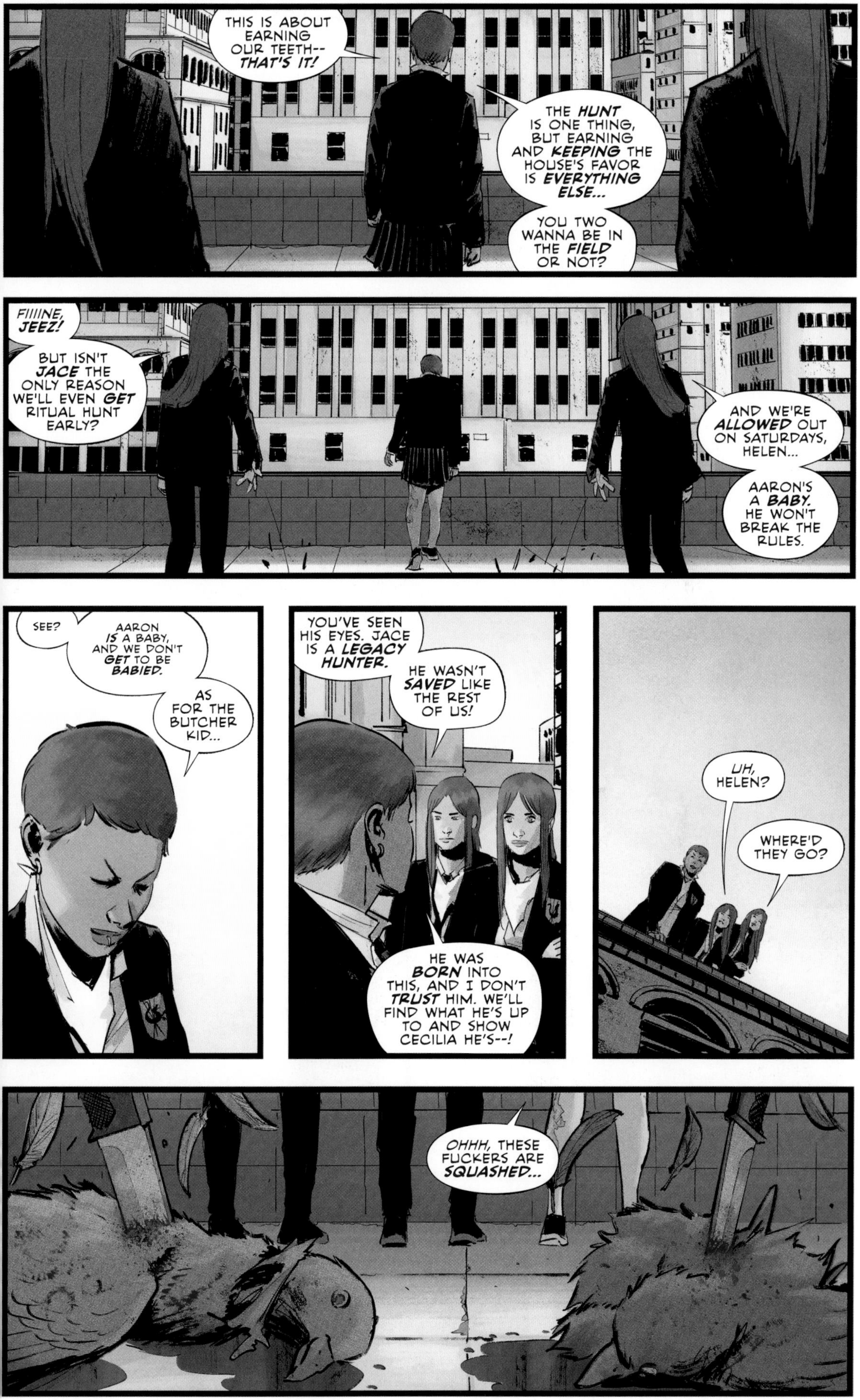
THIS IS ABOUT EARNING OUR TEETH-- THAT'S IT!
THE HUNT IS ONE THING, BUT EARNING AND KEEPING THE HOUSE'S FAVOR IS EVERYTHING ELSE...
YOU TWO WANNA BE IN THE FIELD OR NOT?
FIIIINE, JEEZ!
BUT ISN'T JACE THE ONLY REASON WE'LL EVEN GET RITUAL HUNT EARLY?
AND WE'RE ALLOWED OUT ON SATURDAYS, HELEN...
AARON'S A BABY. HE WON'T BREAK THE RULES.
SEE?
AARON IS A BABY, AND WE DON'T GET TO BE BABIED.
AS FOR THE BUTCHER KID...
YOU'VE SEEN HIS EYES. JACE IS A LEGACY HUNTER.
HE WASN'T SAVED LIKE THE REST OF US!
HE WAS BORN INTO THIS, AND I DON'T TRUST HIM. WE'LL FIND WHAT HE'S UP TO AND SHOW CECILIA HE'S--!
UH, HELEN?
WHERE'D THEY GO?
OHHH, THESE FUCKERS ARE SQUASHED...

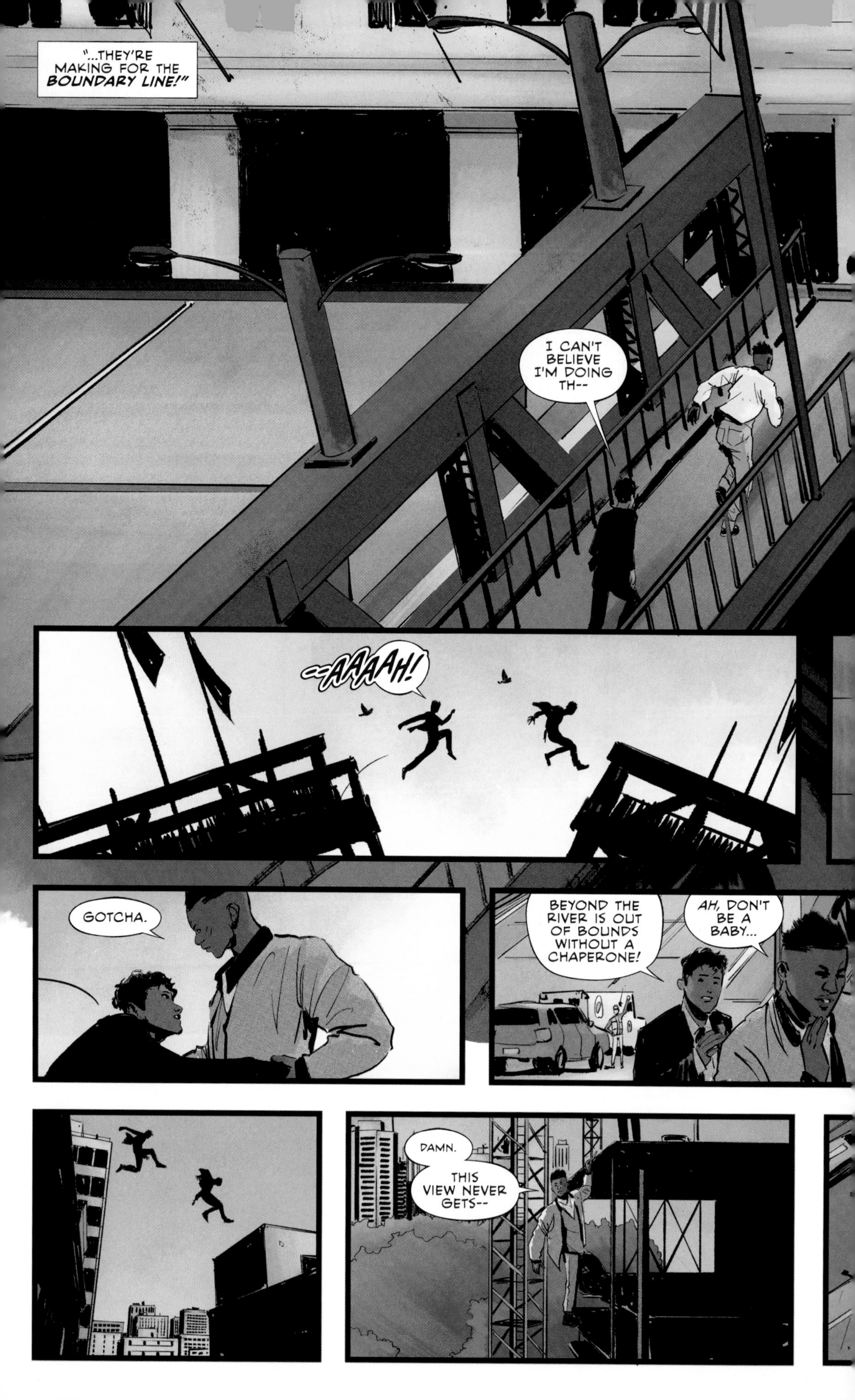
"...THEY'RE MAKING FOR THE *BOUNDARY LINE!*"
I CAN'T BELIEVE I'M DOING TH--
--AAAAAH!
GOTCHA.
BEYOND THE RIVER IS OUT OF BOUNDS WITHOUT A CHAPERONE!
AH, DON'T BE A BABY...
DAMN.
THIS VIEW NEVER GETS--

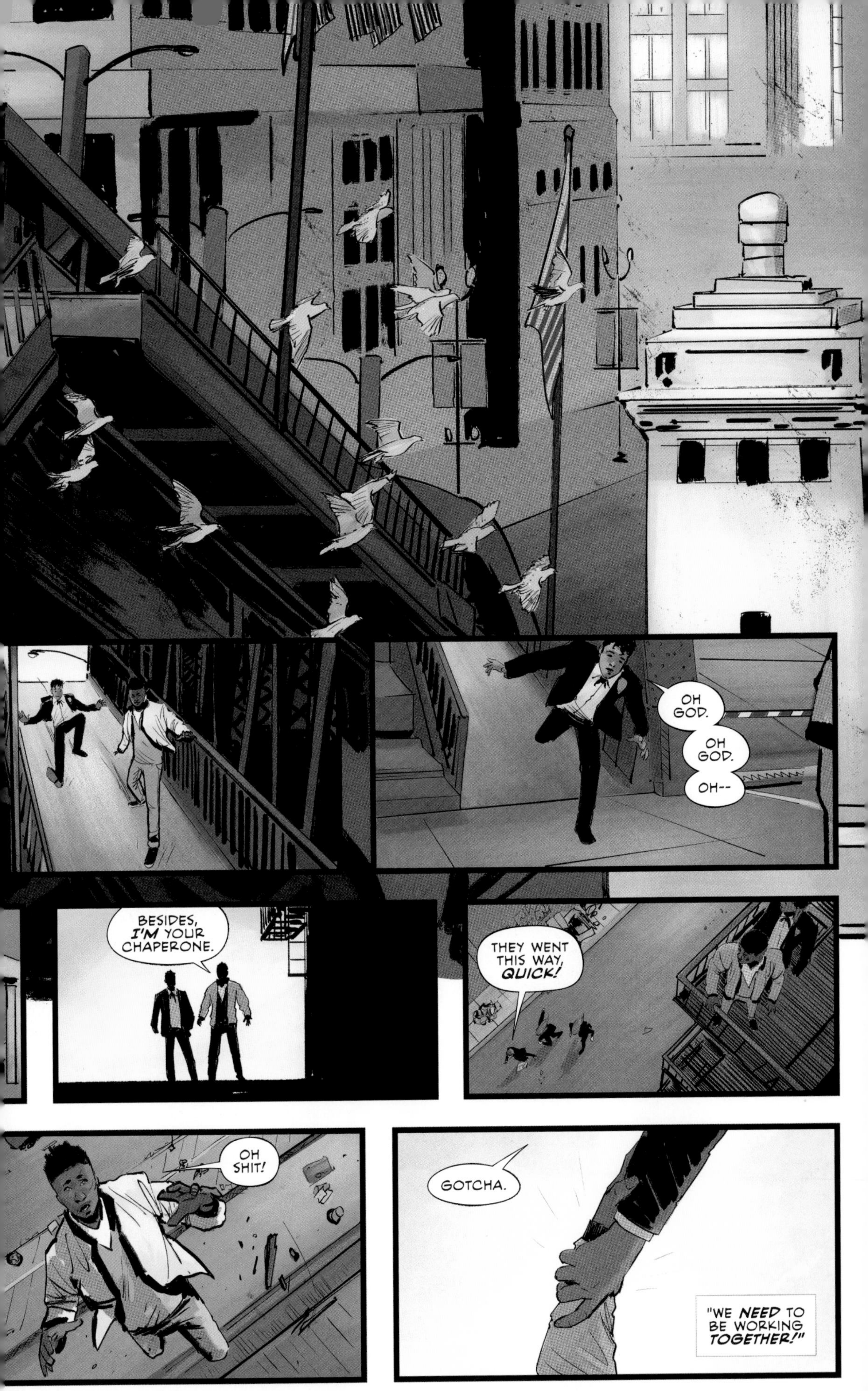
OH GOD.
OH GOD.
OH--
BESIDES, I'M YOUR CHAPERONE.
THEY WENT THIS WAY, QUICK!
OH SHIT!
GOTCHA.
"WE NEED TO BE WORKING TOGETHER!"

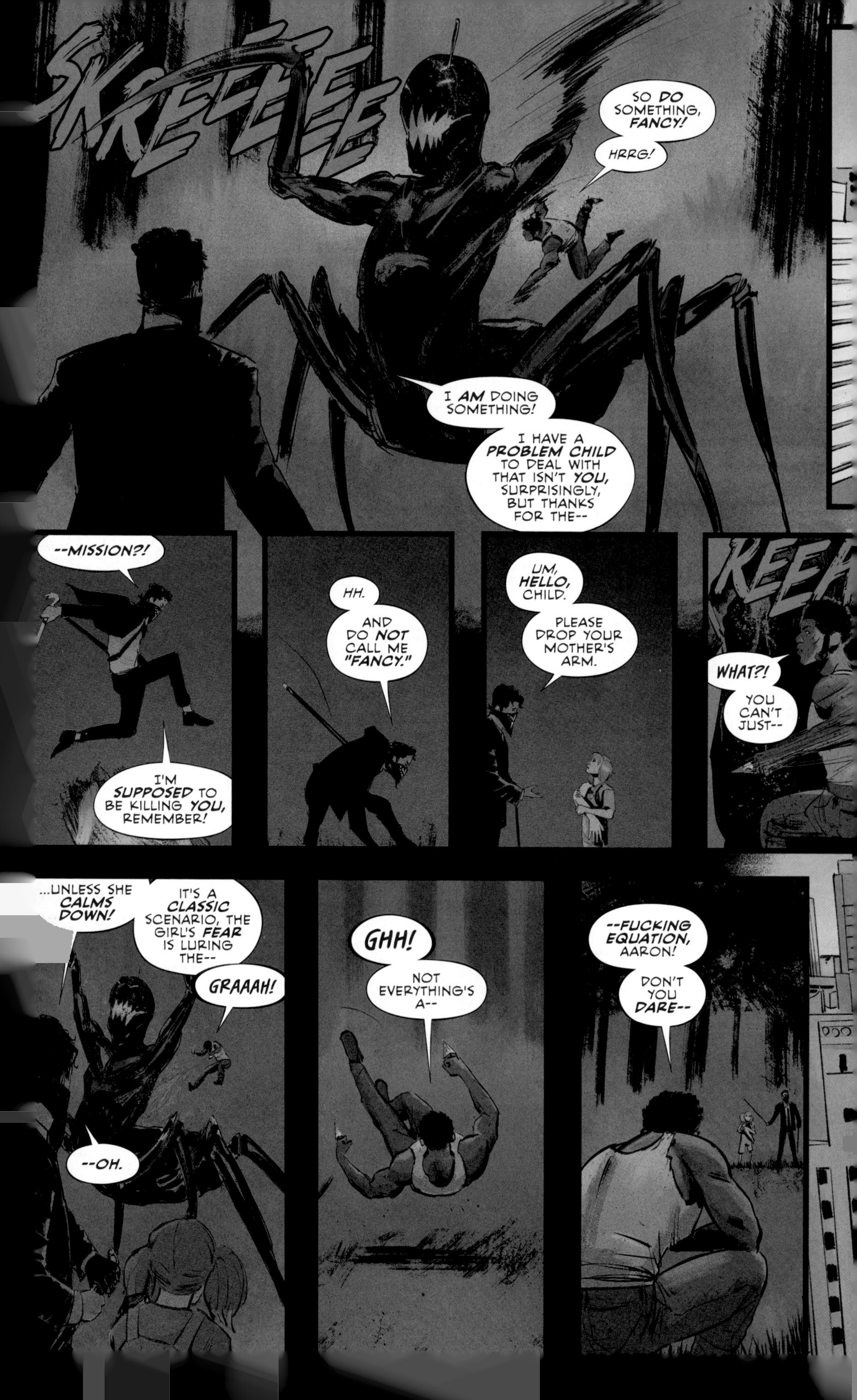
SKREEEE
SO DO SOMETHING, FANCY!
HRRG!
I AM DOING SOMETHING!
I HAVE A PROBLEM CHILD TO DEAL WITH THAT ISN'T YOU, SURPRISINGLY, BUT THANKS FOR THE--
--MISSION?!
I'M SUPPOSED TO BE KILLING YOU, REMEMBER!
HH.
AND DO NOT CALL ME "FANCY."
UM, HELLO, CHILD.
PLEASE DROP YOUR MOTHER'S ARM.
WHAT?!
YOU CAN'T JUST--
IT'S A CLASSIC SCENARIO, THE GIRL'S FEAR IS LURING THE--
...UNLESS SHE CALMS DOWN!
GRAAAH!
--OH.
GHH!
NOT EVERYTHING'S A--
--FUCKING EQUATION, AARON!
DON'T YOU DARE--

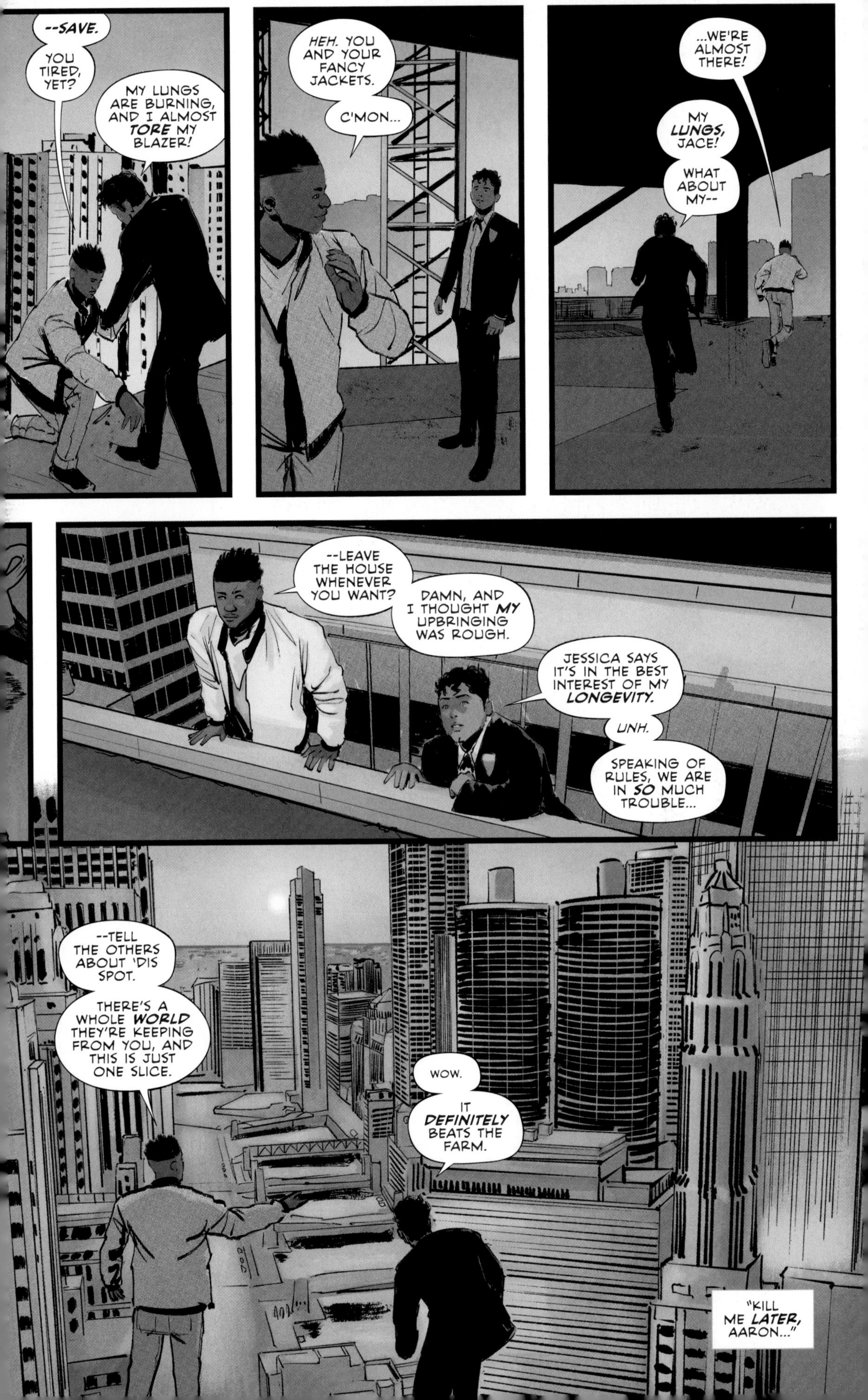
--SAVE.
YOU TIRED, YET?
MY LUNGS ARE BURNING, AND I ALMOST TORE MY BLAZER!
HEH. YOU AND YOUR FANCY JACKETS.
C'MON...
...WE'RE ALMOST THERE!
MY LUNGS, JACE!
WHAT ABOUT MY--
--LEAVE THE HOUSE WHENEVER YOU WANT?
DAMN, AND I THOUGHT MY UPBRINGING WAS ROUGH.
JESSICA SAYS IT'S IN THE BEST INTEREST OF MY LONGEVITY.
UNH.
SPEAKING OF RULES, WE ARE IN SO MUCH TROUBLE...
--TELL THE OTHERS ABOUT 'DIS SPOT.
THERE'S A WHOLE WORLD THEY'RE KEEPING FROM YOU, AND THIS IS JUST ONE SLICE.
WOW.
IT DEFINITELY BEATS THE FARM.
"KILL ME LATER, AARON..."

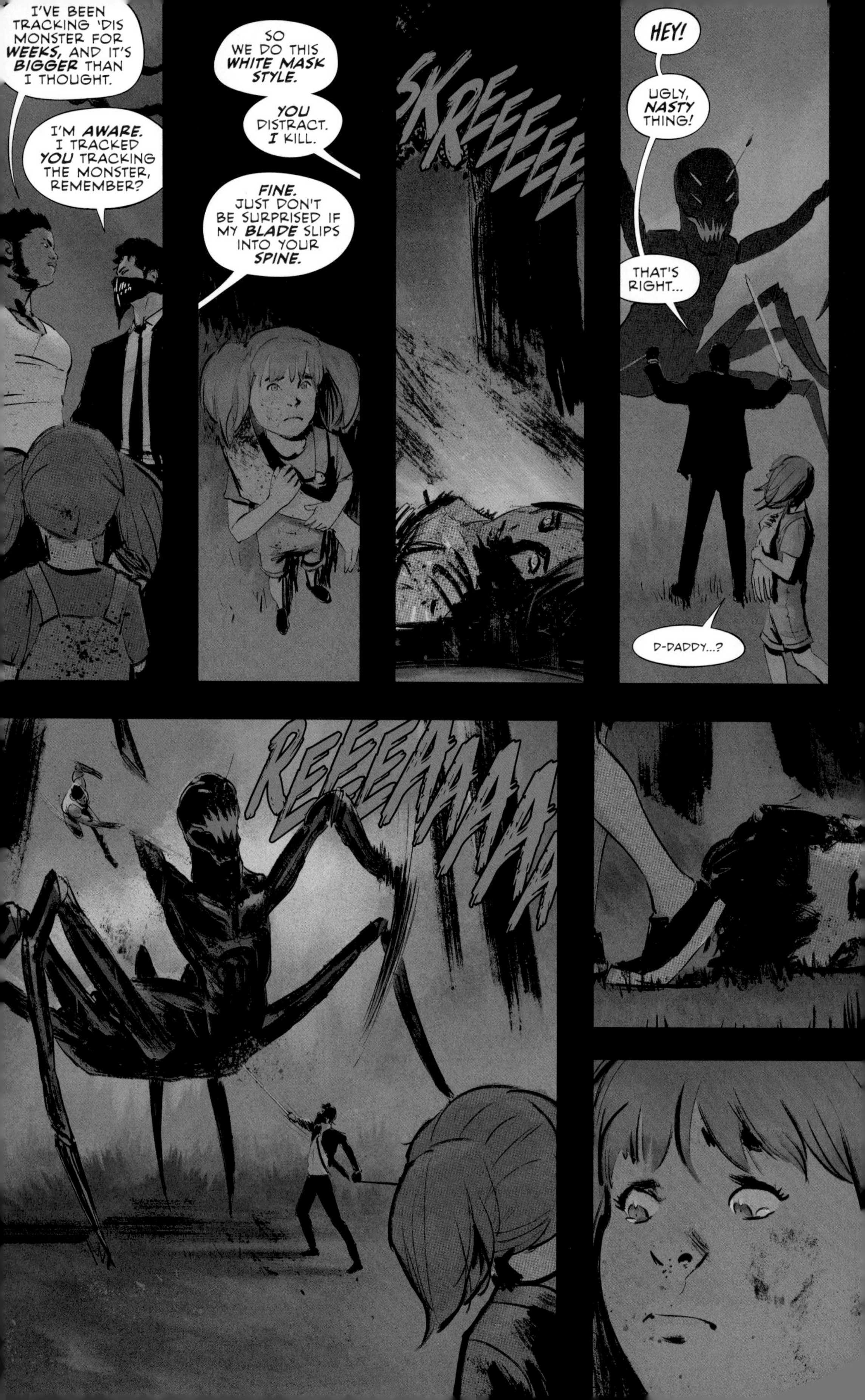
I'VE BEEN TRACKING 'DIS MONSTER FOR WEEKS, AND IT'S BIGGER THAN I THOUGHT.
I'M AWARE. I TRACKED YOU TRACKING THE MONSTER, REMEMBER?
SO WE DO THIS WHITE MASK STYLE.
YOU DISTRACT. I KILL.
FINE. JUST DON'T BE SURPRISED IF MY BLADE SLIPS INTO YOUR SPINE.
SKREEEEEE
HEY!
UGLY, NASTY THING!
THAT'S RIGHT...
D-DADDY...?
REEEAAAA

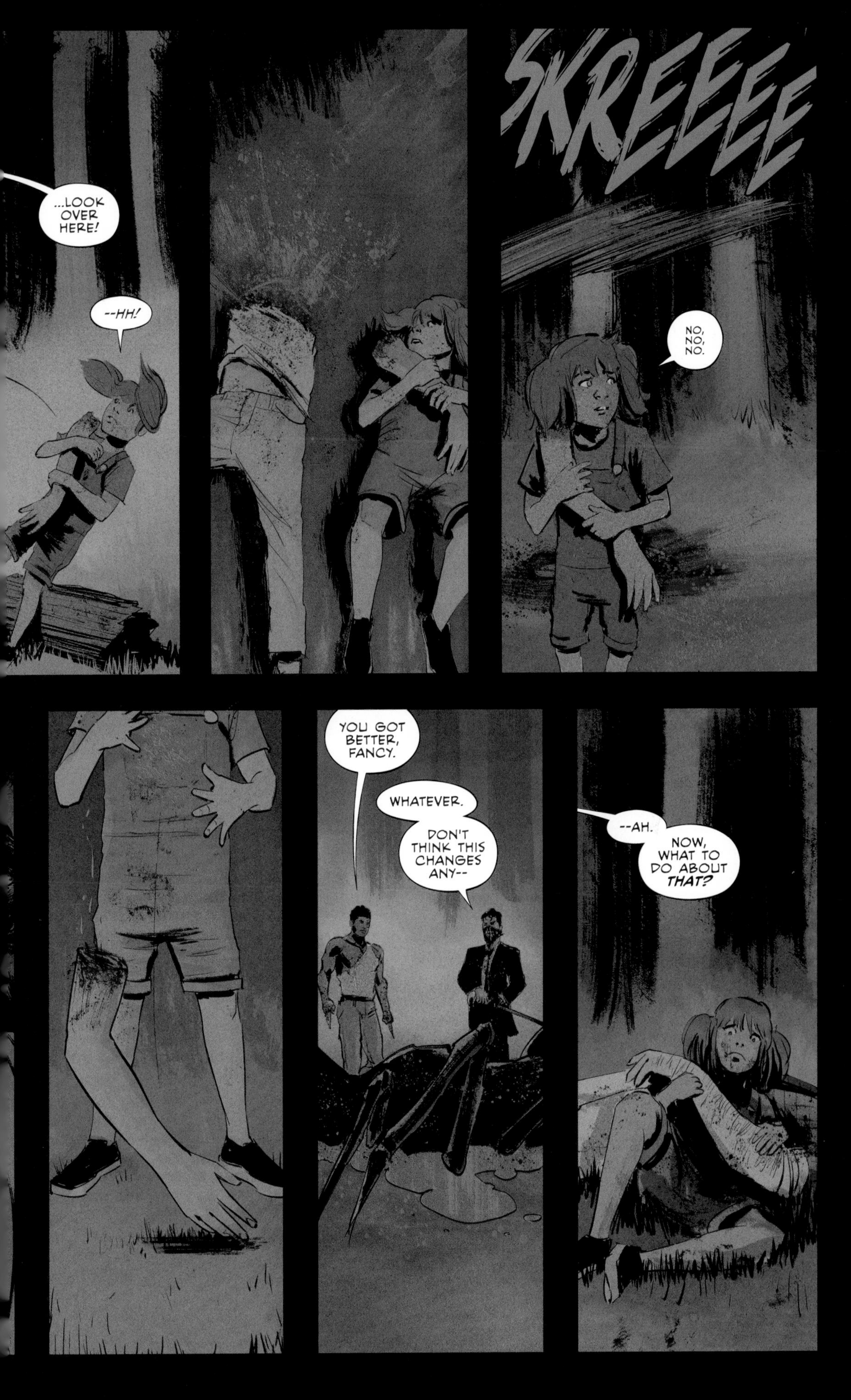
...LOOK OVER HERE!
--HH!
SKREEEE
NO, NO, NO.
YOU GOT BETTER, FANCY.
WHATEVER.
DON'T THINK THIS CHANGES ANY--
--AH.
NOW, WHAT TO DO ABOUT *THAT?*

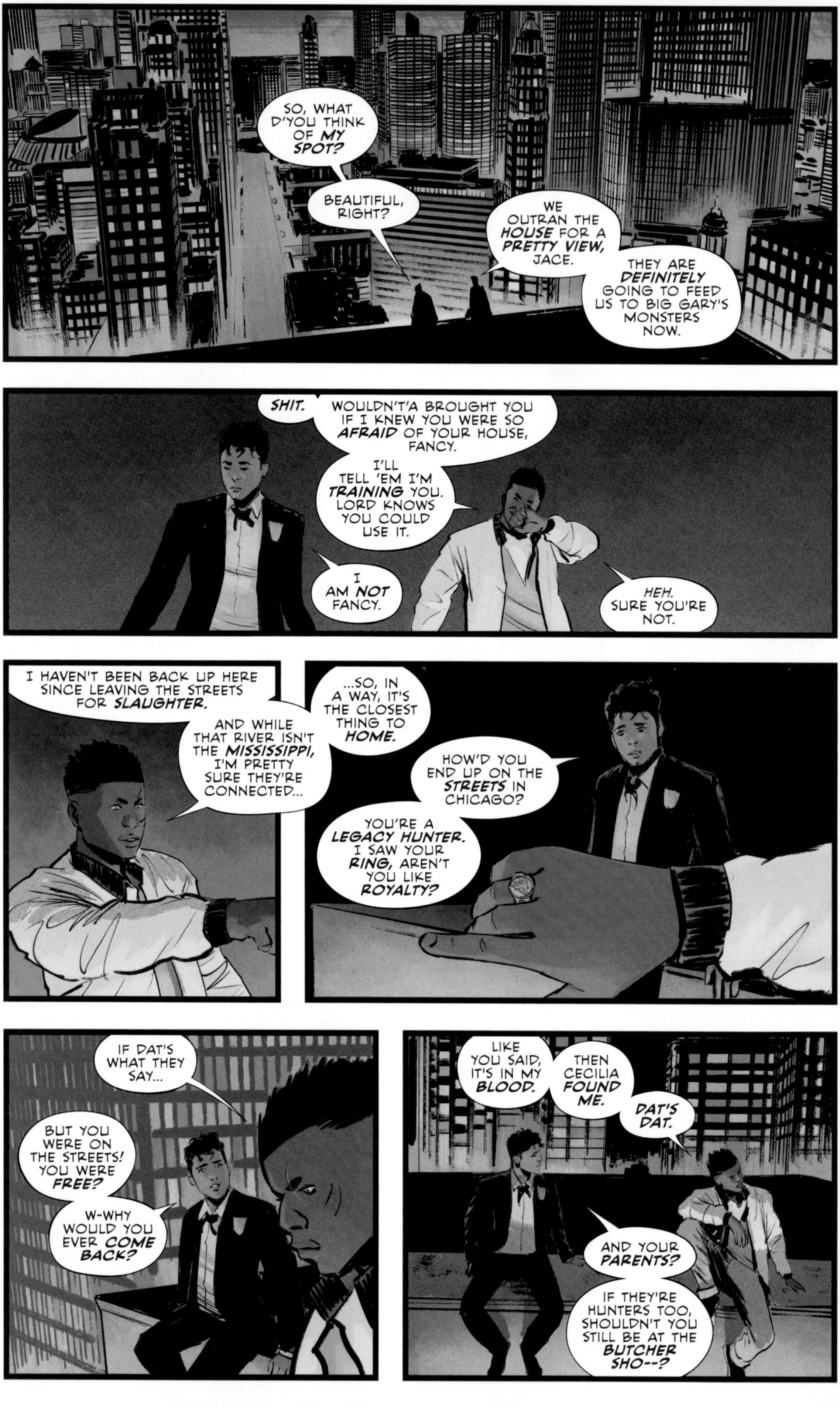

SO, WHAT D'YOU THINK OF MY SPOT?
BEAUTIFUL, RIGHT?
WE OUTRAN THE HOUSE FOR A PRETTY VIEW, JACE.
THEY ARE DEFINITELY GOING TO FEED US TO BIG GARY'S MONSTERS NOW.
SHIT.
WOULDN'T'A BROUGHT YOU IF I KNEW YOU WERE SO AFRAID OF YOUR HOUSE, FANCY.
I'LL TELL 'EM I'M TRAINING YOU. LORD KNOWS YOU COULD USE IT.
I AM NOT FANCY.
HEH. SURE YOU'RE NOT.
I HAVEN'T BEEN BACK UP HERE SINCE LEAVING THE STREETS FOR SLAUGHTER.
AND WHILE THAT RIVER ISN'T THE MISSISSIPPI, I'M PRETTY SURE THEY'RE CONNECTED...
...SO, IN A WAY, IT'S THE CLOSEST THING TO HOME.
HOW'D YOU END UP ON THE STREETS IN CHICAGO?
YOU'RE A LEGACY HUNTER. I SAW YOUR RING, AREN'T YOU LIKE ROYALTY?
IF DAT'S WHAT THEY SAY...
BUT YOU WERE ON THE STREETS! YOU WERE FREE?
W-WHY WOULD YOU EVER COME BACK?
LIKE YOU SAID, IT'S IN MY BLOOD.
THEN CECILIA FOUND ME.
DAT'S DAT.
AND YOUR PARENTS?
IF THEY'RE HUNTERS TOO, SHOULDN'T YOU STILL BE AT THE BUTCHER SHO--?

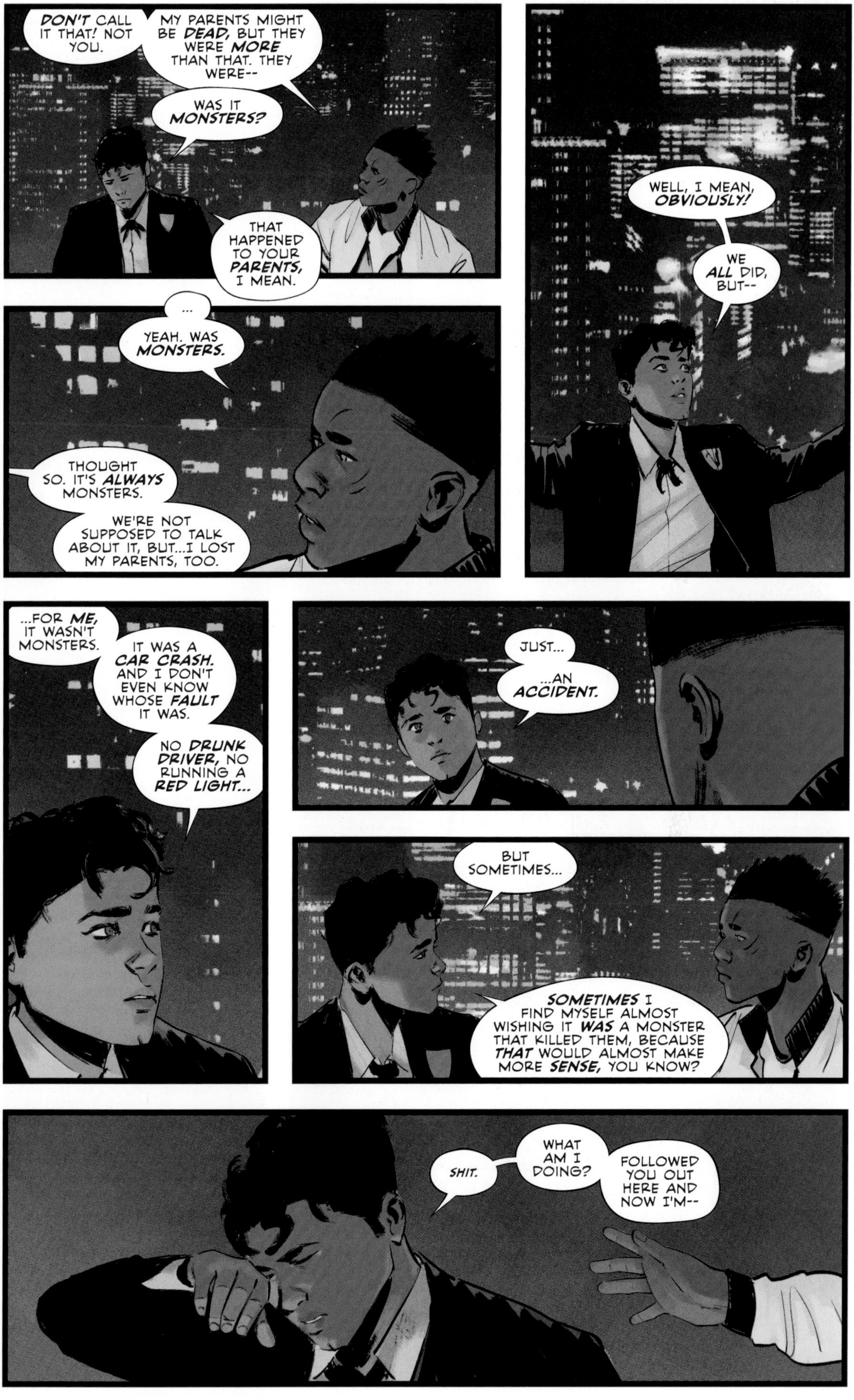
DON'T CALL IT THAT! NOT YOU.
MY PARENTS MIGHT BE DEAD, BUT THEY WERE MORE THAN THAT. THEY WERE--
WAS IT MONSTERS?
THAT HAPPENED TO YOUR PARENTS, I MEAN.
WELL, I MEAN, OBVIOUSLY!
WE ALL DID, BUT--
...
YEAH. WAS MONSTERS.
THOUGHT SO. IT'S ALWAYS MONSTERS.
WE'RE NOT SUPPOSED TO TALK ABOUT IT, BUT...I LOST MY PARENTS, TOO.
...FOR ME, IT WASN'T MONSTERS.
IT WAS A CAR CRASH. AND I DON'T EVEN KNOW WHOSE FAULT IT WAS.
NO DRUNK DRIVER, NO RUNNING A RED LIGHT...
JUST...
...AN ACCIDENT.
BUT SOMETIMES...
SOMETIMES I FIND MYSELF ALMOST WISHING IT WAS A MONSTER THAT KILLED THEM, BECAUSE THAT WOULD ALMOST MAKE MORE SENSE, YOU KNOW?
SHIT.
WHAT AM I DOING?
FOLLOWED YOU OUT HERE AND NOW I'M--

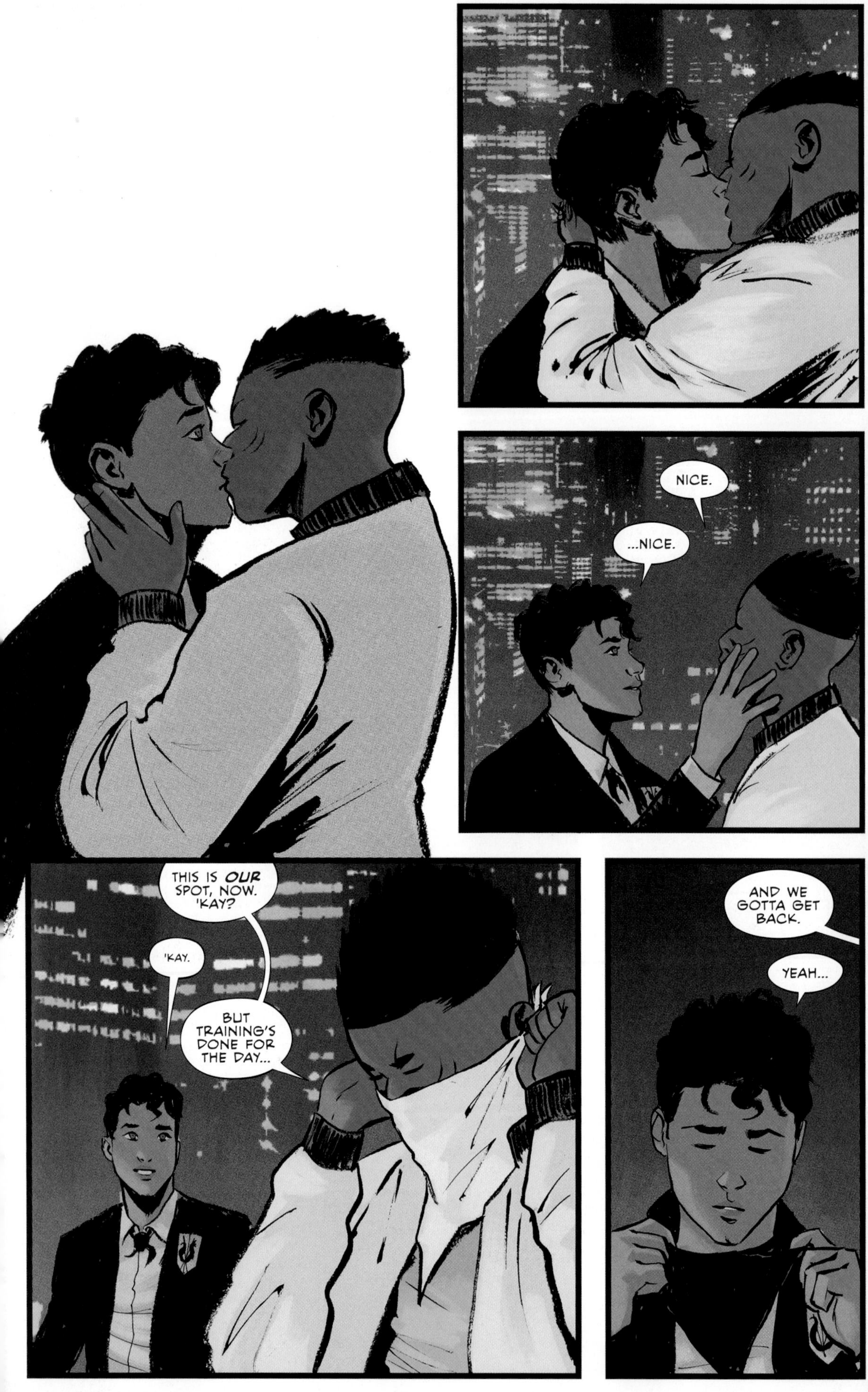
NICE.
...NICE.
THIS IS OUR SPOT, NOW. 'KAY?
'KAY.
BUT TRAINING'S DONE FOR THE DAY...
AND WE GOTTA GET BACK.
YEAH...

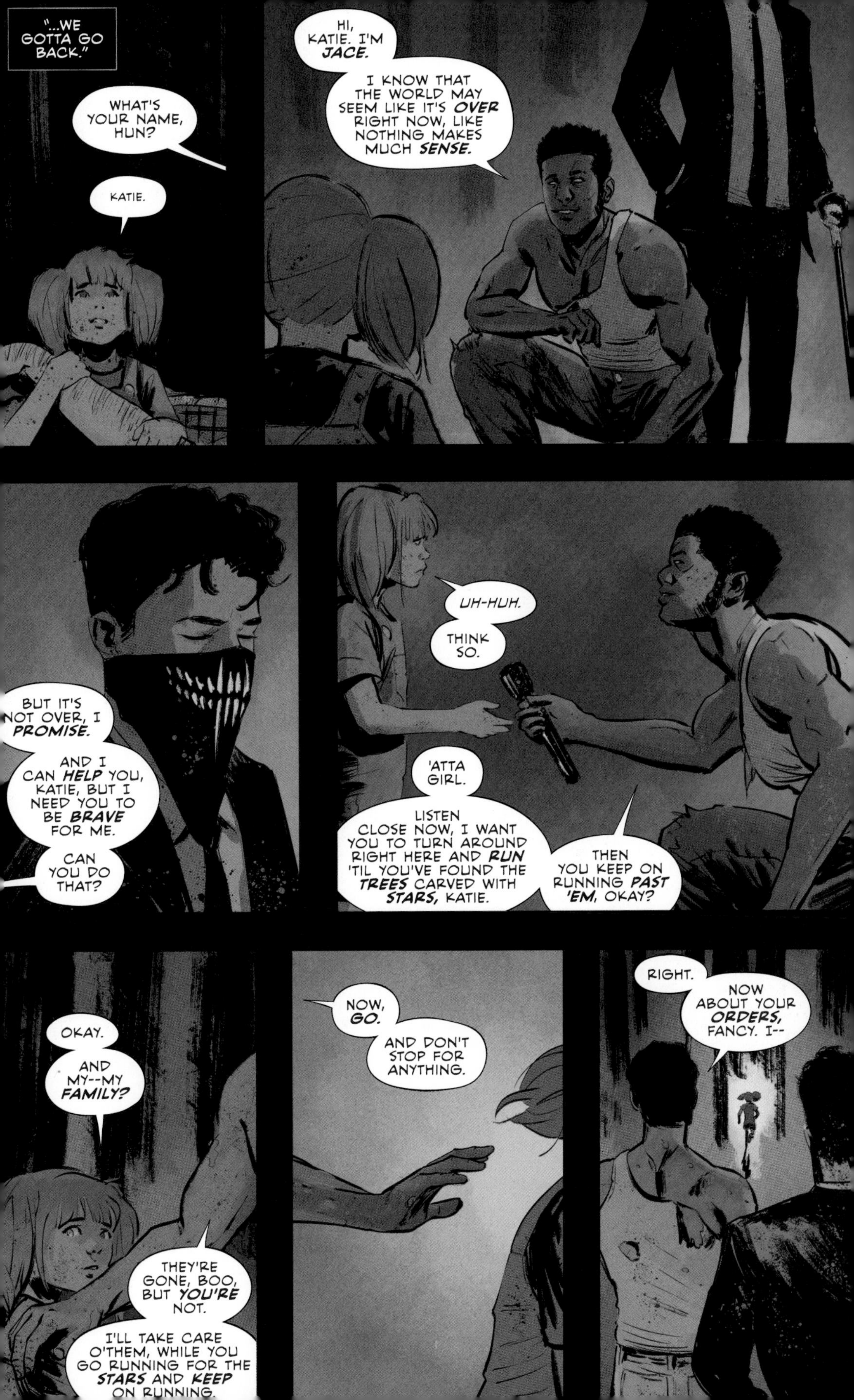
"...WE GOTTA GO BACK."
WHAT'S YOUR NAME, HUN?
KATIE.
HI, KATIE. I'M JACE.
I KNOW THAT THE WORLD MAY SEEM LIKE IT'S OVER RIGHT NOW, LIKE NOTHING MAKES MUCH SENSE.
BUT IT'S NOT OVER, I PROMISE.
AND I CAN HELP YOU, KATIE, BUT I NEED YOU TO BE BRAVE FOR ME.
CAN YOU DO THAT?
UH-HUH.
THINK SO.
'ATTA GIRL.
LISTEN CLOSE NOW, I WANT YOU TO TURN AROUND RIGHT HERE AND RUN 'TIL YOU'VE FOUND THE TREES CARVED WITH STARS, KATIE.
THEN YOU KEEP ON RUNNING PAST 'EM, OKAY?
OKAY.
AND MY--MY FAMILY?
THEY'RE GONE, BOO, BUT YOU'RE NOT.
I'LL TAKE CARE O'THEM, WHILE YOU GO RUNNING FOR THE STARS AND KEEP ON RUNNING.
NOW, GO.
AND DON'T STOP FOR ANYTHING.
RIGHT.
NOW ABOUT YOUR ORDERS, FANCY. I--

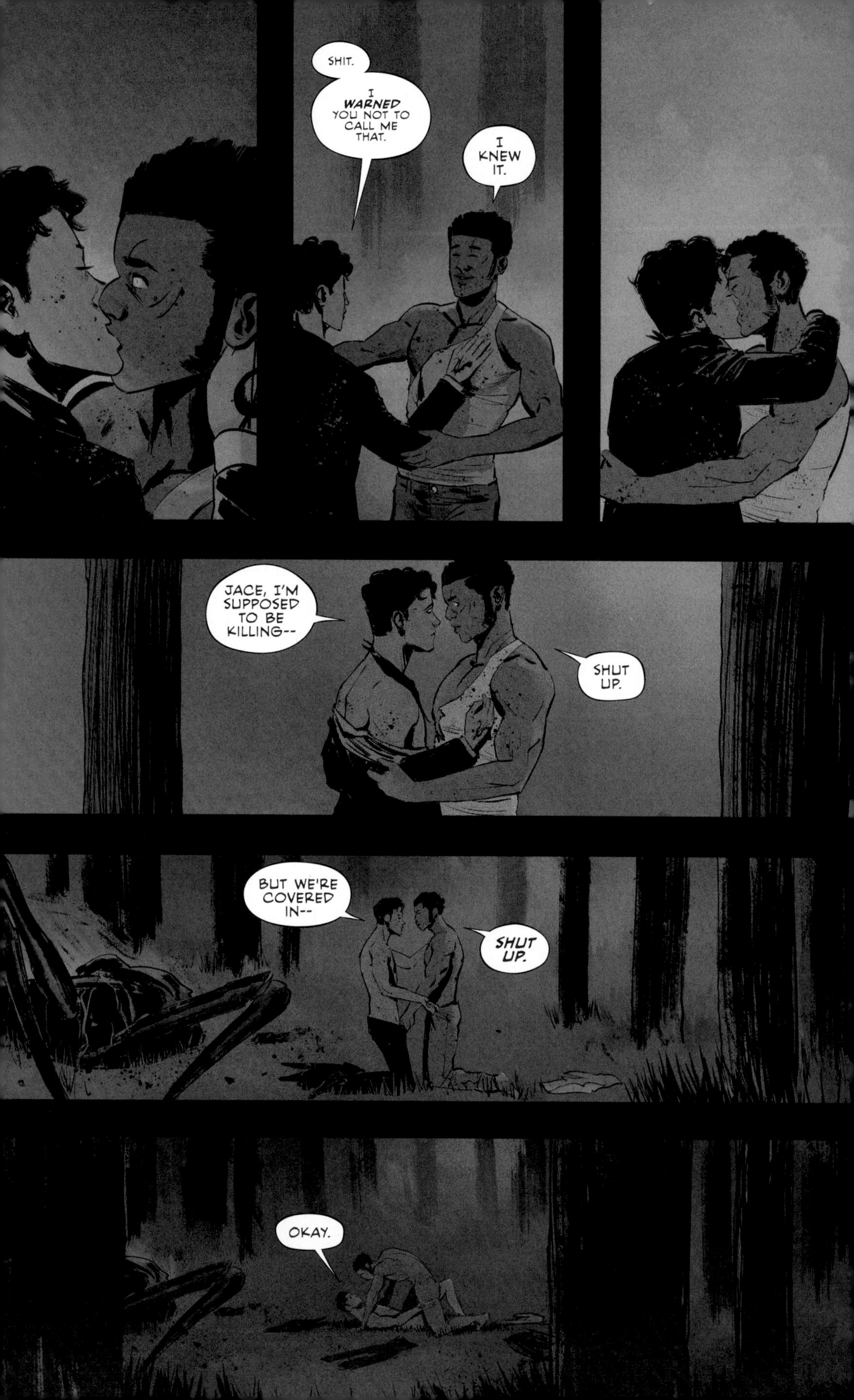
SHIT.
I WARNED YOU NOT TO CALL ME THAT.
I KNEW IT.
JACE, I'M SUPPOSED TO BE KILLING--
SHUT UP.
BUT WE'RE COVERED IN--
SHUT UP.
OKAY.

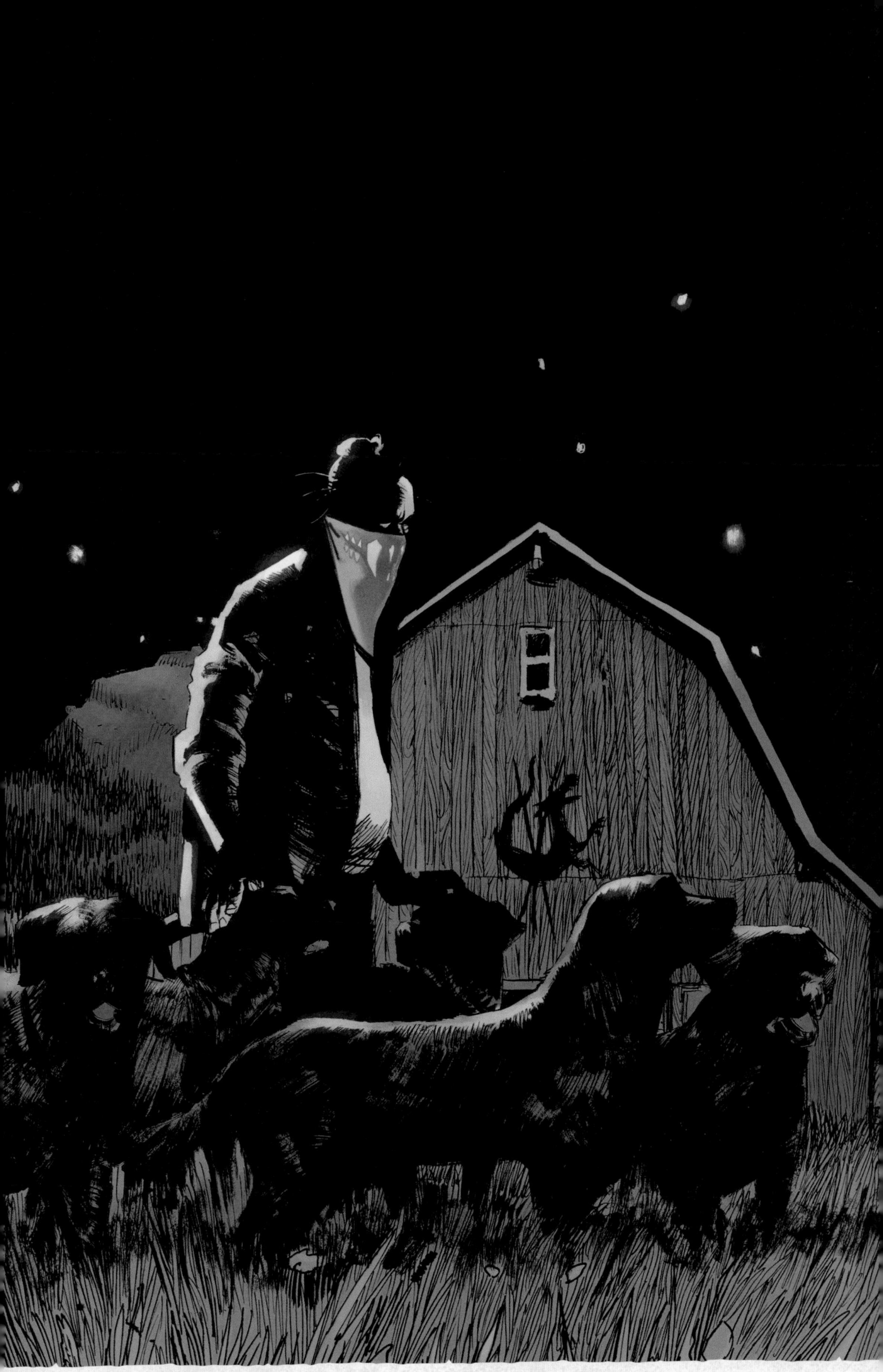

ISSUE THREE COVER BY WERTHER DELL'EDERA WITH COLORS BY MIQUEL MUERTO

PART FOUR

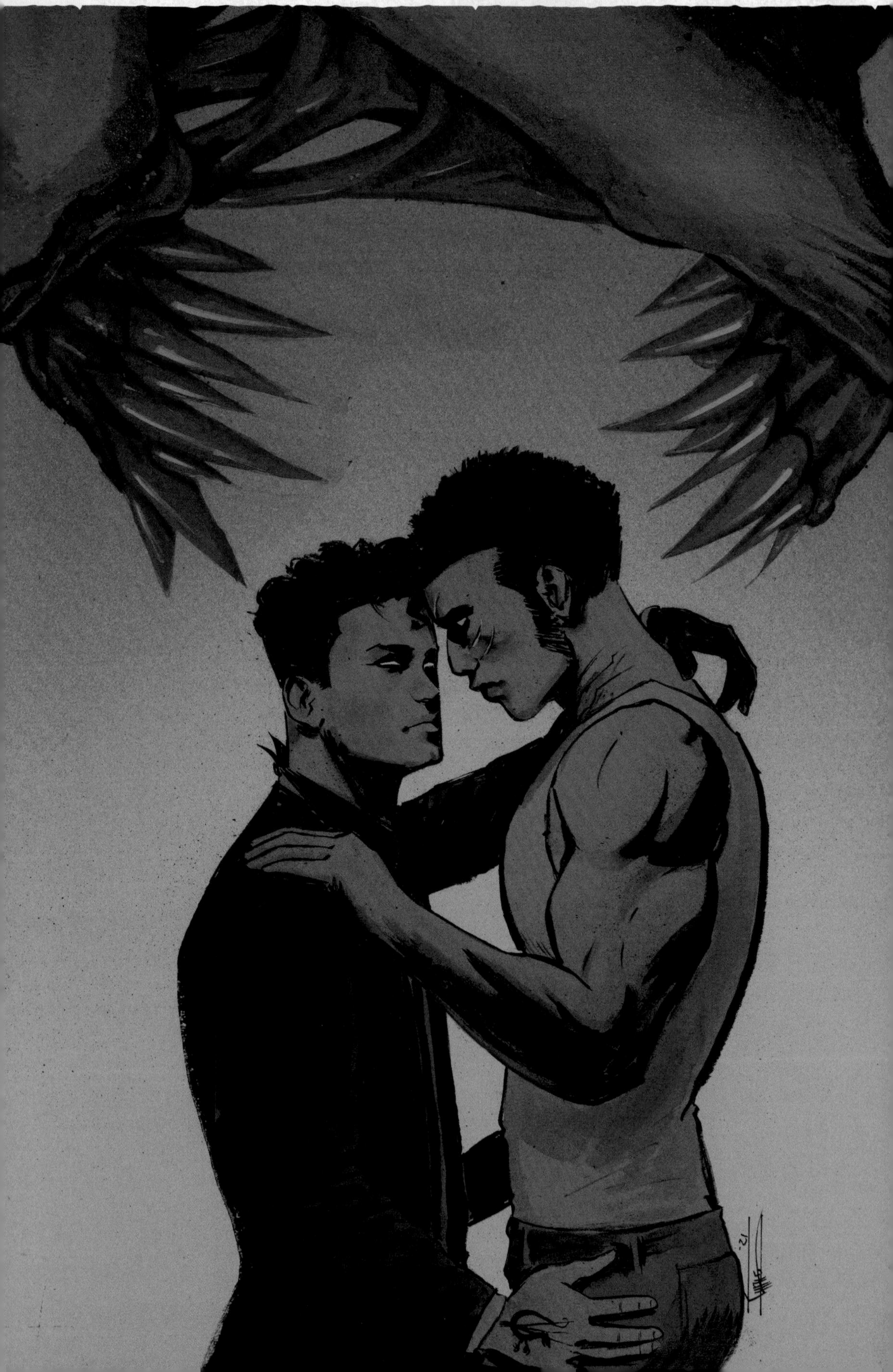

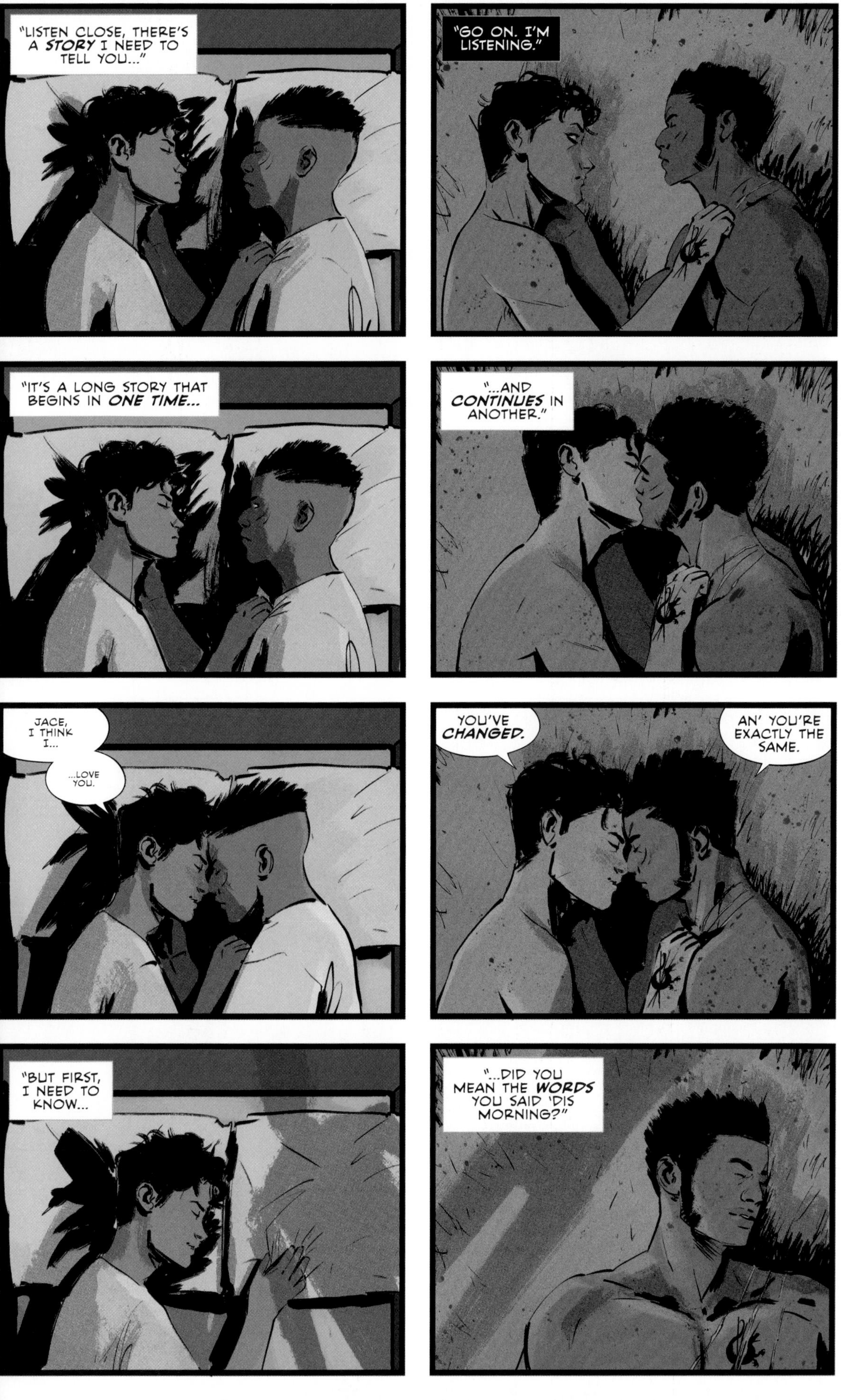
"LISTEN CLOSE, THERE'S A STORY I NEED TO TELL YOU..."
"GO ON. I'M LISTENING."
"IT'S A LONG STORY THAT BEGINS IN ONE TIME...
"...AND CONTINUES IN ANOTHER."
JACE, I THINK I...
...LOVE YOU.
YOU'VE CHANGED.
AN' YOU'RE EXACTLY THE SAME.
"BUT FIRST, I NEED TO KNOW...
"...DID YOU MEAN THE WORDS YOU SAID 'DIS MORNING?"

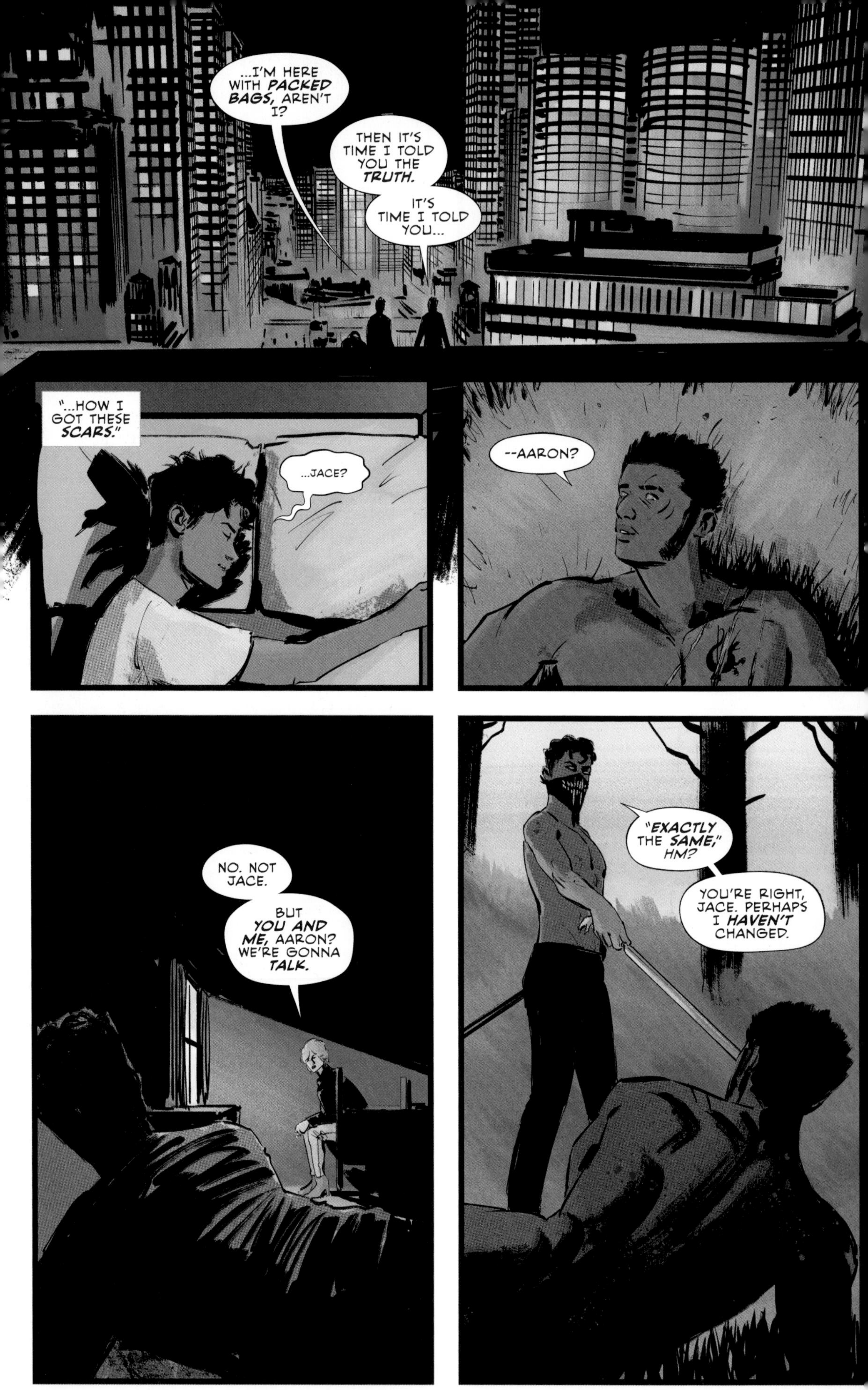
...I'M HERE WITH PACKED BAGS, AREN'T I?
THEN IT'S TIME I TOLD YOU THE TRUTH.
IT'S TIME I TOLD YOU...
"...HOW I GOT THESE SCARS."
...JACE?
--AARON?
NO. NOT JACE.
BUT YOU AND ME, AARON? WE'RE GONNA TALK.
"EXACTLY THE SAME," HM?
YOU'RE RIGHT, JACE. PERHAPS I HAVEN'T CHANGED.

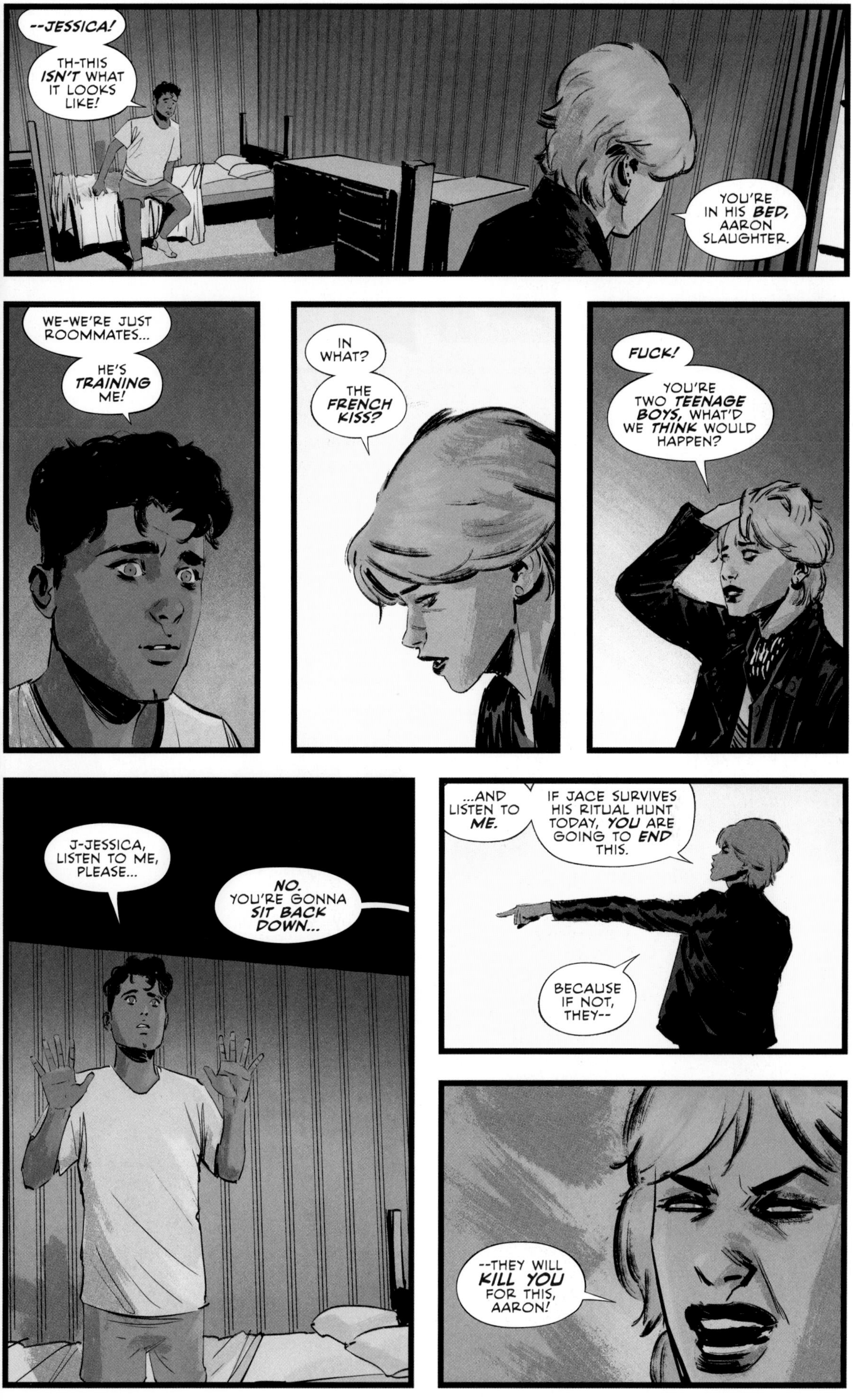
--JESSICA!
TH-THIS ISN'T WHAT IT LOOKS LIKE!
YOU'RE IN HIS BED, AARON SLAUGHTER.
WE-WE'RE JUST ROOMMATES...
HE'S TRAINING ME!
IN WHAT?
THE FRENCH KISS?
FUCK!
YOU'RE TWO TEENAGE BOYS, WHAT'D WE THINK WOULD HAPPEN?
J-JESSICA, LISTEN TO ME, PLEASE...
NO. YOU'RE GONNA SIT BACK DOWN...
...AND LISTEN TO ME.
IF JACE SURVIVES HIS RITUAL HUNT TODAY, YOU ARE GOING TO END THIS.
BECAUSE IF NOT, THEY--
--THEY WILL KILL YOU FOR THIS, AARON!

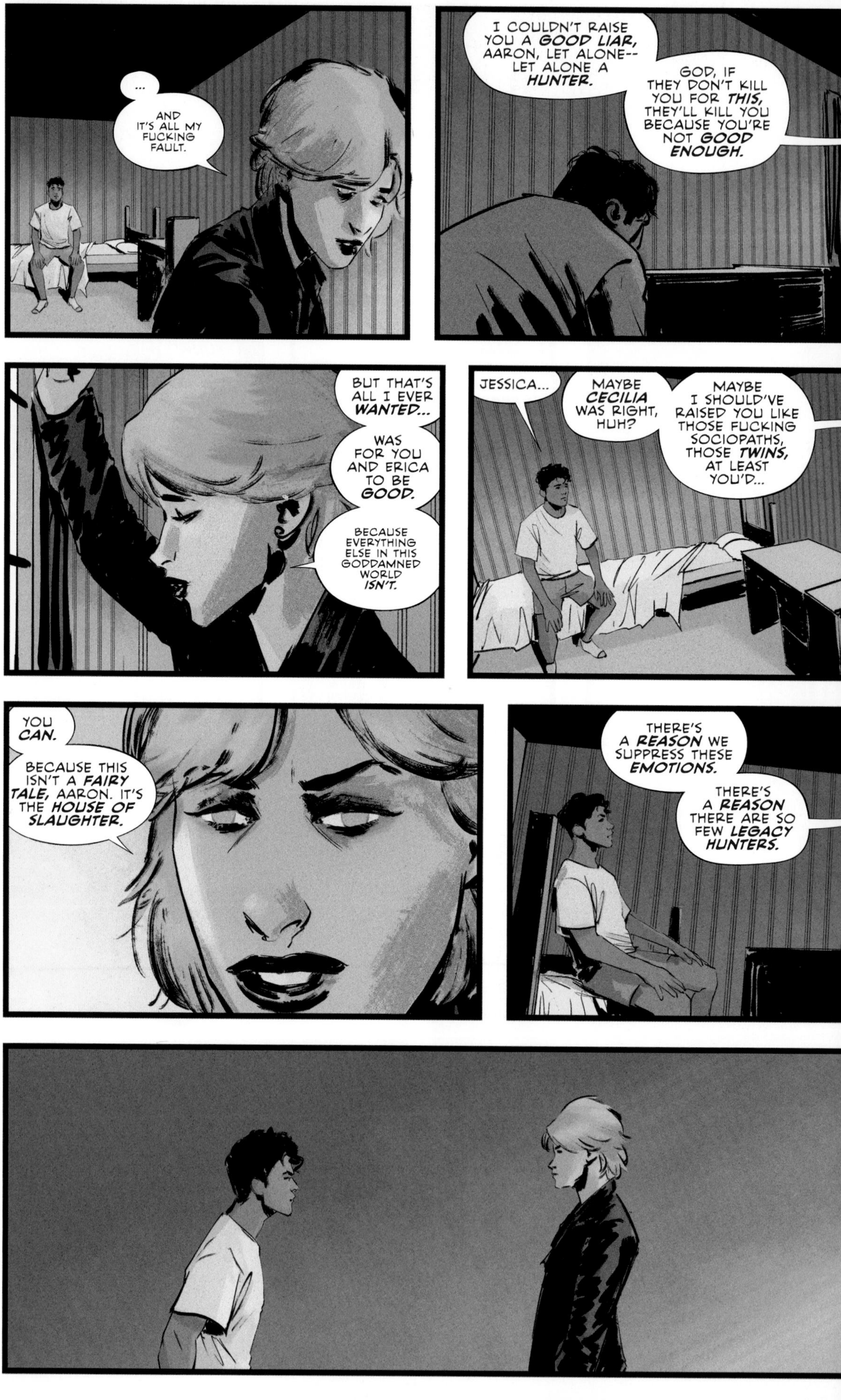
...
AND IT'S ALL MY FUCKING FAULT.
I COULDN'T RAISE YOU A GOOD LIAR, AARON, LET ALONE-- LET ALONE A HUNTER.
GOD, IF THEY DON'T KILL YOU FOR THIS, THEY'LL KILL YOU BECAUSE YOU'RE NOT GOOD ENOUGH.
BUT THAT'S ALL I EVER WANTED...
WAS FOR YOU AND ERICA TO BE GOOD.
BECAUSE EVERYTHING ELSE IN THIS GODDAMNED WORLD ISN'T.
JESSICA...
MAYBE CECILIA WAS RIGHT, HUH?
MAYBE I SHOULD'VE RAISED YOU LIKE THOSE FUCKING SOCIOPATHS, THOSE TWINS, AT LEAST YOU'D...
YOU CAN.
BECAUSE THIS ISN'T A FAIRY TALE, AARON. IT'S THE HOUSE OF SLAUGHTER.
THERE'S A REASON WE SUPPRESS THESE EMOTIONS.
THERE'S A REASON THERE ARE SO FEW LEGACY HUNTERS.

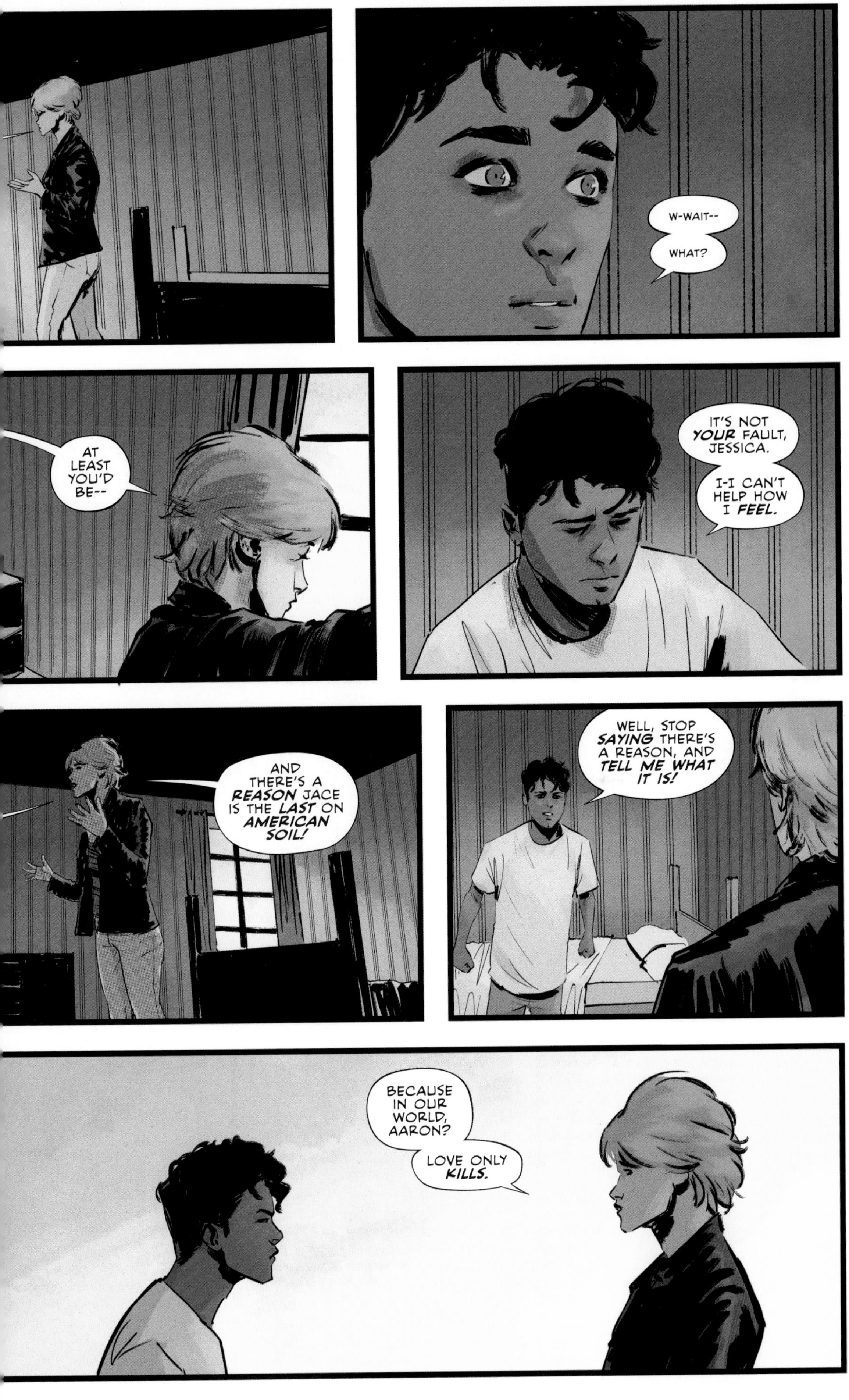

W-WAIT--
WHAT?
AT LEAST YOU'D BE--
IT'S NOT YOUR FAULT, JESSICA.
I-I CAN'T HELP HOW I FEEL.
AND THERE'S A REASON JACE IS THE LAST ON AMERICAN SOIL!
WELL, STOP SAYING THERE'S A REASON, AND TELL ME WHAT IT IS!
BECAUSE IN OUR WORLD, AARON?
LOVE ONLY KILLS.

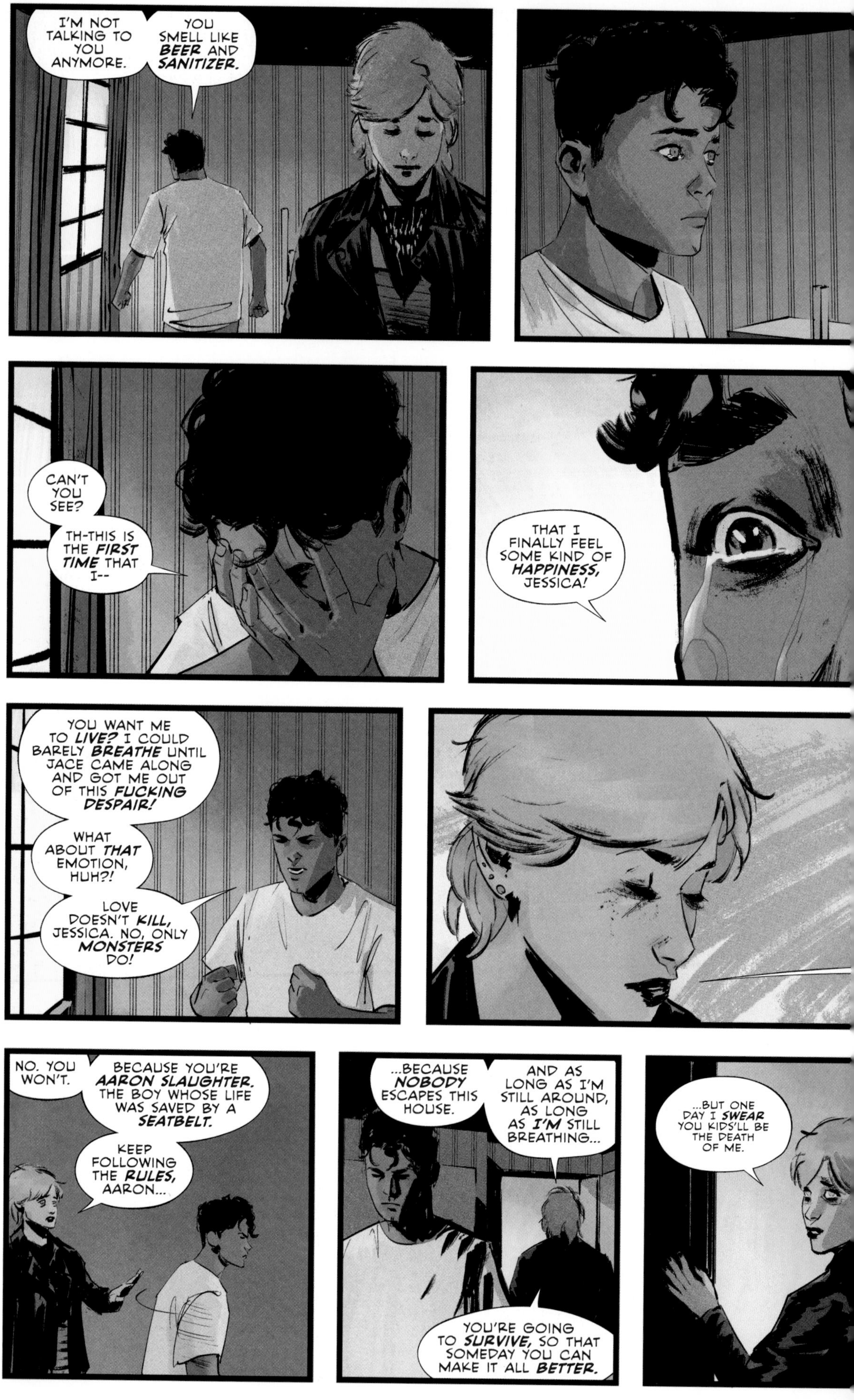
I'M NOT TALKING TO YOU ANYMORE.
YOU SMELL LIKE BEER AND SANITIZER.
CAN'T YOU SEE?
TH-THIS IS THE FIRST TIME THAT I--
THAT I FINALLY FEEL SOME KIND OF HAPPINESS, JESSICA!
YOU WANT ME TO LIVE? I COULD BARELY BREATHE UNTIL JACE CAME ALONG AND GOT ME OUT OF THIS FUCKING DESPAIR!
WHAT ABOUT THAT EMOTION, HUH?!
LOVE DOESN'T KILL, JESSICA. NO, ONLY MONSTERS DO!
NO. YOU WON'T.
BECAUSE YOU'RE AARON SLAUGHTER. THE BOY WHOSE LIFE WAS SAVED BY A SEATBELT.
KEEP FOLLOWING THE RULES, AARON...
...BECAUSE NOBODY ESCAPES THIS HOUSE.
AND AS LONG AS I'M STILL AROUND, AS LONG AS I'M STILL BREATHING...
YOU'RE GOING TO SURVIVE, SO THAT SOMEDAY YOU CAN MAKE IT ALL BETTER.
...BUT ONE DAY I SWEAR YOU KIDS'LL BE THE DEATH OF ME.

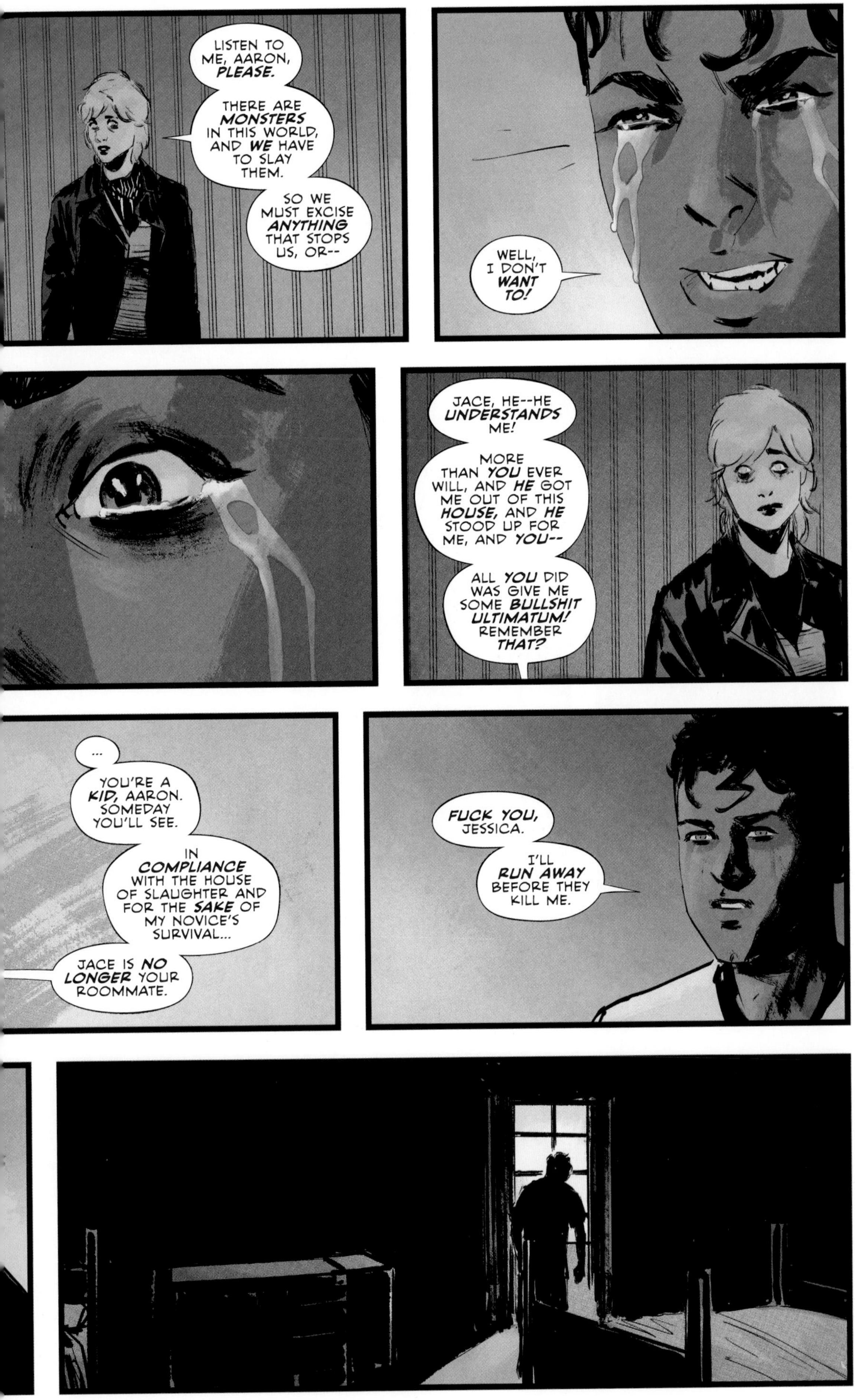
LISTEN TO ME, AARON, PLEASE.
THERE ARE MONSTERS IN THIS WORLD, AND WE HAVE TO SLAY THEM.
SO WE MUST EXCISE ANYTHING THAT STOPS US, OR--
WELL, I DON'T WANT TO!
JACE, HE--HE UNDERSTANDS ME!
MORE THAN YOU EVER WILL, AND HE GOT ME OUT OF THIS HOUSE, AND HE STOOD UP FOR ME, AND YOU--
ALL YOU DID WAS GIVE ME SOME BULLSHIT ULTIMATUM! REMEMBER THAT?
...
YOU'RE A KID, AARON. SOMEDAY YOU'LL SEE.
IN COMPLIANCE WITH THE HOUSE OF SLAUGHTER AND FOR THE SAKE OF MY NOVICE'S SURVIVAL...
JACE IS NO LONGER YOUR ROOMMATE.
FUCK YOU, JESSICA.
I'LL RUN AWAY BEFORE THEY KILL ME.

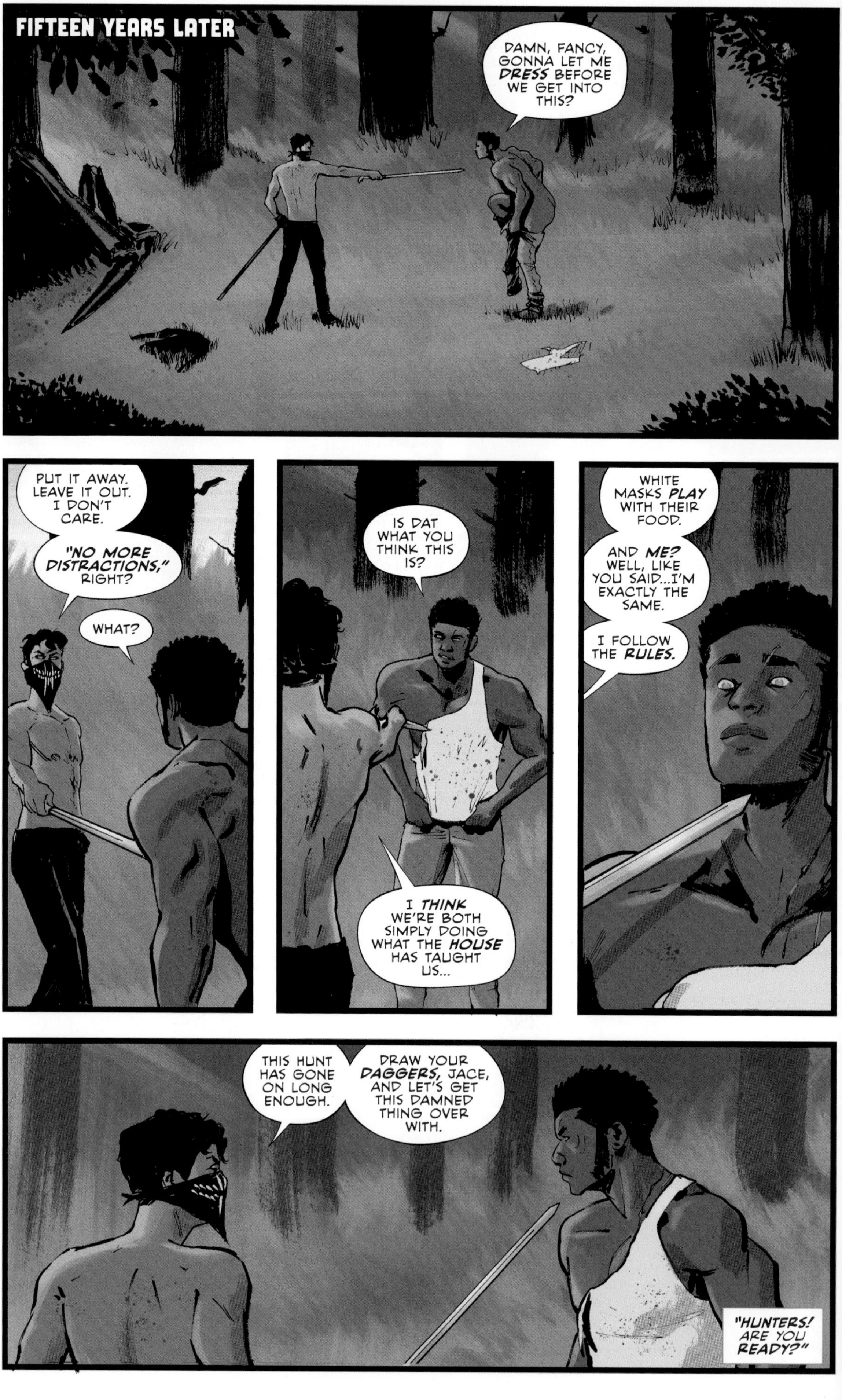
FIFTEEN YEARS LATER
DAMN, FANCY, GONNA LET ME DRESS BEFORE WE GET INTO THIS?
PUT IT AWAY. LEAVE IT OUT. I DON'T CARE.
"NO MORE DISTRACTIONS," RIGHT?
WHAT?
IS DAT WHAT YOU THINK THIS IS?
I THINK WE'RE BOTH SIMPLY DOING WHAT THE HOUSE HAS TAUGHT US...
WHITE MASKS PLAY WITH THEIR FOOD.
AND ME? WELL, LIKE YOU SAID...I'M EXACTLY THE SAME.
I FOLLOW THE RULES.
THIS HUNT HAS GONE ON LONG ENOUGH.
DRAW YOUR DAGGERS, JACE, AND LET'S GET THIS DAMNED THING OVER WITH.
"HUNTERS! ARE YOU READY?"

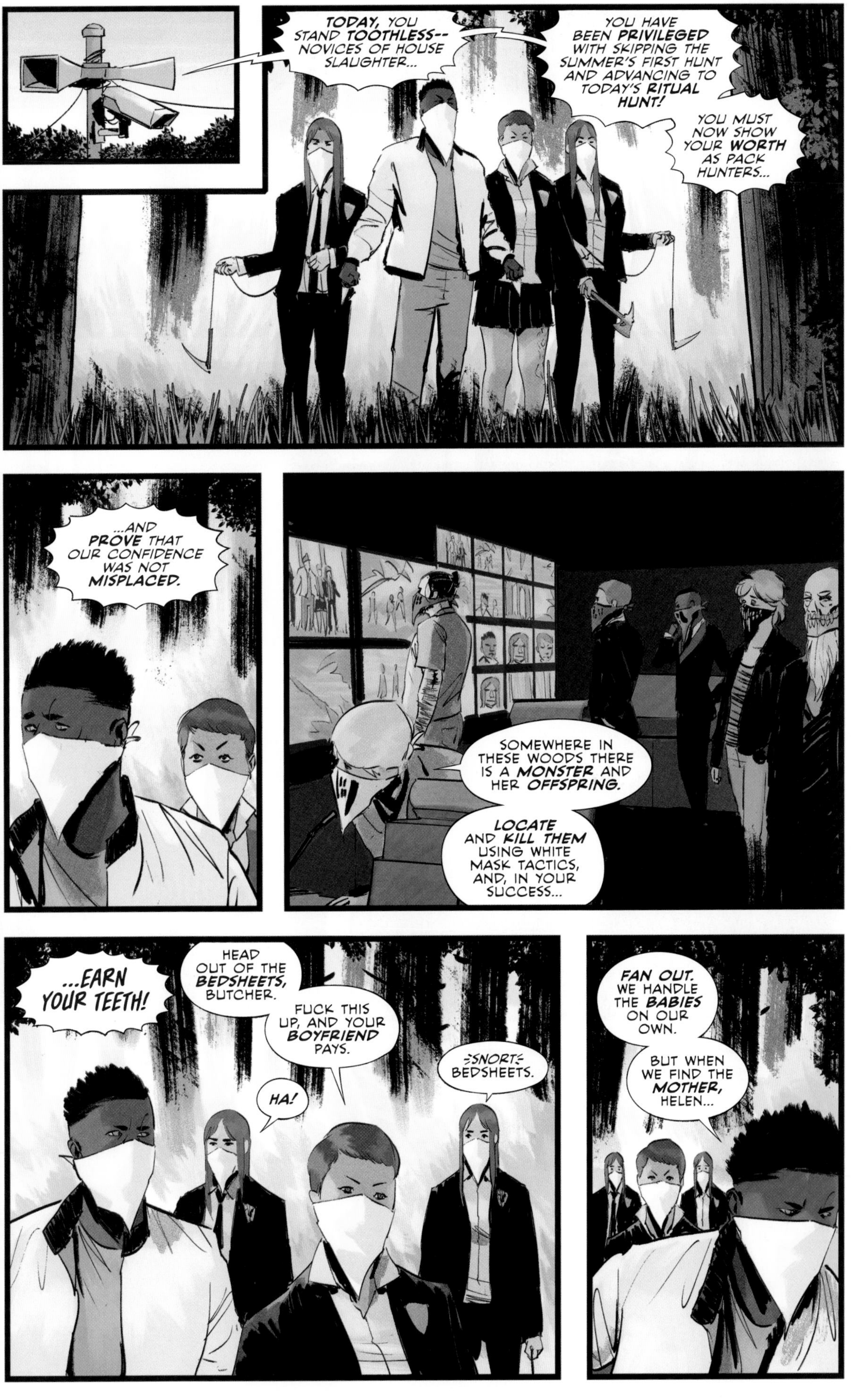
TODAY, YOU STAND TOOTHLESS-- NOVICES OF HOUSE SLAUGHTER...
YOU HAVE BEEN PRIVILEGED WITH SKIPPING THE SUMMER'S FIRST HUNT AND ADVANCING TO TODAY'S RITUAL HUNT!
YOU MUST NOW SHOW YOUR WORTH AS PACK HUNTERS...
...AND PROVE THAT OUR CONFIDENCE WAS NOT MISPLACED.
SOMEWHERE IN THESE WOODS THERE IS A MONSTER AND HER OFFSPRING.
LOCATE AND KILL THEM USING WHITE MASK TACTICS, AND, IN YOUR SUCCESS...
...EARN YOUR TEETH!
HEAD OUT OF THE BEDSHEETS, BUTCHER.
FUCK THIS UP, AND YOUR BOYFRIEND PAYS.
HA!
SNORT BEDSHEETS.
FAN OUT. WE HANDLE THE BABIES ON OUR OWN.
BUT WHEN WE FIND THE MOTHER, HELEN...

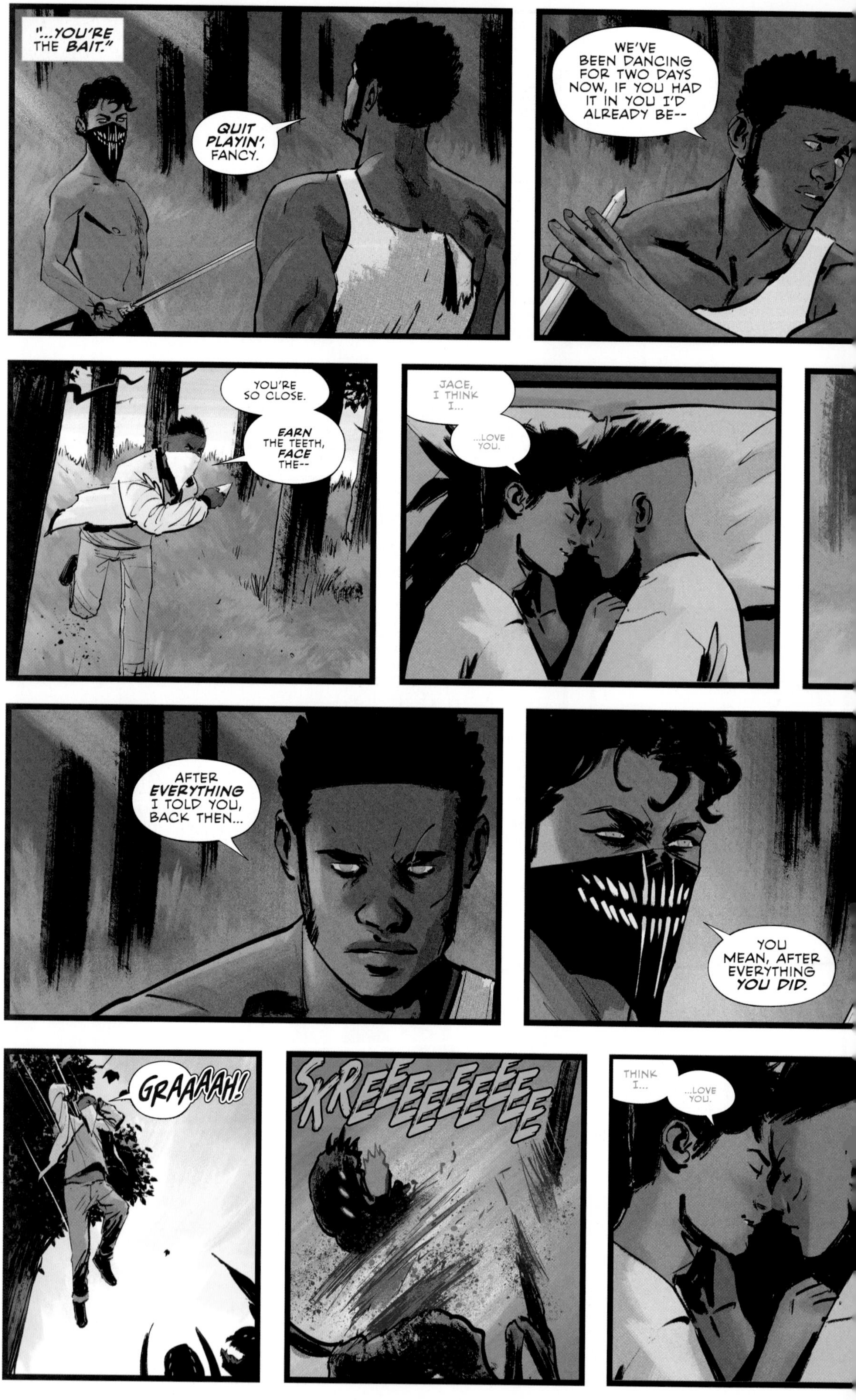
"...YOU'RE THE BAIT."
QUIT PLAYIN', FANCY.
WE'VE BEEN DANCING FOR TWO DAYS NOW, IF YOU HAD IT IN YOU I'D ALREADY BE--
YOU'RE SO CLOSE.
EARN THE TEETH, FACE THE--
JACE, I THINK I...
...LOVE YOU.
AFTER EVERYTHING I TOLD YOU, BACK THEN...
YOU MEAN, AFTER EVERYTHING YOU DID.
GRAAAAH!
SKREEEEEEEEEE
THINK I...
...LOVE YOU.

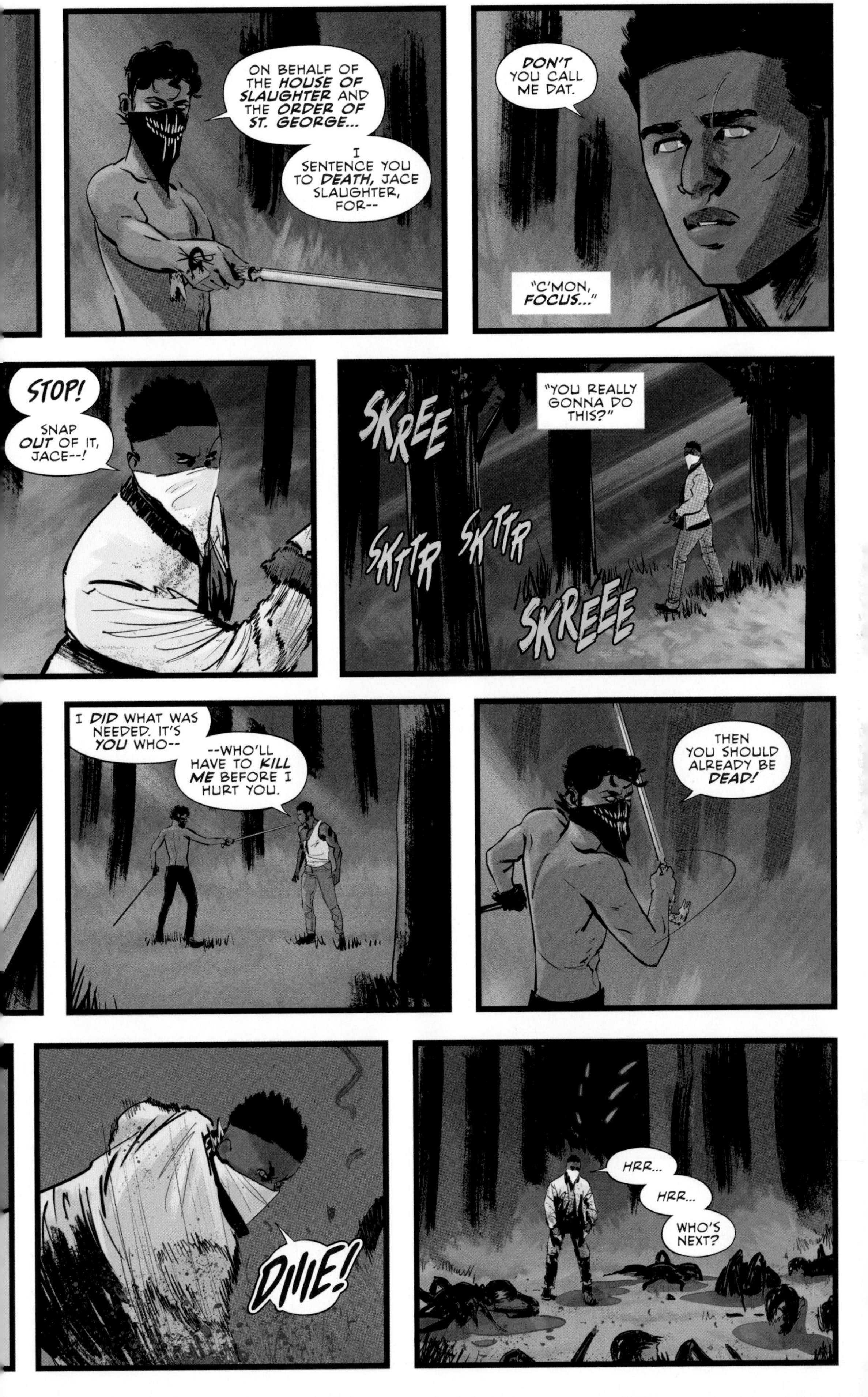

ON BEHALF OF THE HOUSE OF SLAUGHTER AND THE ORDER OF ST. GEORGE...
I SENTENCE YOU TO DEATH, JACE SLAUGHTER, FOR--
DON'T YOU CALL ME DAT.
"C'MON, FOCUS..."
STOP!
SNAP OUT OF IT, JACE--!
SKREE
"YOU REALLY GONNA DO THIS?"
SKTTR SKTTR
SKREEE
I DID WHAT WAS NEEDED. IT'S YOU WHO--
--WHO'LL HAVE TO KILL ME BEFORE I HURT YOU.
THEN YOU SHOULD ALREADY BE DEAD!
DIIIE!
HRR...
HRR...
WHO'S NEXT?

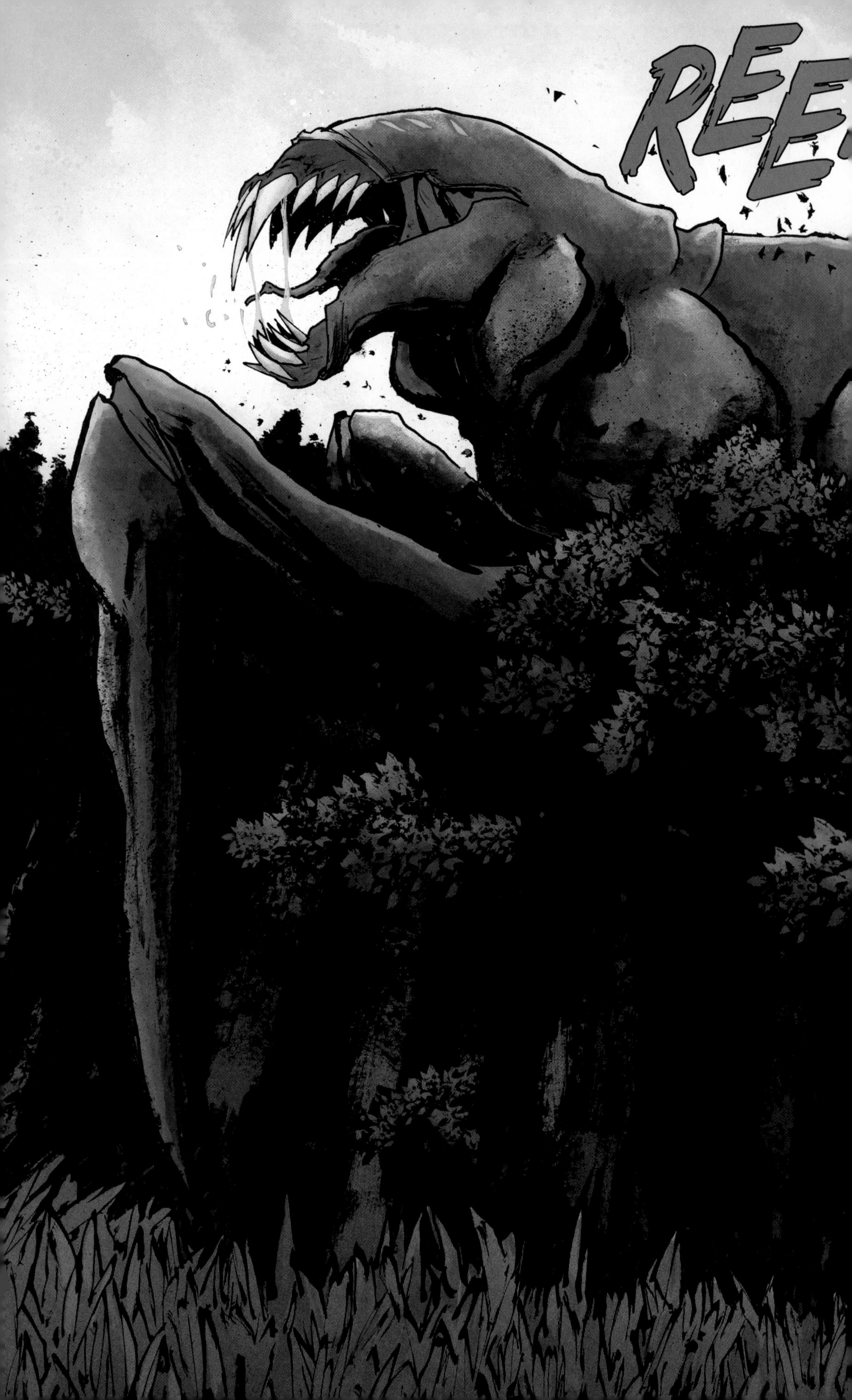
REE

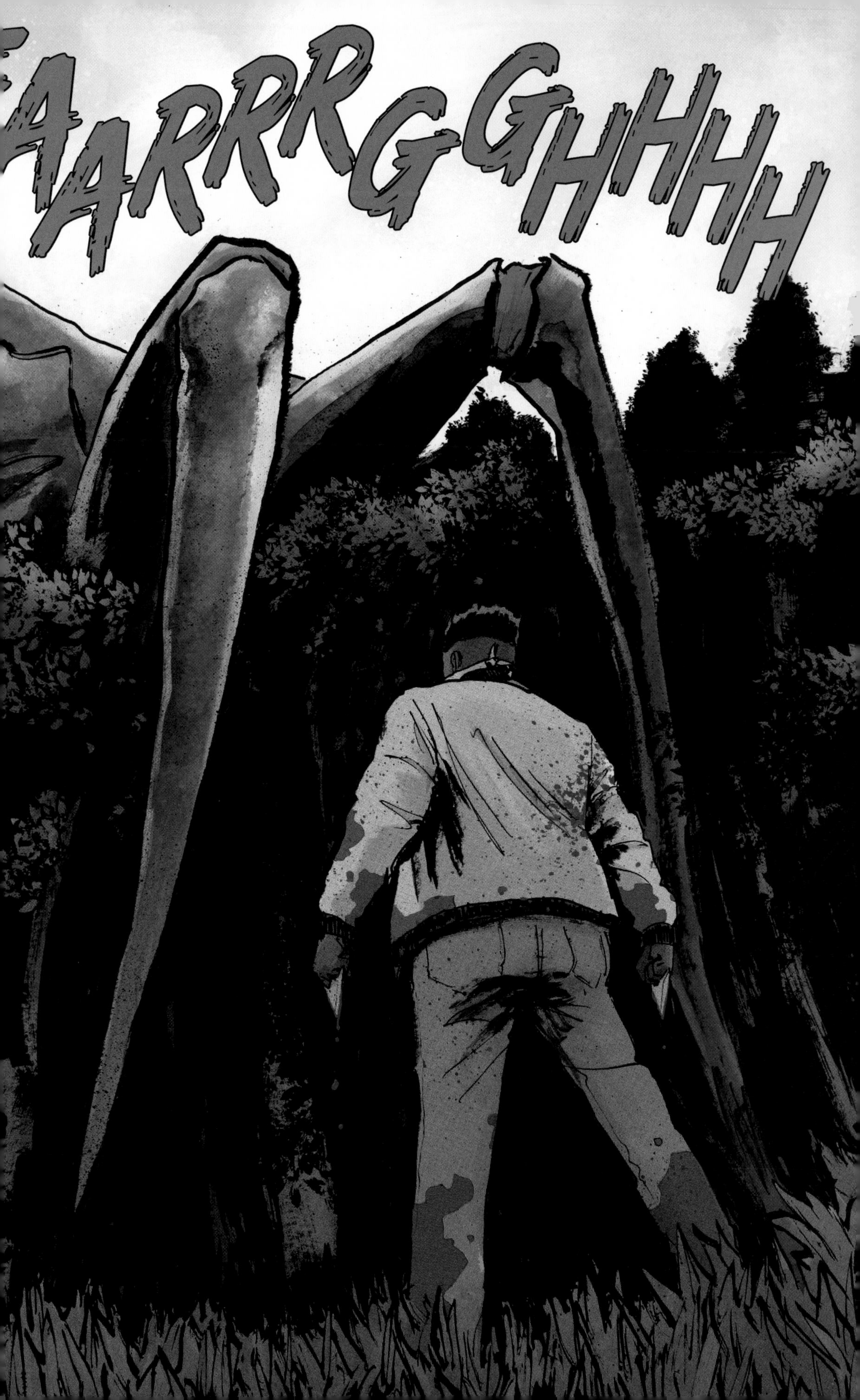
AARRRGGHHHHH

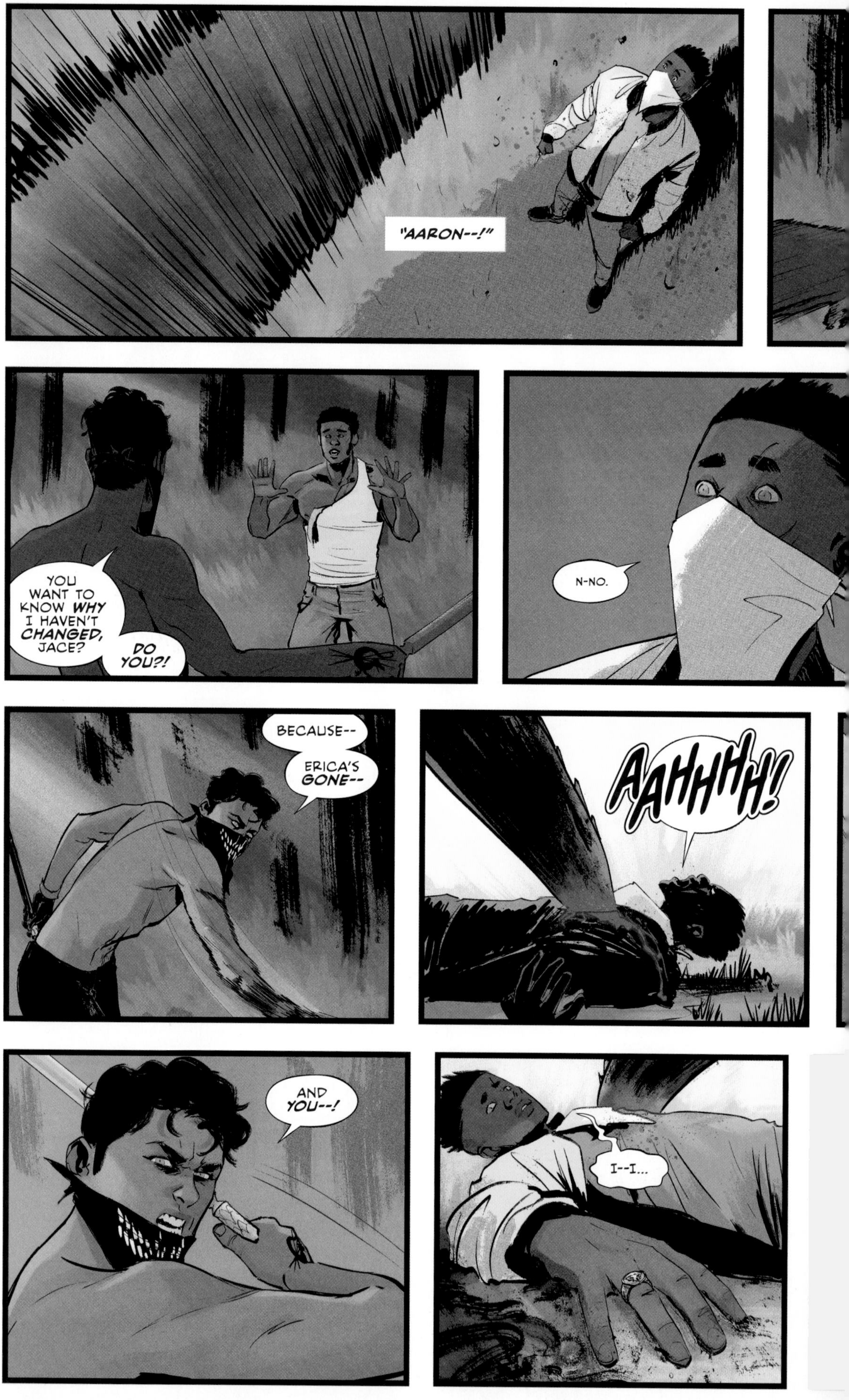
"AARON--!"
YOU WANT TO KNOW WHY I HAVEN'T CHANGED, JACE?
DO YOU?!
N-NO.
BECAUSE--
ERICA'S GONE--
AAHHHH!
AND YOU--!
I--I...

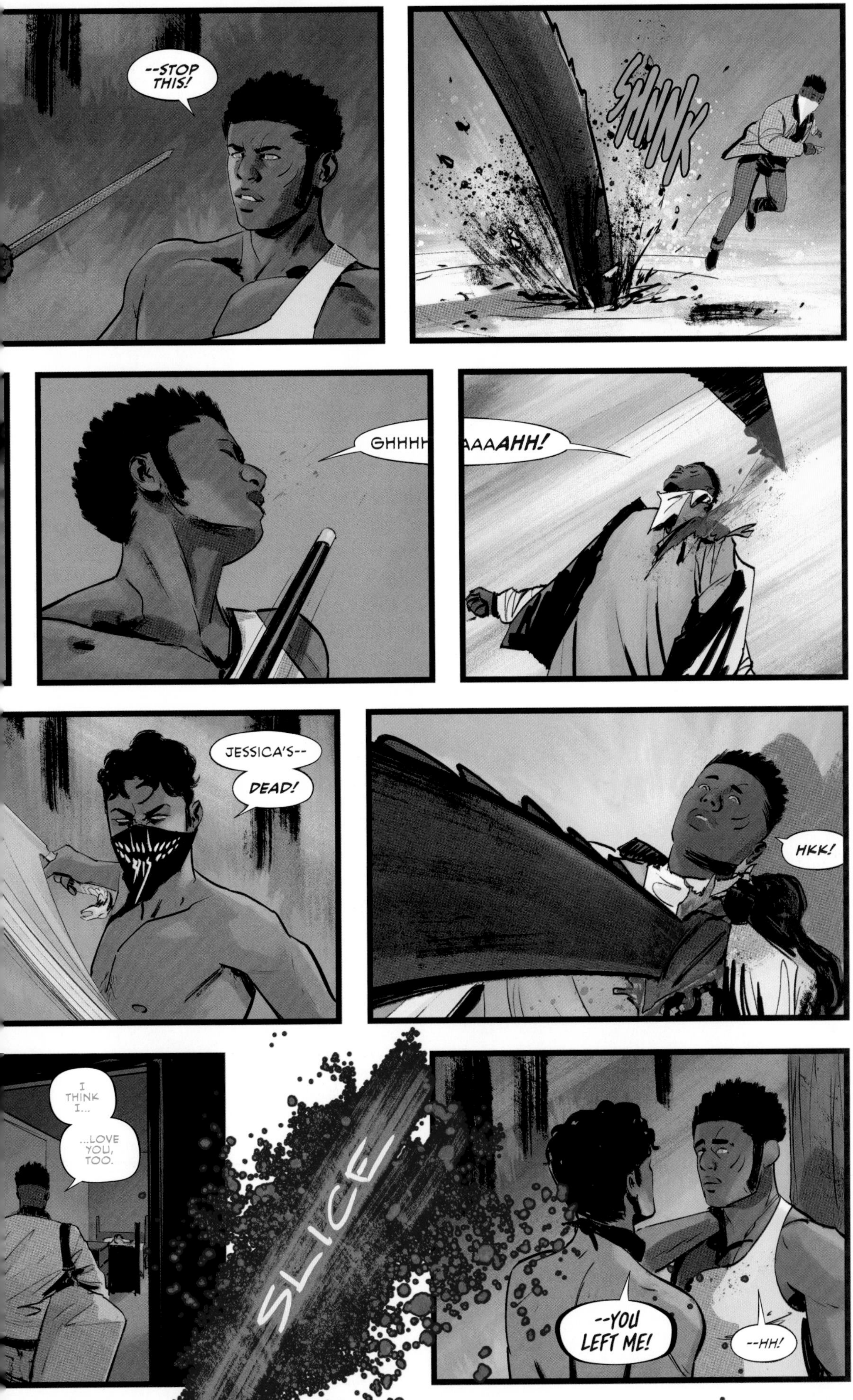
--STOP THIS!
SHNNK
GHHHHAAAAAHH!
JESSICA'S--
DEAD!
HKK!
I THINK I...
...LOVE YOU, TOO.
SLICE
--YOU LEFT ME!
--HH!

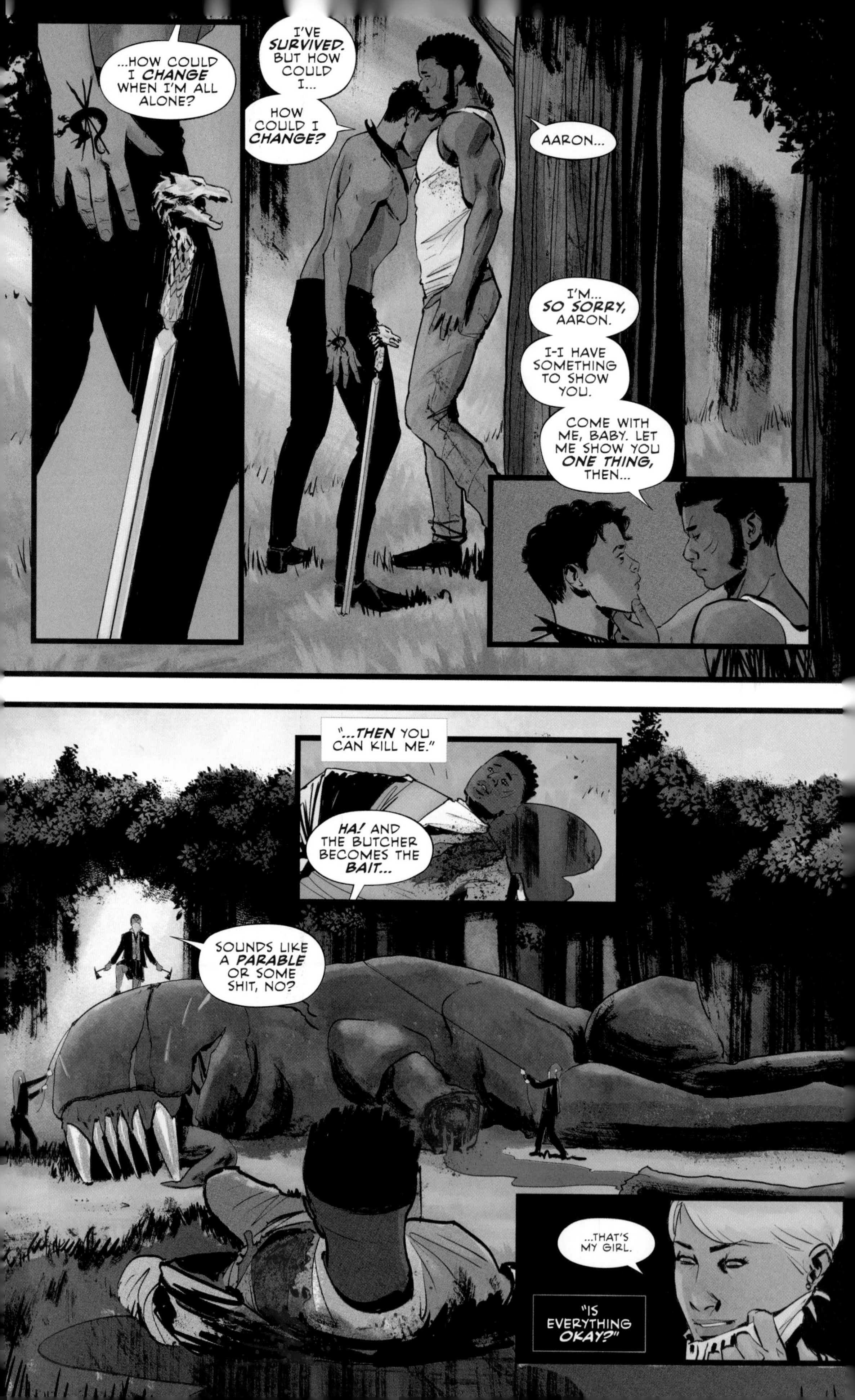
...HOW COULD I CHANGE WHEN I'M ALL ALONE?
I'VE SURVIVED. BUT HOW COULD I...
HOW COULD I CHANGE?
AARON...
I'M... SO SORRY, AARON.
I-I HAVE SOMETHING TO SHOW YOU.
COME WITH ME, BABY. LET ME SHOW YOU ONE THING, THEN...
"...THEN YOU CAN KILL ME."
HA! AND THE BUTCHER BECOMES THE BAIT...
SOUNDS LIKE A PARABLE OR SOME SHIT, NO?
...THAT'S MY GIRL.
"IS EVERYTHING OKAY?"

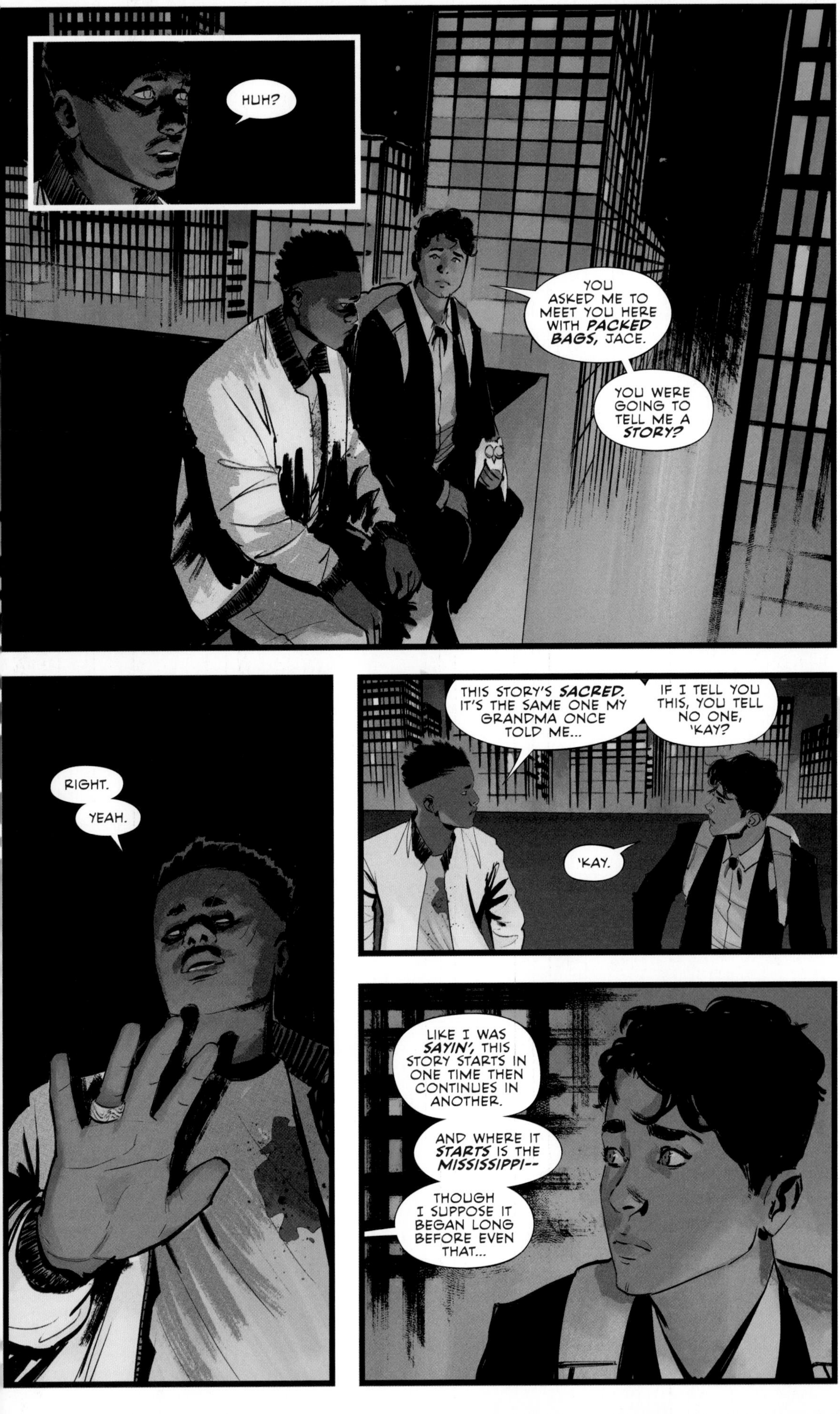
HUH?
YOU ASKED ME TO MEET YOU HERE WITH PACKED BAGS, JACE.
YOU WERE GOING TO TELL ME A STORY?
RIGHT.
YEAH.
THIS STORY'S SACRED. IT'S THE SAME ONE MY GRANDMA ONCE TOLD ME...
IF I TELL YOU THIS, YOU TELL NO ONE, 'KAY?
'KAY.
LIKE I WAS SAYIN', THIS STORY STARTS IN ONE TIME THEN CONTINUES IN ANOTHER.
AND WHERE IT STARTS IS THE MISSISSIPPI--
THOUGH I SUPPOSE IT BEGAN LONG BEFORE EVEN THAT...

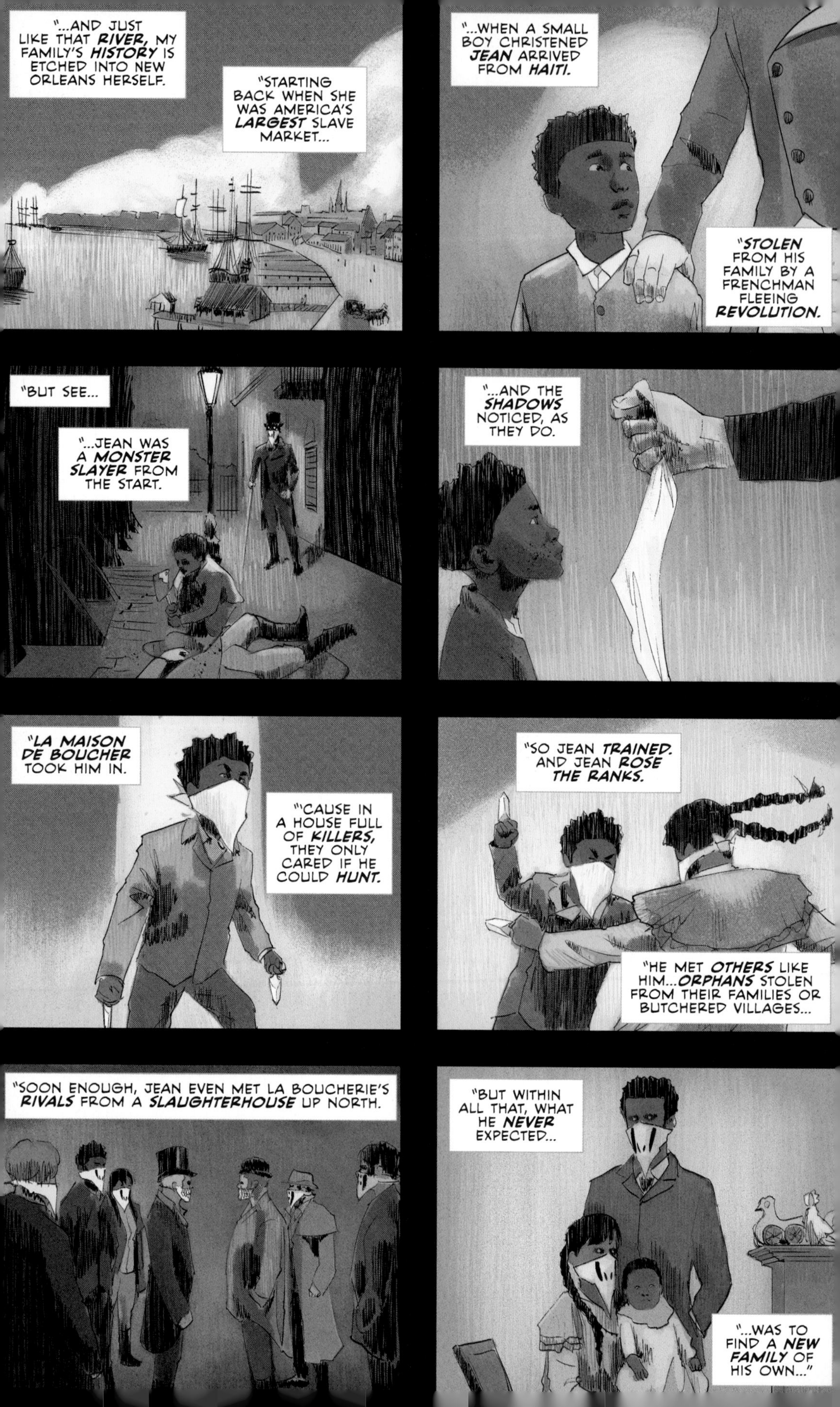
"...AND JUST LIKE THAT RIVER, MY FAMILY'S HISTORY IS ETCHED INTO NEW ORLEANS HERSELF.
"STARTING BACK WHEN SHE WAS AMERICA'S LARGEST SLAVE MARKET...
"...WHEN A SMALL BOY CHRISTENED JEAN ARRIVED FROM HAITI.
"STOLEN FROM HIS FAMILY BY A FRENCHMAN FLEEING REVOLUTION.
"BUT SEE...
"...JEAN WAS A MONSTER SLAYER FROM THE START.
"...AND THE SHADOWS NOTICED, AS THEY DO.
"LA MAISON DE BOUCHER TOOK HIM IN.
"'CAUSE IN A HOUSE FULL OF KILLERS, THEY ONLY CARED IF HE COULD HUNT.
"SO JEAN TRAINED. AND JEAN ROSE THE RANKS.
"HE MET OTHERS LIKE HIM...ORPHANS STOLEN FROM THEIR FAMILIES OR BUTCHERED VILLAGES...
"SOON ENOUGH, JEAN EVEN MET LA BOUCHERIE'S RIVALS FROM A SLAUGHTERHOUSE UP NORTH.
"BUT WITHIN ALL THAT, WHAT HE NEVER EXPECTED...
"...WAS TO FIND A NEW FAMILY OF HIS OWN..."

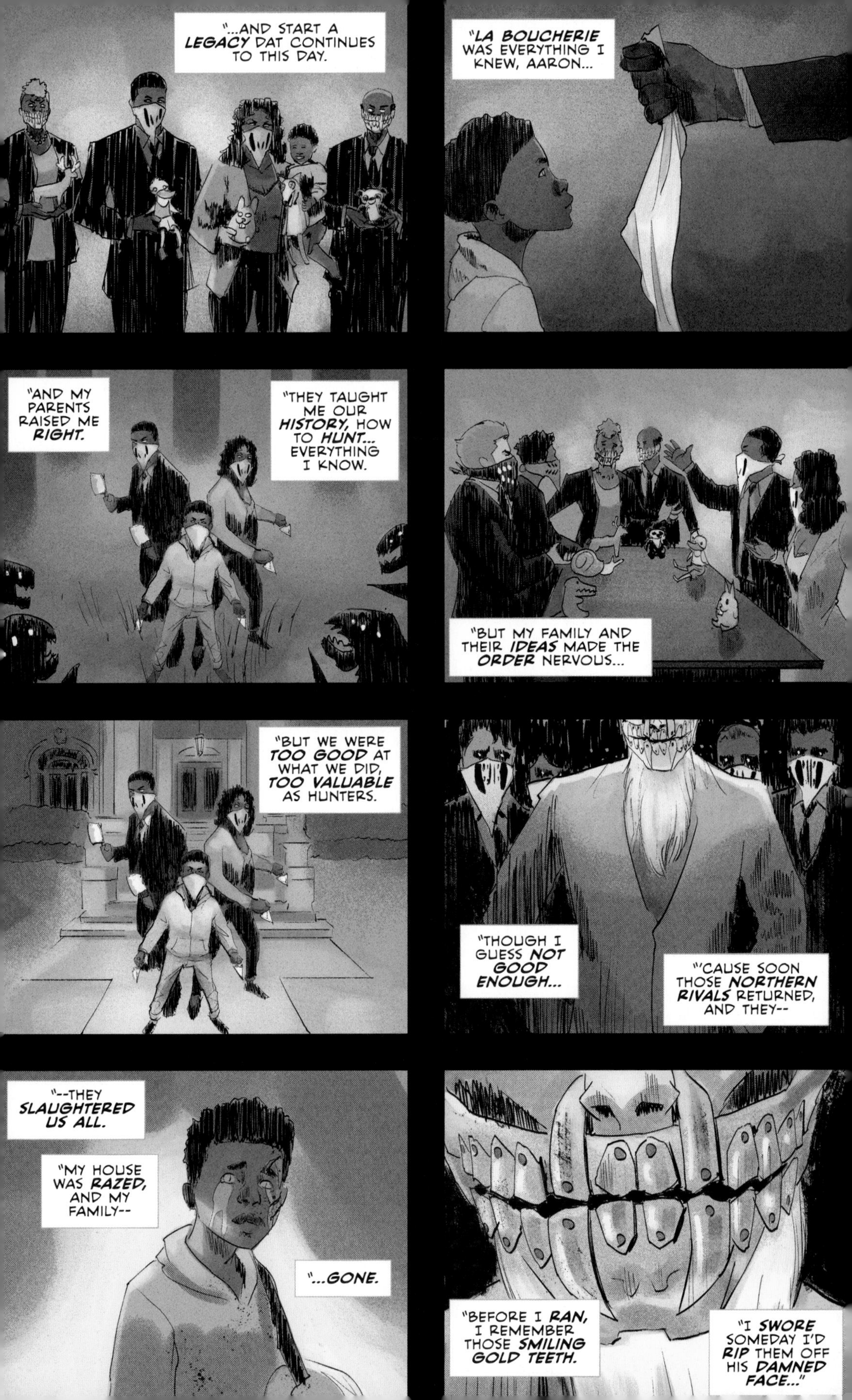
"...AND START A LEGACY DAT CONTINUES TO THIS DAY.
"LA BOUCHERIE WAS EVERYTHING I KNEW, AARON...
"AND MY PARENTS RAISED ME RIGHT.
"THEY TAUGHT ME OUR HISTORY, HOW TO HUNT... EVERYTHING I KNOW.
"BUT MY FAMILY AND THEIR IDEAS MADE THE ORDER NERVOUS...
"BUT WE WERE TOO GOOD AT WHAT WE DID, TOO VALUABLE AS HUNTERS.
"THOUGH I GUESS NOT GOOD ENOUGH...
"'CAUSE SOON THOSE NORTHERN RIVALS RETURNED, AND THEY--
"--THEY SLAUGHTERED US ALL.
"MY HOUSE WAS RAZED, AND MY FAMILY--
"...GONE.
"BEFORE I RAN, I REMEMBER THOSE SMILING GOLD TEETH.
"I SWORE SOMEDAY I'D RIP THEM OFF HIS DAMNED FACE..."

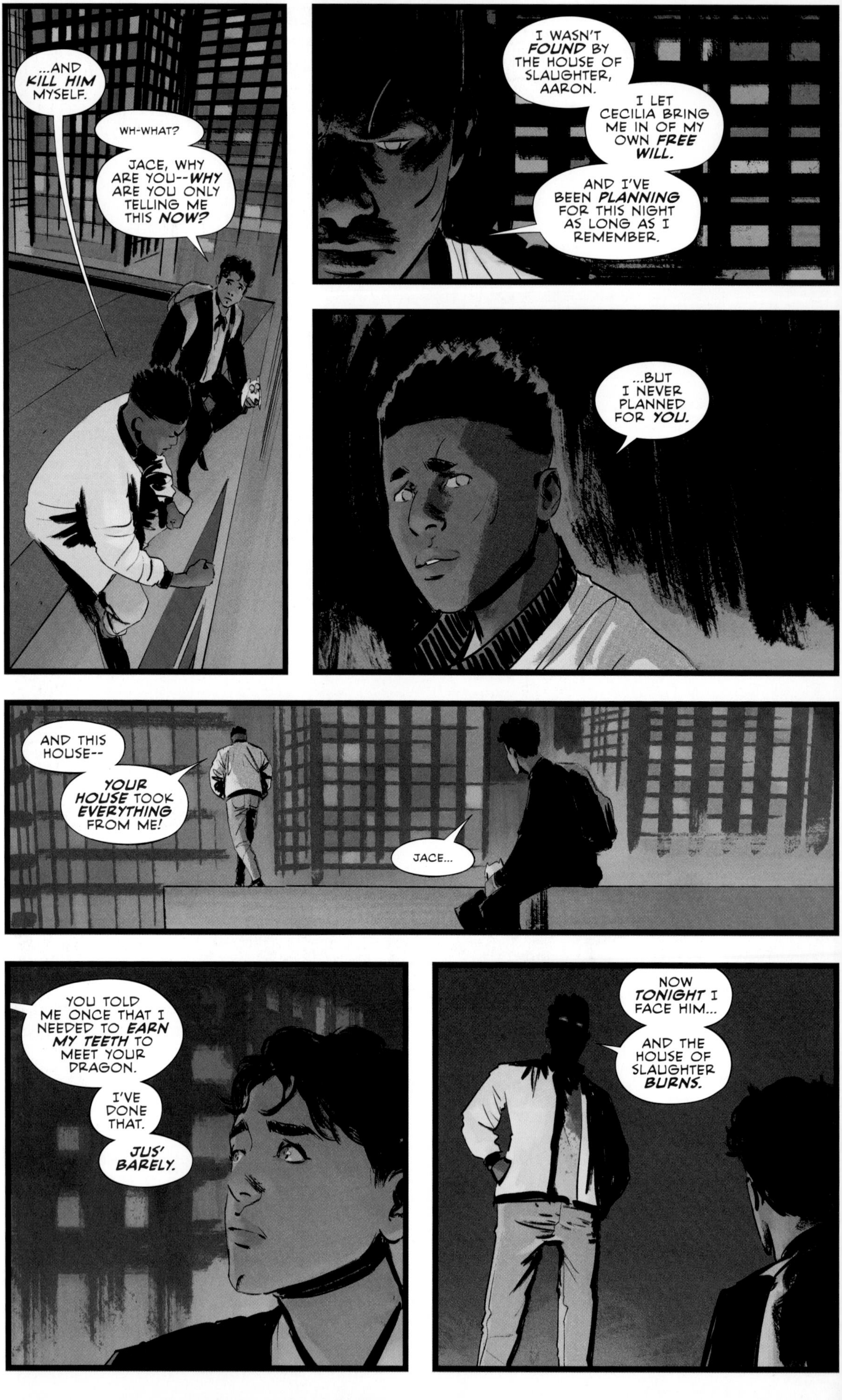

...AND KILL HIM MYSELF.
WH-WHAT?
JACE, WHY ARE YOU--WHY ARE YOU ONLY TELLING ME THIS NOW?
I WASN'T FOUND BY THE HOUSE OF SLAUGHTER, AARON.
I LET CECILIA BRING ME IN OF MY OWN FREE WILL.
AND I'VE BEEN PLANNING FOR THIS NIGHT AS LONG AS I REMEMBER.
...BUT I NEVER PLANNED FOR YOU.
AND THIS HOUSE--
YOUR HOUSE TOOK EVERYTHING FROM ME!
JACE...
YOU TOLD ME ONCE THAT I NEEDED TO EARN MY TEETH TO MEET YOUR DRAGON.
I'VE DONE THAT.
JUS' BARELY.
NOW TONIGHT I FACE HIM...
AND THE HOUSE OF SLAUGHTER BURNS.

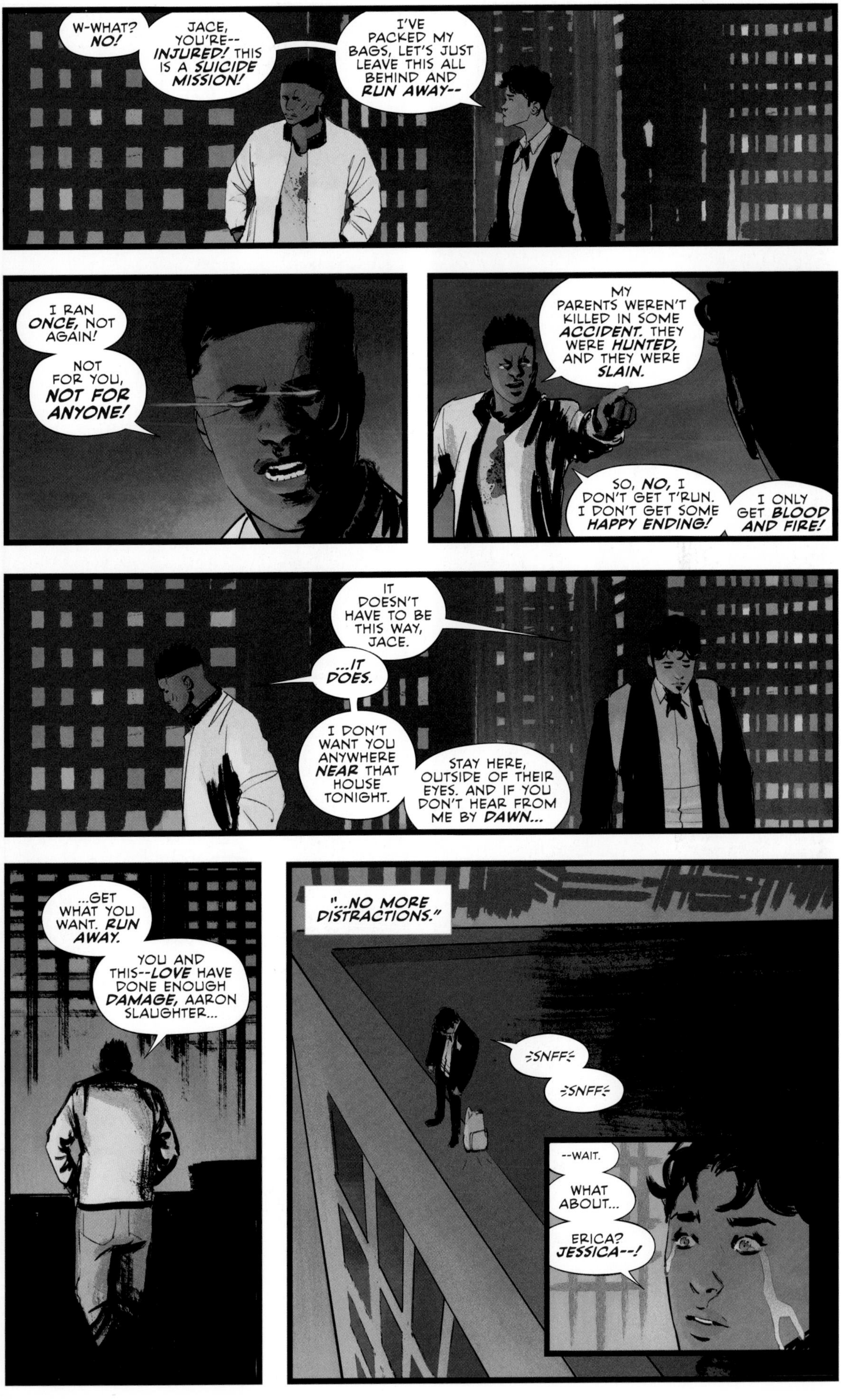
W-WHAT? NO!
JACE, YOU'RE-- INJURED! THIS IS A SUICIDE MISSION!
I'VE PACKED MY BAGS, LET'S JUST LEAVE THIS ALL BEHIND AND RUN AWAY--
I RAN ONCE, NOT AGAIN!
NOT FOR YOU, NOT FOR ANYONE!
MY PARENTS WEREN'T KILLED IN SOME ACCIDENT. THEY WERE HUNTED, AND THEY WERE SLAIN.
SO, NO, I DON'T GET T'RUN. I DON'T GET SOME HAPPY ENDING!
I ONLY GET BLOOD AND FIRE!
IT DOESN'T HAVE TO BE THIS WAY, JACE.
...IT DOES.
I DON'T WANT YOU ANYWHERE NEAR THAT HOUSE TONIGHT.
STAY HERE, OUTSIDE OF THEIR EYES. AND IF YOU DON'T HEAR FROM ME BY DAWN...
...GET WHAT YOU WANT. RUN AWAY.
YOU AND THIS--LOVE HAVE DONE ENOUGH DAMAGE, AARON SLAUGHTER...
"...NO MORE DISTRACTIONS."
SNFF
SNFF
--WAIT.
WHAT ABOUT...
ERICA? JESSICA--!

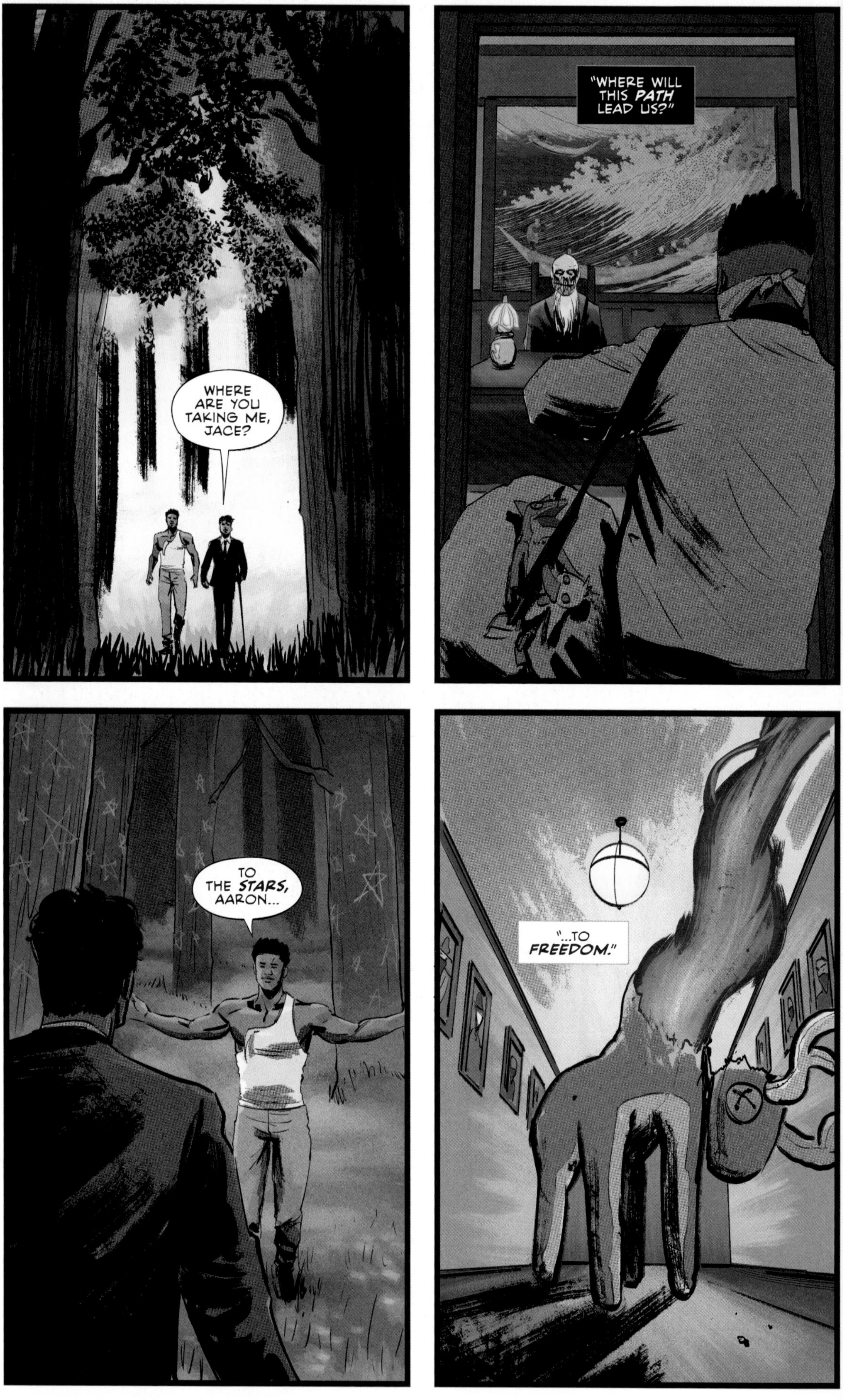
WHERE ARE YOU TAKING ME, JACE?
"WHERE WILL THIS PATH LEAD US?"
TO THE STARS, AARON...
"...TO FREEDOM."

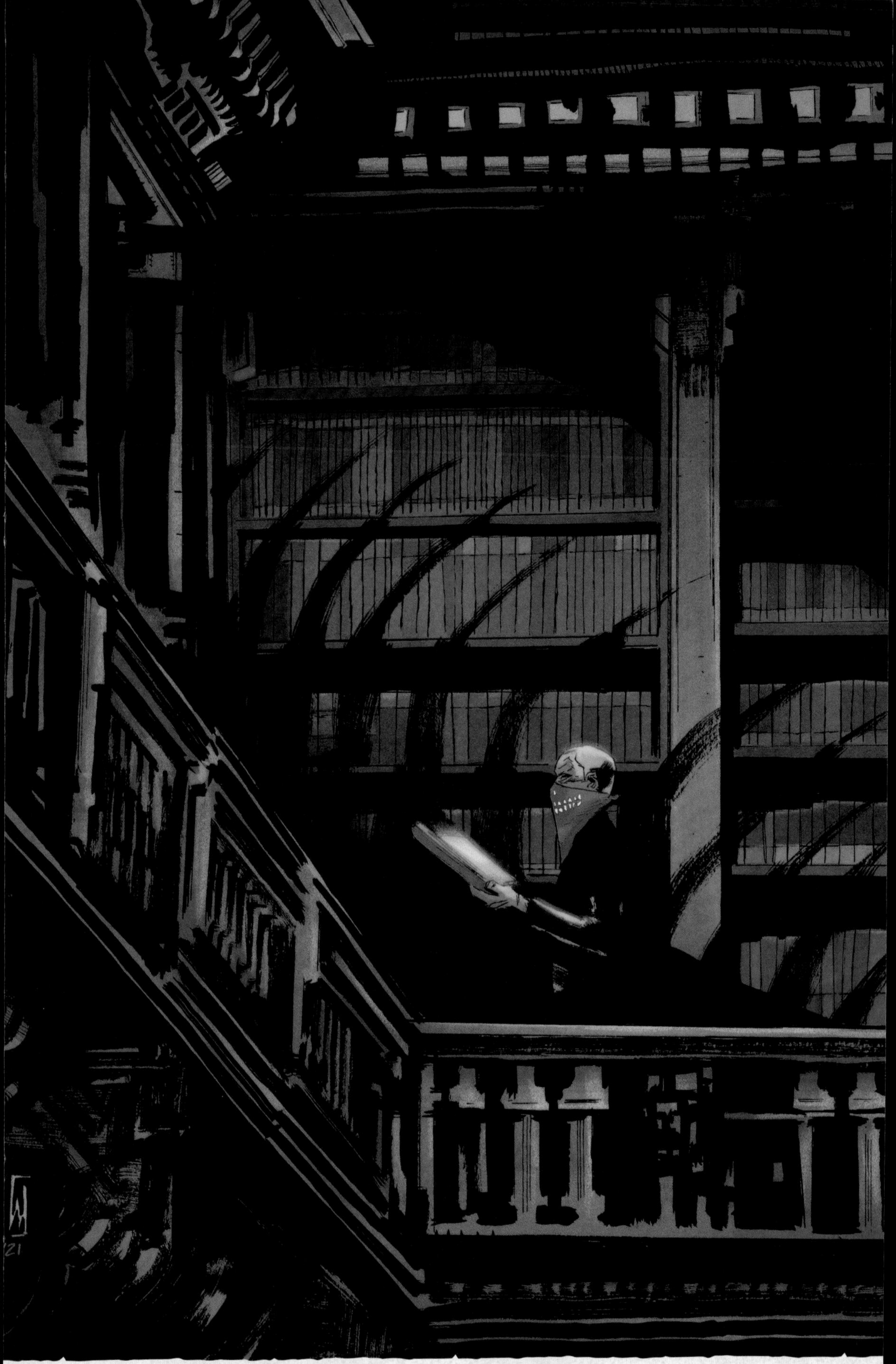

ISSUE FOUR COVER BY WERTHER DELL'EDERA WITH COLORS BY MIQUEL MUERTO

PART FIVE

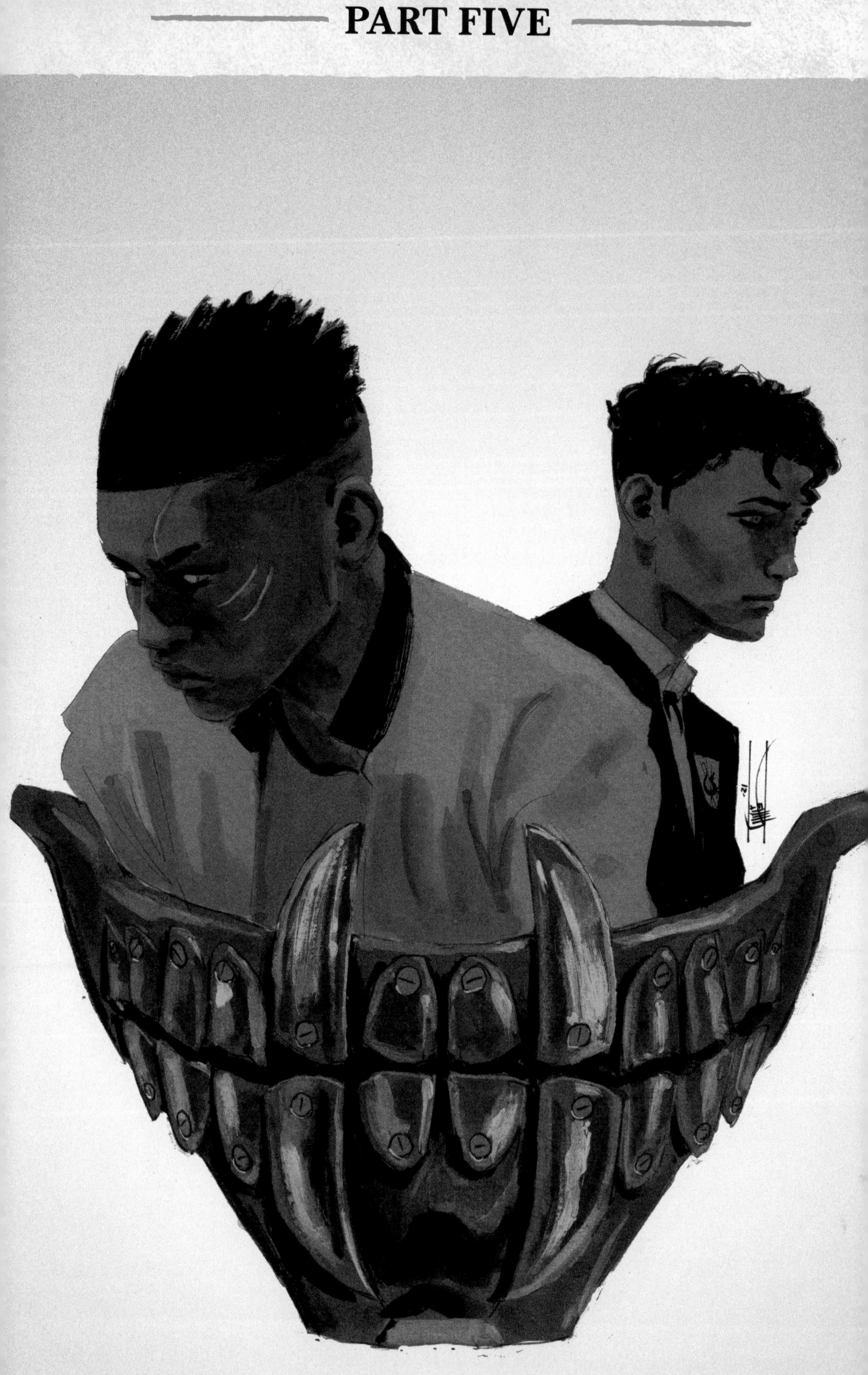

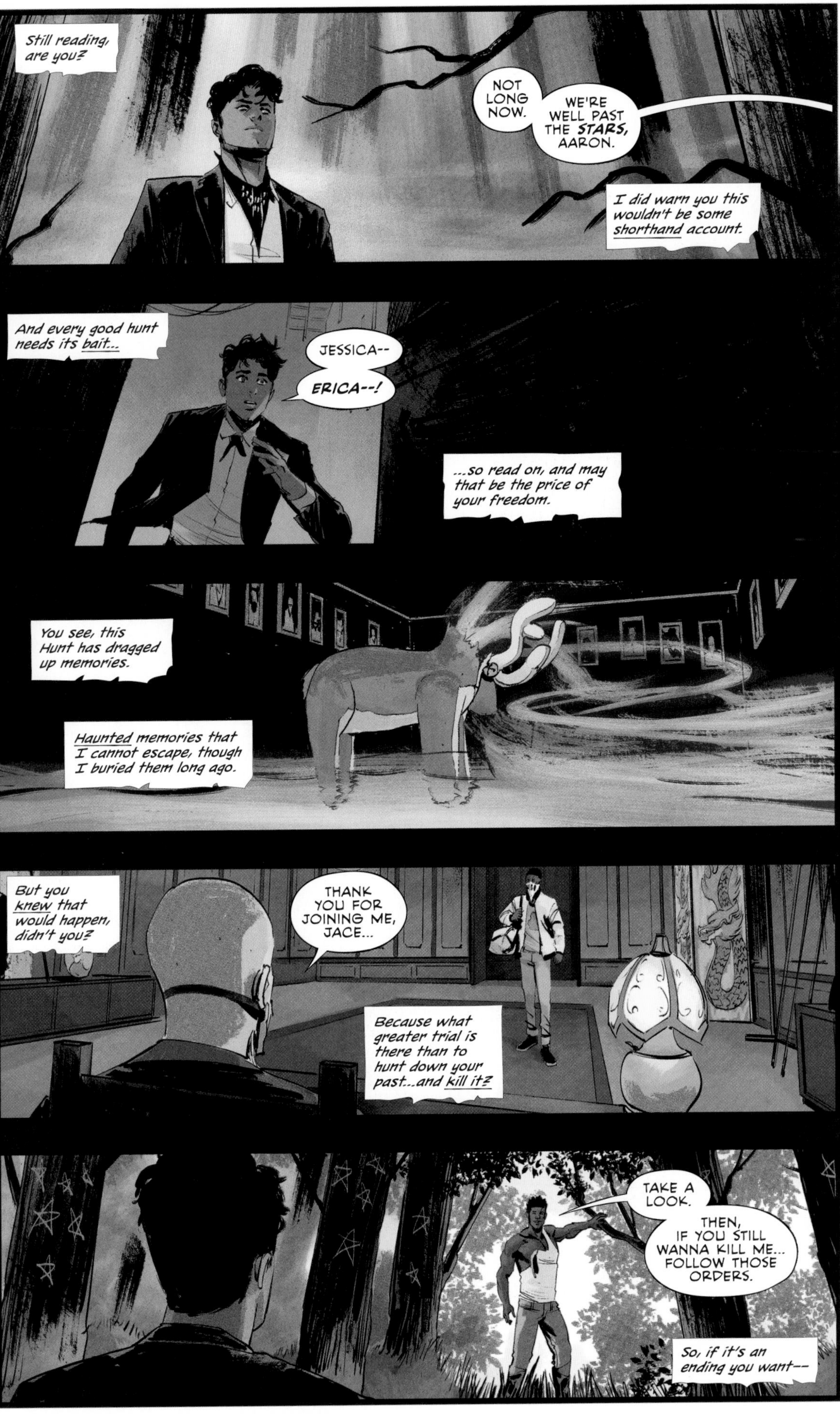
Still reading, are you?
NOT LONG NOW.
WE'RE WELL PAST THE STARS, AARON.
I did warn you this wouldn't be some shorthand account.
And every good hunt needs its bait...
JESSICA--
ERICA--!
...so read on, and may that be the price of your freedom.
You see, this Hunt has dragged up memories.
Haunted memories that I cannot escape, though I buried them long ago.
But you knew that would happen, didn't you?
THANK YOU FOR JOINING ME, JACE...
Because what greater trial is there than to hunt down your past...and kill it?
TAKE A LOOK.
THEN, IF YOU STILL WANNA KILL ME... FOLLOW THOSE ORDERS.
So, if it's an ending you want--

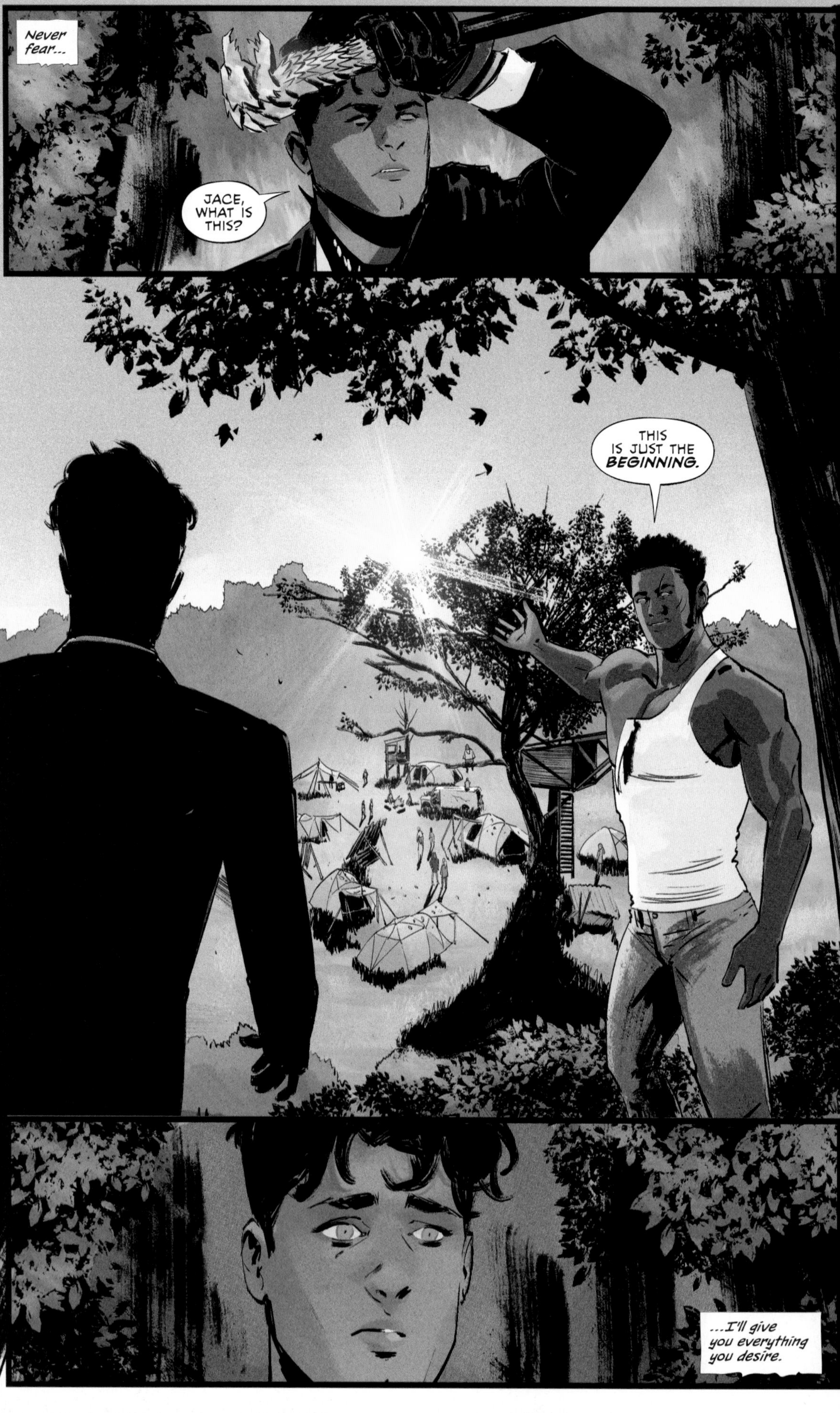
Never fear...
JACE, WHAT IS THIS?
THIS IS JUST THE BEGINNING.
...I'll give you everything you desire.

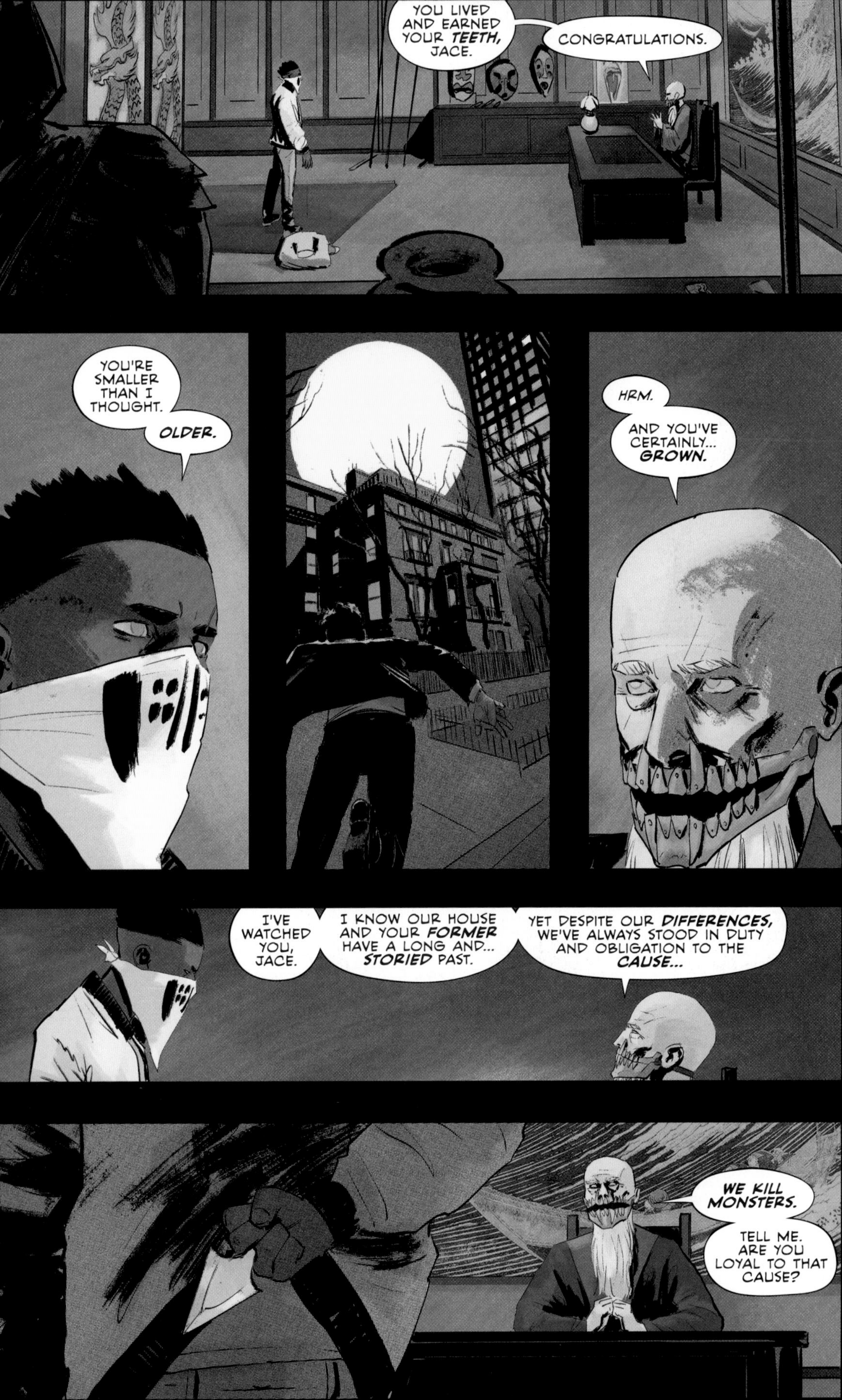
YOU LIVED AND EARNED YOUR *TEETH,* JACE.
CONGRATULATIONS.
YOU'RE SMALLER THAN I THOUGHT.
OLDER.
HRM.
AND YOU'VE CERTAINLY... ***GROWN.***
I'VE WATCHED YOU, JACE.
I KNOW OUR HOUSE AND YOUR ***FORMER*** HAVE A LONG AND... ***STORIED*** PAST.
YET DESPITE OUR ***DIFFERENCES,*** WE'VE ALWAYS STOOD IN DUTY AND OBLIGATION TO THE ***CAUSE...***
WE KILL MONSTERS.
TELL ME. ARE YOU LOYAL TO THAT CAUSE?

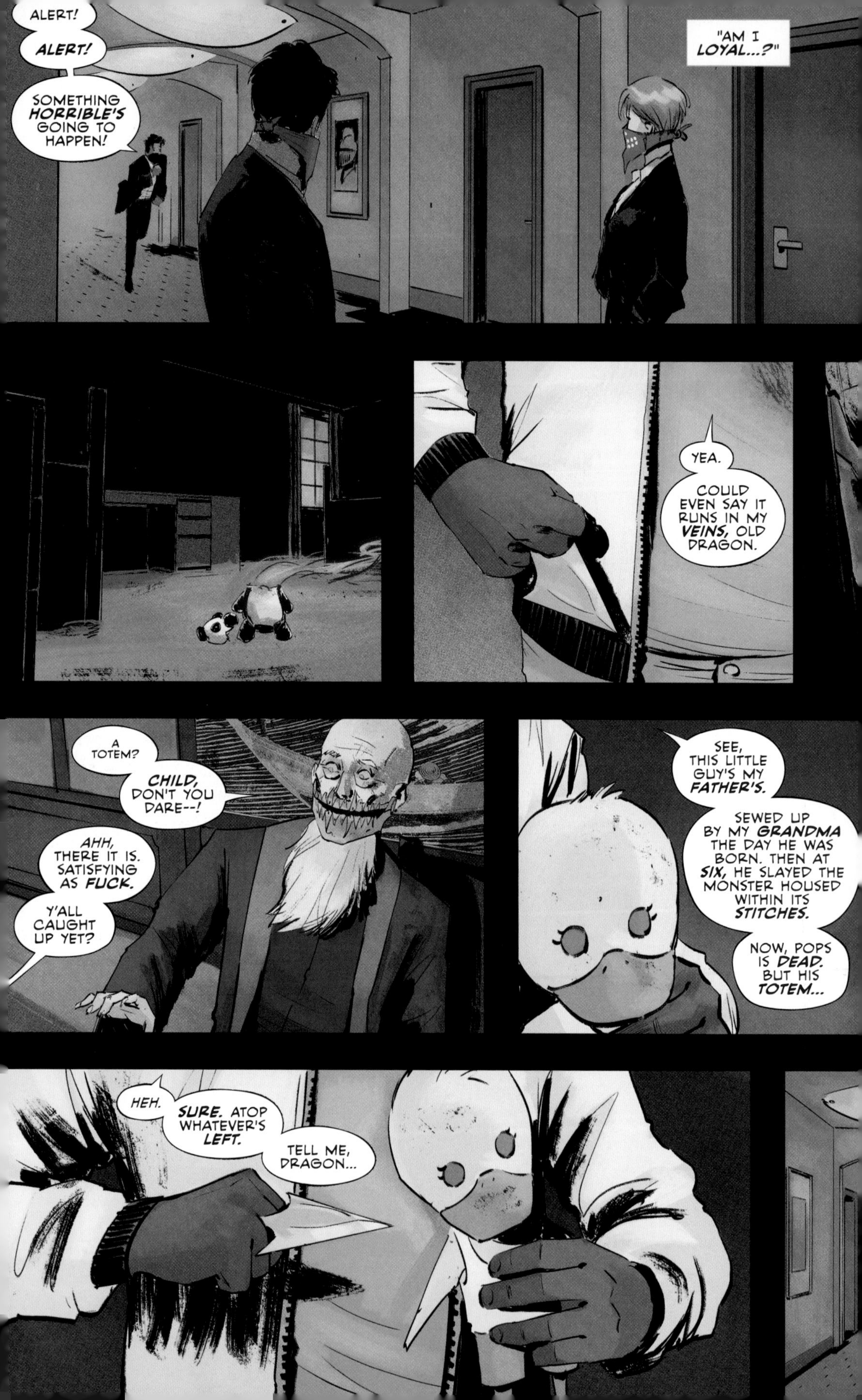

ALERT!
ALERT!
SOMETHING HORRIBLE'S GOING TO HAPPEN!
"AM I LOYAL...?"
YEA.
COULD EVEN SAY IT RUNS IN MY VEINS, OLD DRAGON.
A TOTEM?
CHILD, DON'T YOU DARE--!
AHH, THERE IT IS. SATISFYING AS FUCK.
Y'ALL CAUGHT UP YET?
SEE, THIS LITTLE GUY'S MY FATHER'S.
SEWED UP BY MY GRANDMA THE DAY HE WAS BORN. THEN AT SIX, HE SLAYED THE MONSTER HOUSED WITHIN ITS STITCHES.
NOW, POPS IS DEAD. BUT HIS TOTEM...
HEH.
SURE. ATOP WHATEVER'S LEFT.
TELL ME, DRAGON...

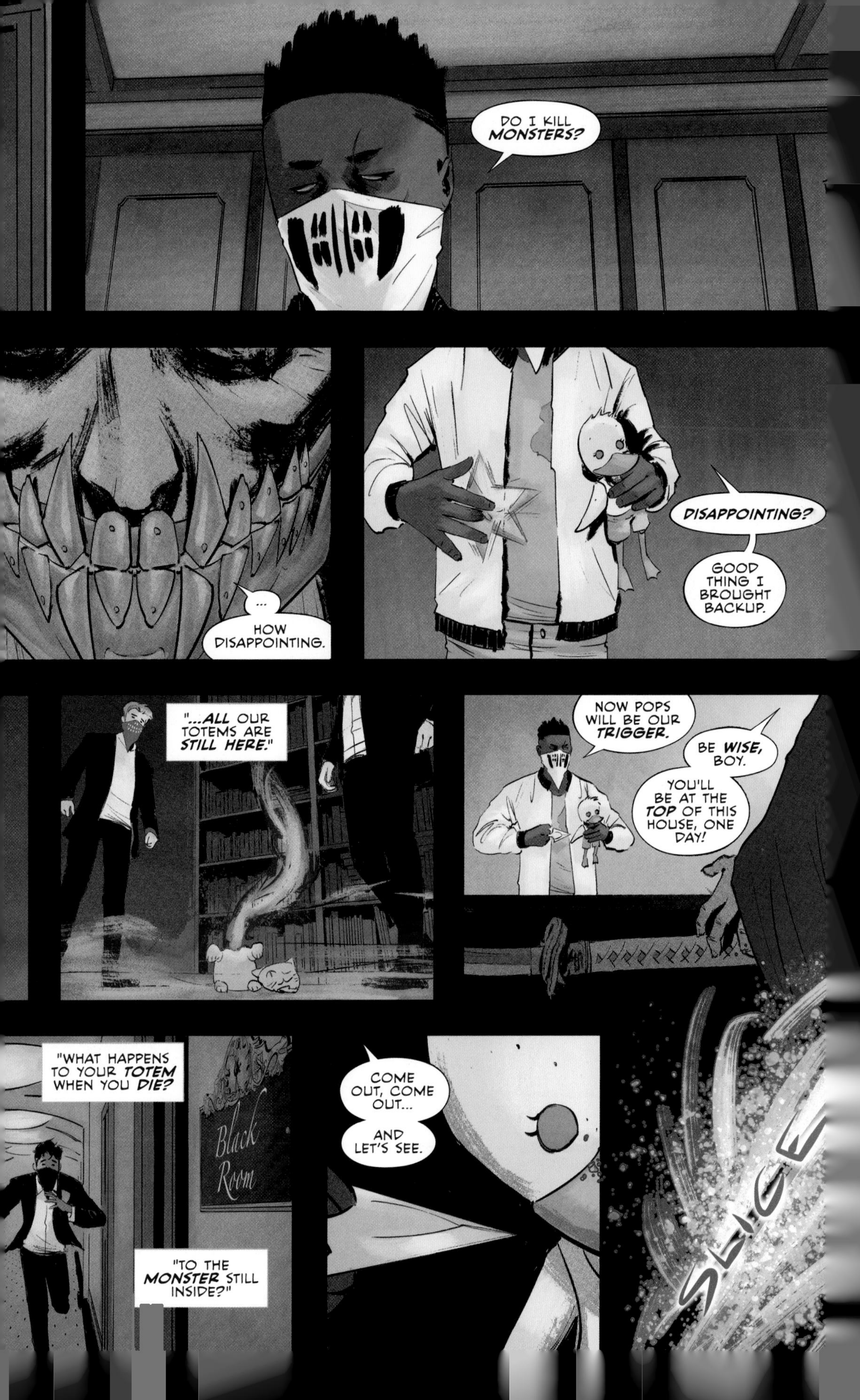
DO I KILL MONSTERS?
...
HOW DISAPPOINTING.
DISAPPOINTING?
GOOD THING I BROUGHT BACKUP.
"...ALL OUR TOTEMS ARE STILL HERE."
NOW POPS WILL BE OUR TRIGGER.
BE WISE, BOY.
YOU'LL BE AT THE TOP OF THIS HOUSE, ONE DAY!
"WHAT HAPPENS TO YOUR TOTEM WHEN YOU DIE?
Black Room
"TO THE MONSTER STILL INSIDE?"
COME OUT, COME OUT...
AND LET'S SEE.
SLICE

SKREEEEEEEEEE

REEAARGH

EOOOOOOOW!!

HUH. LOOKS LIKE OUR MONSTERS *LIVE ON.*

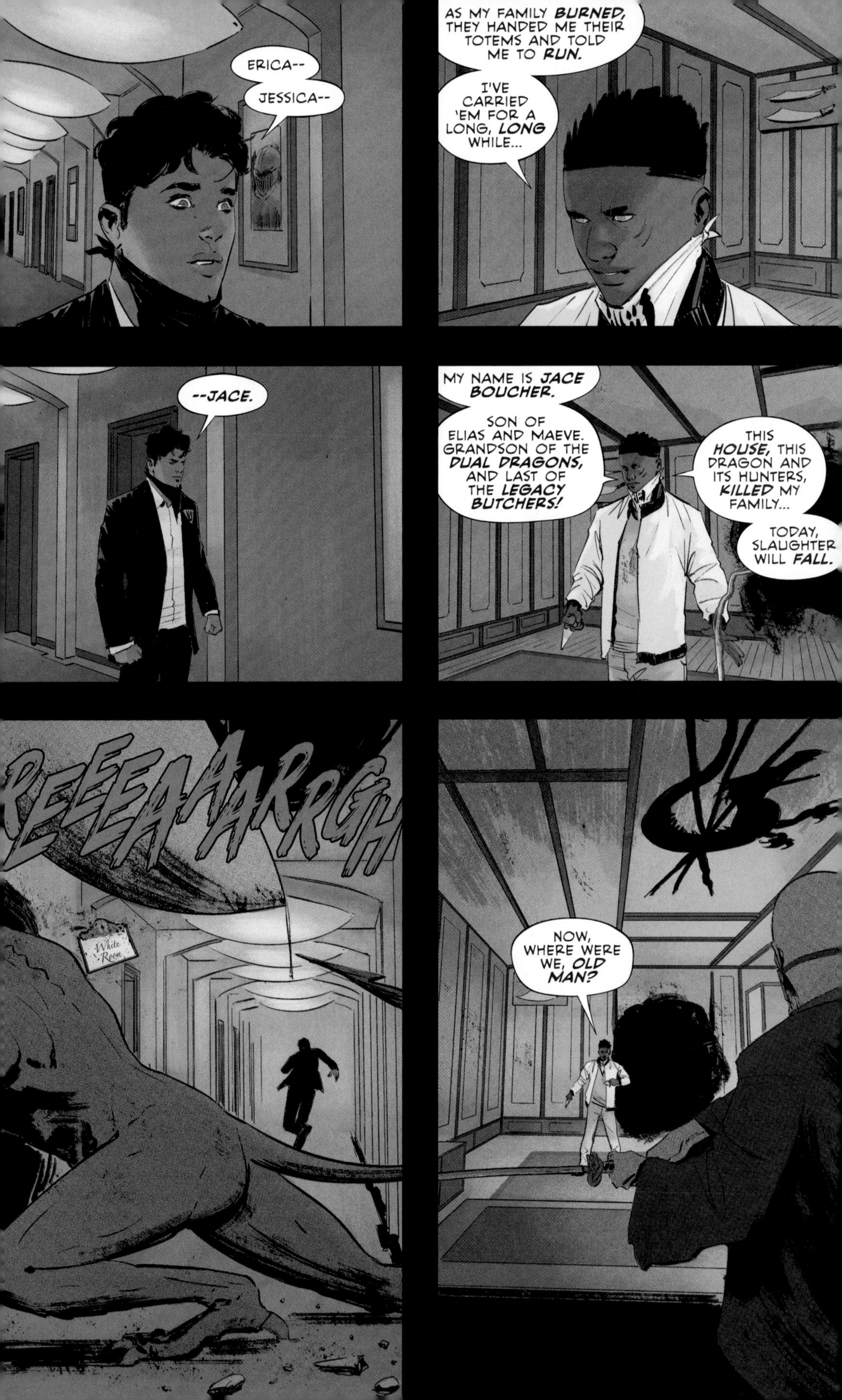
ERICA--
JESSICA--
AS MY FAMILY BURNED, THEY HANDED ME THEIR TOTEMS AND TOLD ME TO RUN.
I'VE CARRIED 'EM FOR A LONG, LONG WHILE...
--JACE.
MY NAME IS JACE BOUCHER.
SON OF ELIAS AND MAEVE. GRANDSON OF THE DUAL DRAGONS, AND LAST OF THE LEGACY BUTCHERS!
THIS HOUSE, THIS DRAGON AND ITS HUNTERS, KILLED MY FAMILY...
TODAY, SLAUGHTER WILL FALL.
REEEAAARRGH
White Room
NOW, WHERE WERE WE, OLD MAN?

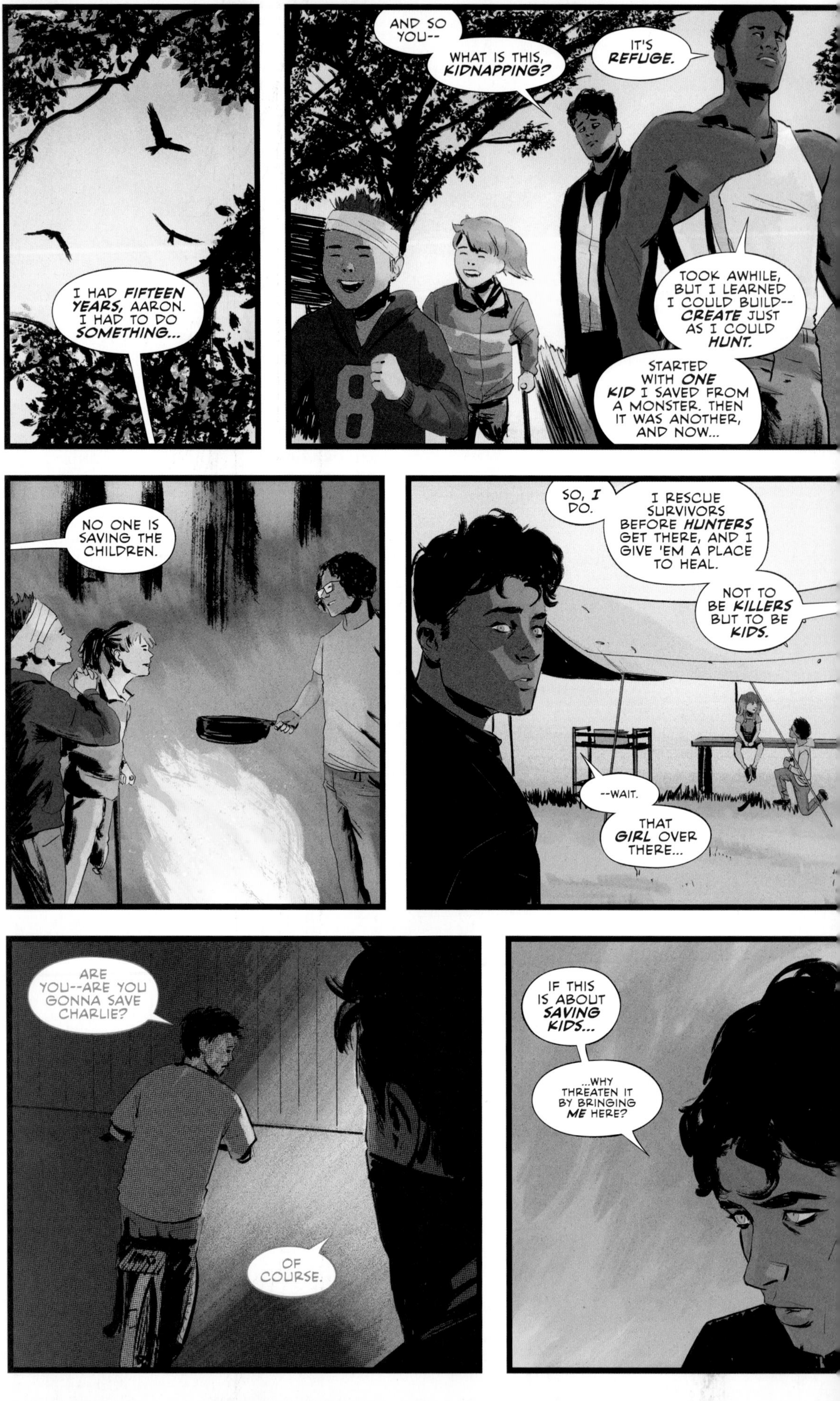
I HAD FIFTEEN YEARS, AARON. I HAD TO DO SOMETHING...
AND SO YOU--
WHAT IS THIS, KIDNAPPING?
IT'S REFUGE.
TOOK AWHILE, BUT I LEARNED I COULD BUILD-- CREATE JUST AS I COULD HUNT.
STARTED WITH ONE KID I SAVED FROM A MONSTER. THEN IT WAS ANOTHER, AND NOW...
NO ONE IS SAVING THE CHILDREN.
SO, I DO.
I RESCUE SURVIVORS BEFORE HUNTERS GET THERE, AND I GIVE 'EM A PLACE TO HEAL.
NOT TO BE KILLERS BUT TO BE KIDS.
--WAIT.
THAT GIRL OVER THERE...
ARE YOU--ARE YOU GONNA SAVE CHARLIE?
OF COURSE.
IF THIS IS ABOUT SAVING KIDS...
...WHY THREATEN IT BY BRINGING ME HERE?

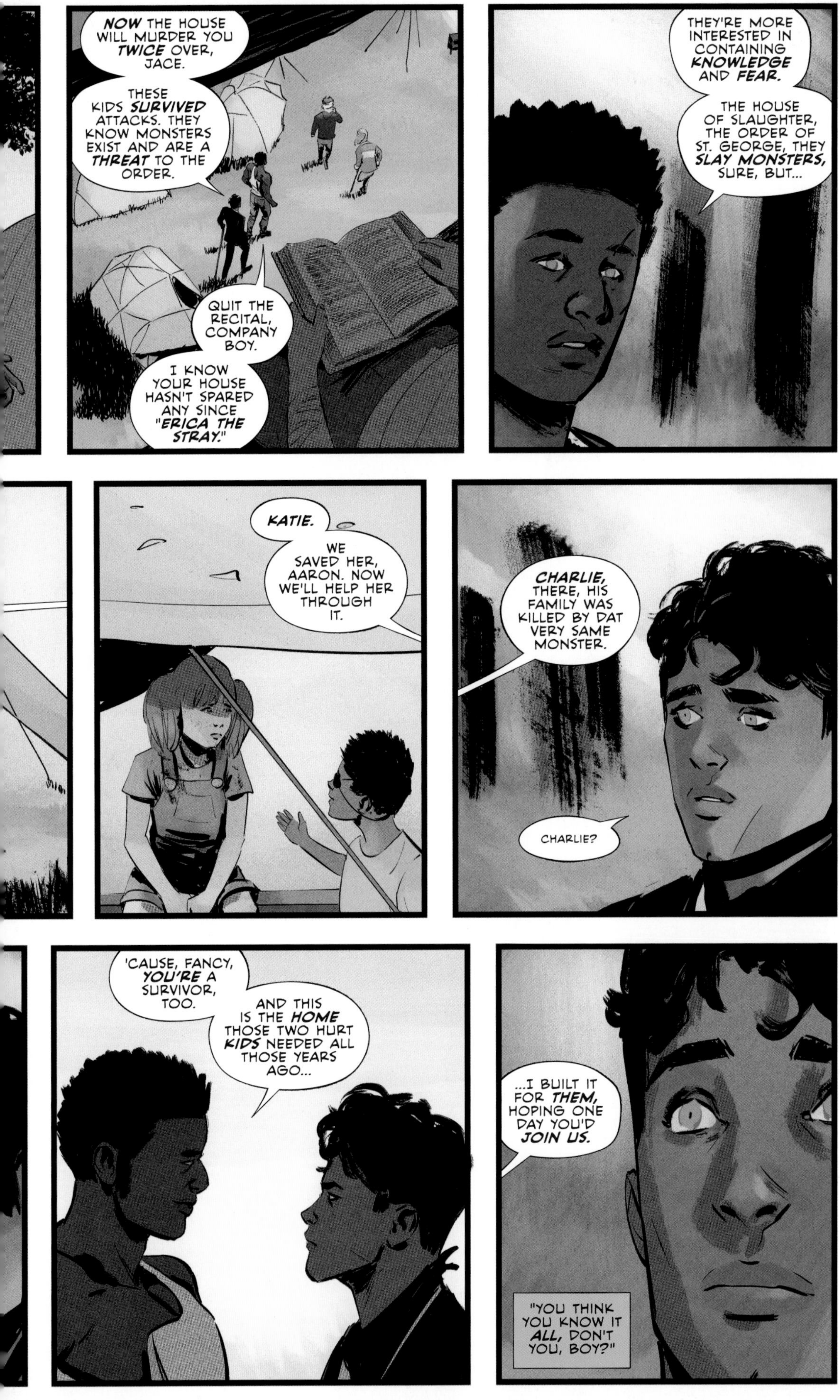
NOW THE HOUSE WILL MURDER YOU TWICE OVER, JACE.
THESE KIDS SURVIVED ATTACKS. THEY KNOW MONSTERS EXIST AND ARE A THREAT TO THE ORDER.
QUIT THE RECITAL, COMPANY BOY.
I KNOW YOUR HOUSE HASN'T SPARED ANY SINCE "ERICA THE STRAY."
THEY'RE MORE INTERESTED IN CONTAINING KNOWLEDGE AND FEAR.
THE HOUSE OF SLAUGHTER, THE ORDER OF ST. GEORGE, THEY SLAY MONSTERS, SURE, BUT...
KATIE.
WE SAVED HER, AARON. NOW WE'LL HELP HER THROUGH IT.
CHARLIE, THERE, HIS FAMILY WAS KILLED BY DAT VERY SAME MONSTER.
CHARLIE?
'CAUSE, FANCY, YOU'RE A SURVIVOR, TOO.
AND THIS IS THE HOME THOSE TWO HURT KIDS NEEDED ALL THOSE YEARS AGO...
...I BUILT IT FOR THEM, HOPING ONE DAY YOU'D JOIN US.
"YOU THINK YOU KNOW IT ALL, DON'T YOU, BOY?"

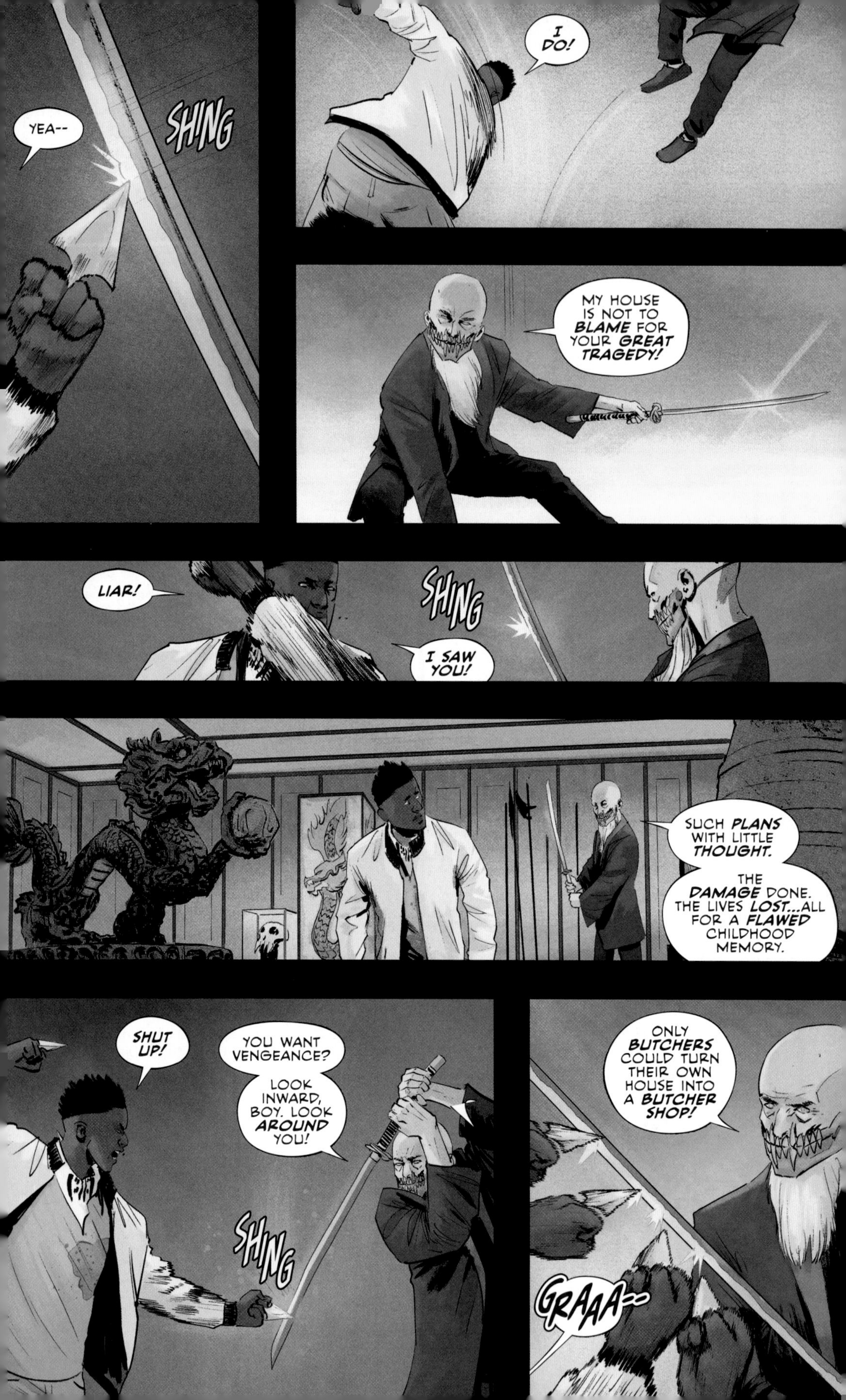
YEA--
SHING
I DO!
MY HOUSE IS NOT TO BLAME FOR YOUR GREAT TRAGEDY!
LIAR!
SHING
I SAW YOU!
SUCH PLANS WITH LITTLE THOUGHT.
THE DAMAGE DONE. THE LIVES LOST...ALL FOR A FLAWED CHILDHOOD MEMORY.
SHUT UP!
YOU WANT VENGEANCE?
LOOK INWARD, BOY. LOOK AROUND YOU!
SHING
ONLY BUTCHERS COULD TURN THEIR OWN HOUSE INTO A BUTCHER SHOP!
GRAAA--

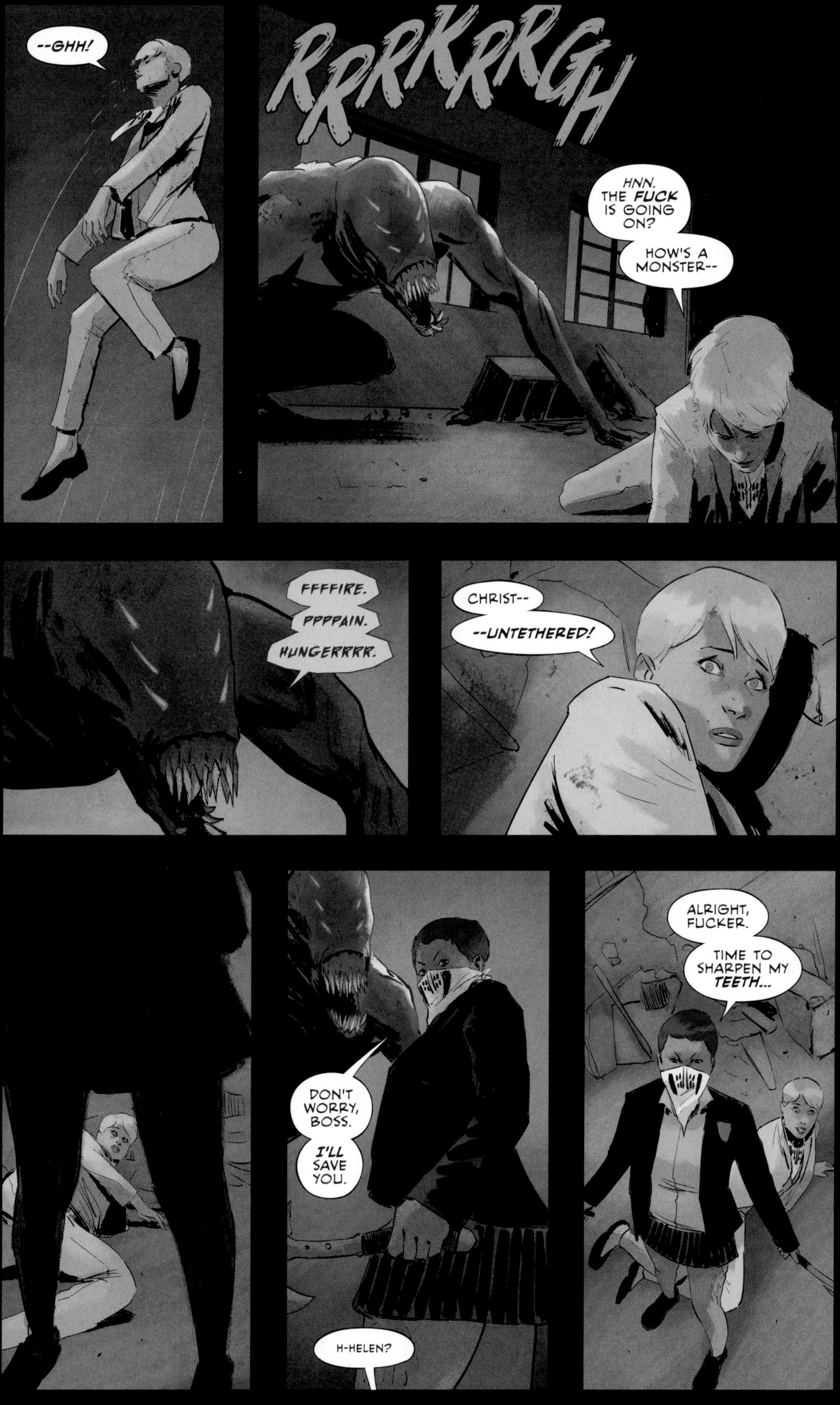
--GHH!
RRRKRRGH
HNN. THE FUCK IS GOING ON?
HOW'S A MONSTER--
FFFFIRE.
PPPPAIN.
HUNGERRRR.
CHRIST--
--UNTETHERED!
DON'T WORRY, BOSS.
I'LL SAVE YOU.
H-HELEN?
ALRIGHT, FUCKER.
TIME TO SHARPEN MY TEETH...

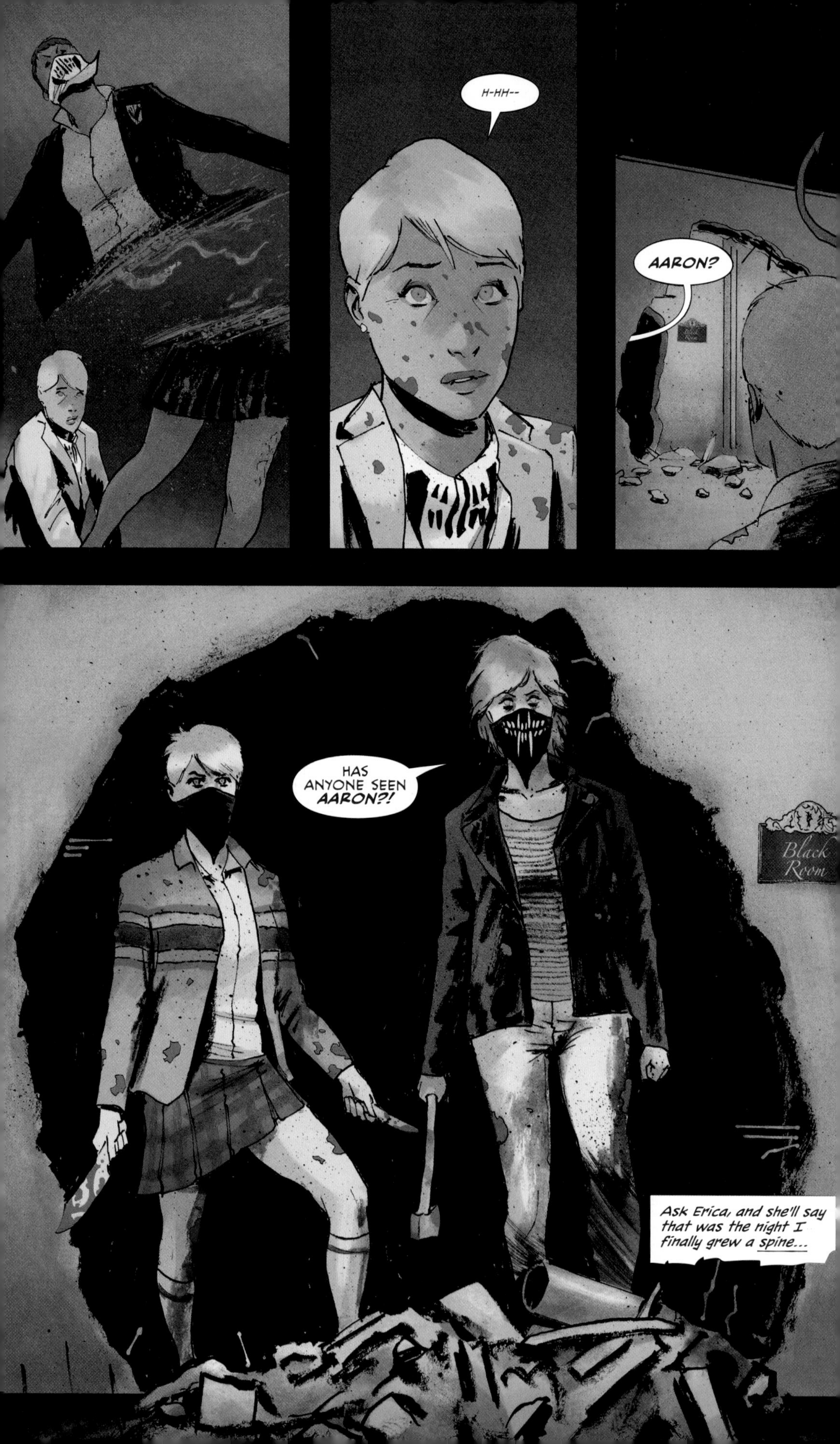
H-HH--
AARON?
HAS ANYONE SEEN AARON?!
Ask Erica, and she'll say that was the night I finally grew a spine...
Black Room

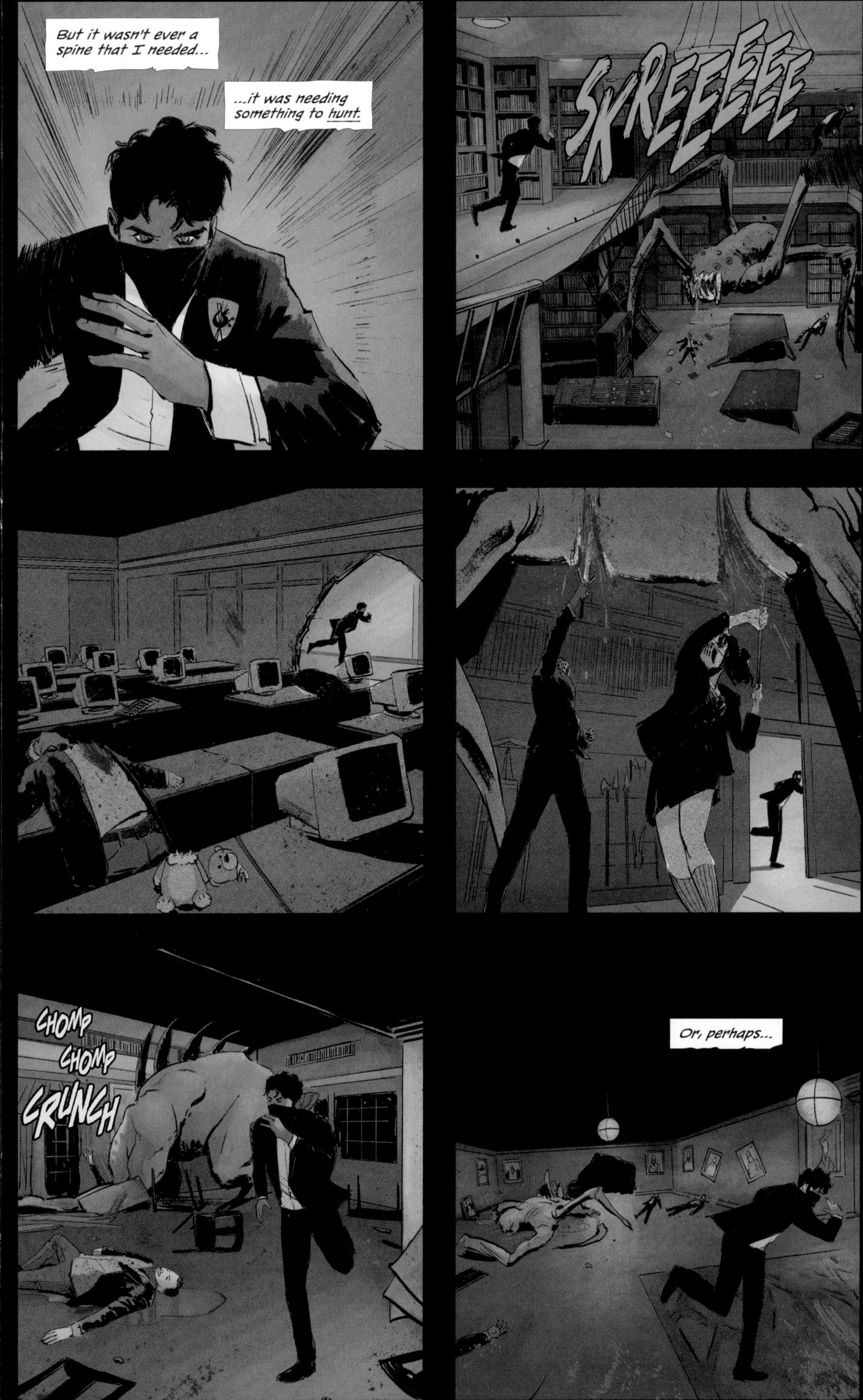
But it wasn't ever a spine that I needed...
...it was needing something to hunt.
SKREEEEEE
CHOMP
CHOMP
CRUNCH
Or, perhaps...

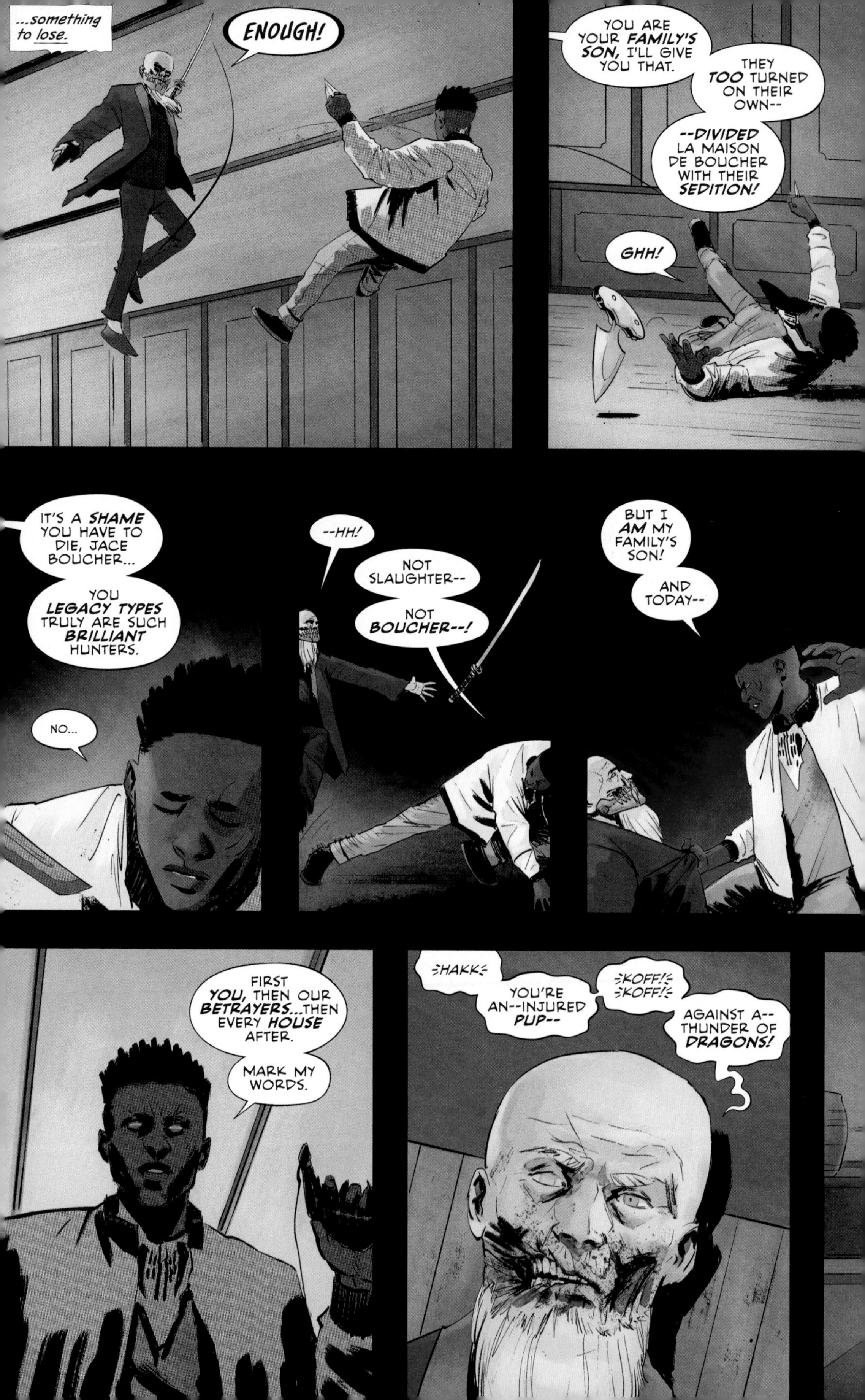
...something to lose.
ENOUGH!
YOU ARE YOUR FAMILY'S SON, I'LL GIVE YOU THAT.
THEY TOO TURNED ON THEIR OWN--
--DIVIDED LA MAISON DE BOUCHER WITH THEIR SEDITION!
GHH!
IT'S A SHAME YOU HAVE TO DIE, JACE BOUCHER...
YOU LEGACY TYPES TRULY ARE SUCH BRILLIANT HUNTERS.
NO...
--HH!
NOT SLAUGHTER--
NOT BOUCHER--!
BUT I AM MY FAMILY'S SON!
AND TODAY--
FIRST YOU, THEN OUR BETRAYERS...THEN EVERY HOUSE AFTER.
MARK MY WORDS.
HAKK
YOU'RE AN--INJURED PUP--
KOFF! KOFF!
AGAINST A--THUNDER OF DRAGONS!

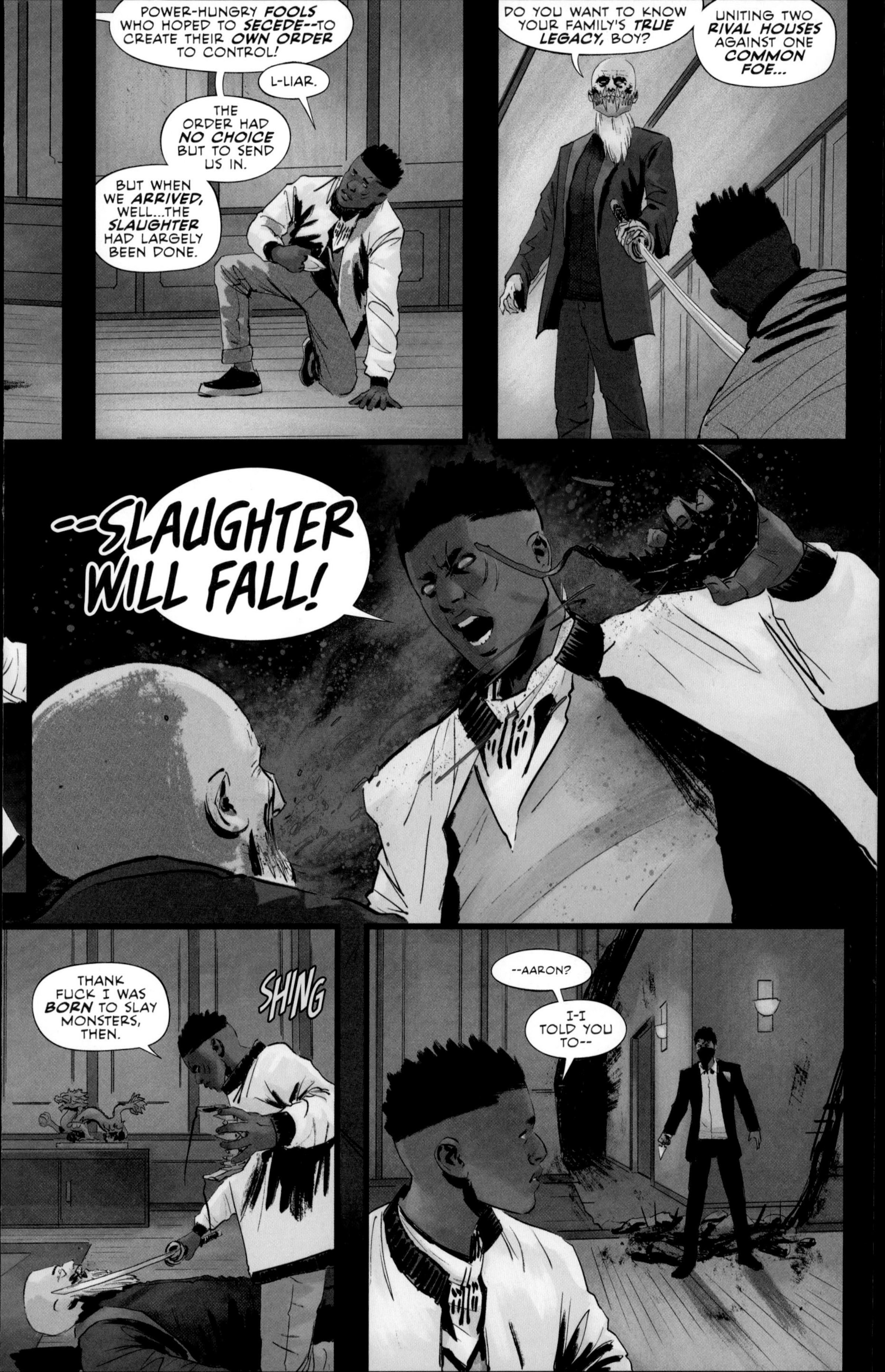

POWER-HUNGRY FOOLS WHO HOPED TO SECEDE--TO CREATE THEIR OWN ORDER TO CONTROL!
L-LIAR.
THE ORDER HAD NO CHOICE BUT TO SEND US IN.
BUT WHEN WE ARRIVED, WELL...THE SLAUGHTER HAD LARGELY BEEN DONE.
DO YOU WANT TO KNOW YOUR FAMILY'S TRUE LEGACY, BOY?
UNITING TWO RIVAL HOUSES AGAINST ONE COMMON FOE...
--SLAUGHTER WILL FALL!
THANK FUCK I WAS BORN TO SLAY MONSTERS, THEN.
SHING
--AARON?
I-I TOLD YOU TO--

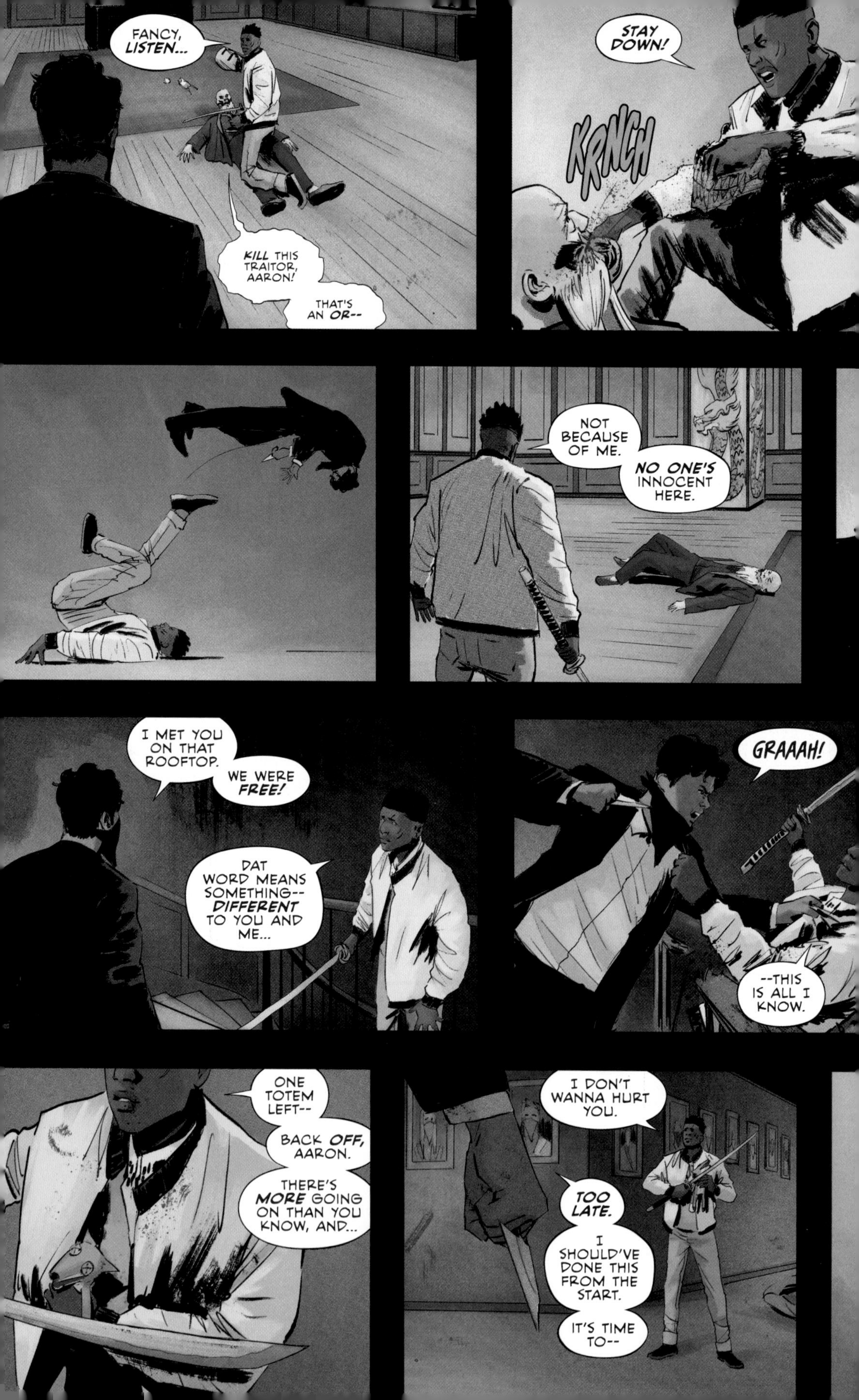
FANCY, LISTEN...
KILL THIS TRAITOR, AARON!
THAT'S AN OR--
STAY DOWN!
KRNCH
NOT BECAUSE OF ME.
NO ONE'S INNOCENT HERE.
I MET YOU ON THAT ROOFTOP.
WE WERE FREE!
DAT WORD MEANS SOMETHING-- DIFFERENT TO YOU AND ME...
GRAAAH!
--THIS IS ALL I KNOW.
ONE TOTEM LEFT--
BACK OFF, AARON.
THERE'S MORE GOING ON THAN YOU KNOW, AND...
I DON'T WANNA HURT YOU.
TOO LATE.
I SHOULD'VE DONE THIS FROM THE START.
IT'S TIME TO--

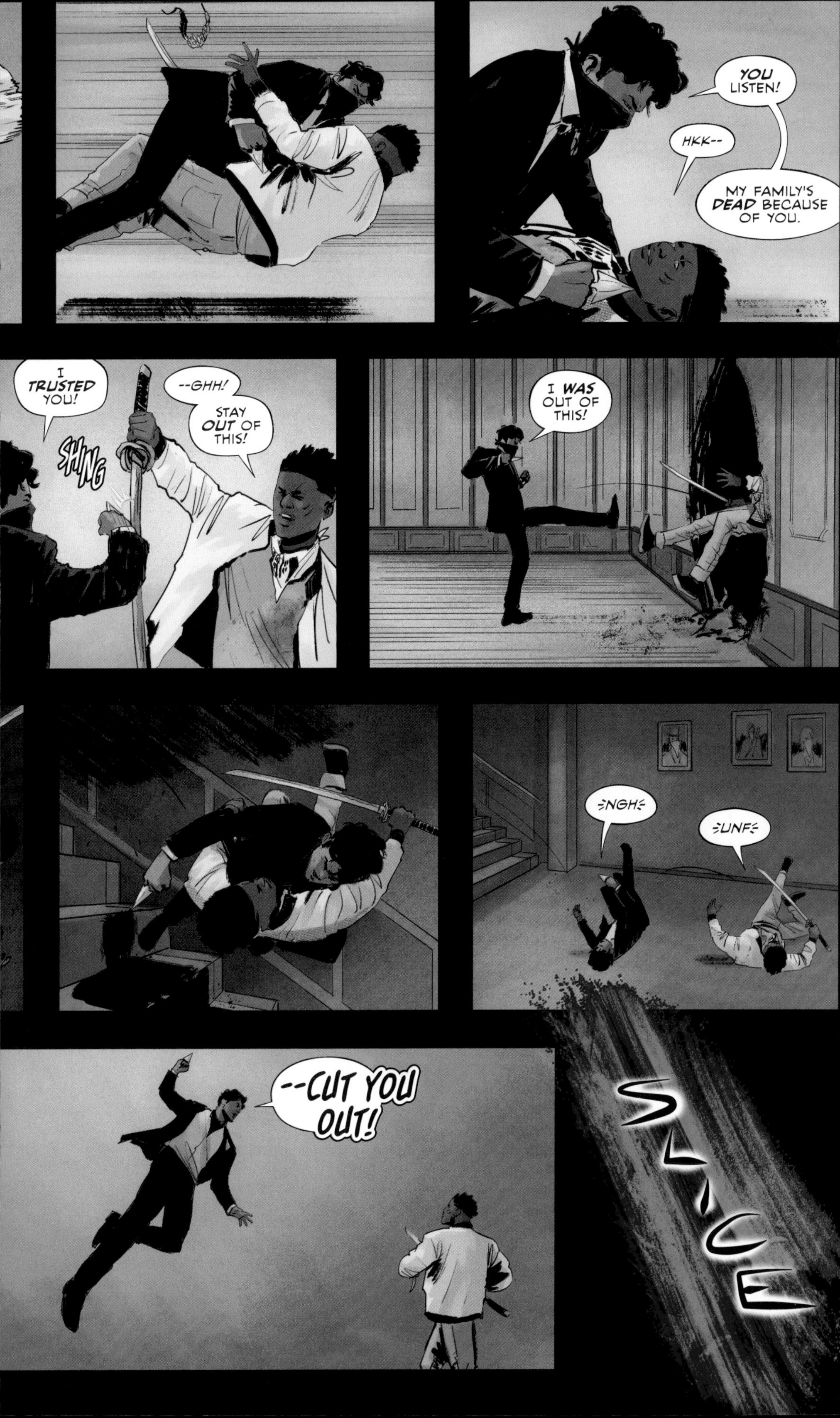
YOU LISTEN!
HKK--
MY FAMILY'S DEAD BECAUSE OF YOU.
I TRUSTED YOU!
SHING
--GHH!
STAY OUT OF THIS!
I WAS OUT OF THIS!
NGH
UNF
--CUT YOU OUT!
SLICE

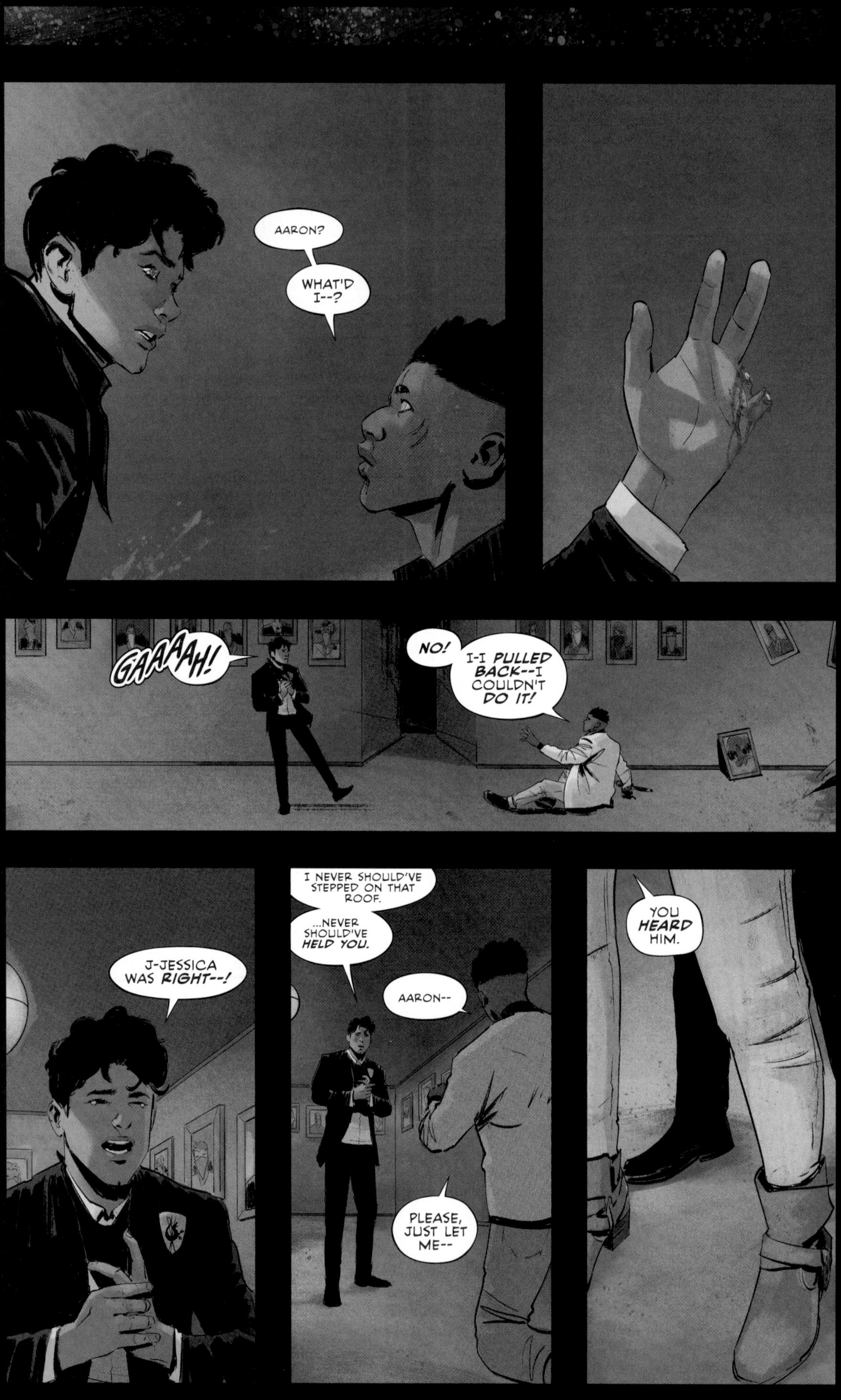
AARON?
WHAT'D I--?
GAAAAAH!
NO!
I-I PULLED BACK--I COULDN'T DO IT!
J-JESSICA WAS RIGHT--!
I NEVER SHOULD'VE STEPPED ON THAT ROOF.
...NEVER SHOULD'VE HELD YOU.
AARON--
PLEASE, JUST LET ME--
YOU HEARD HIM.

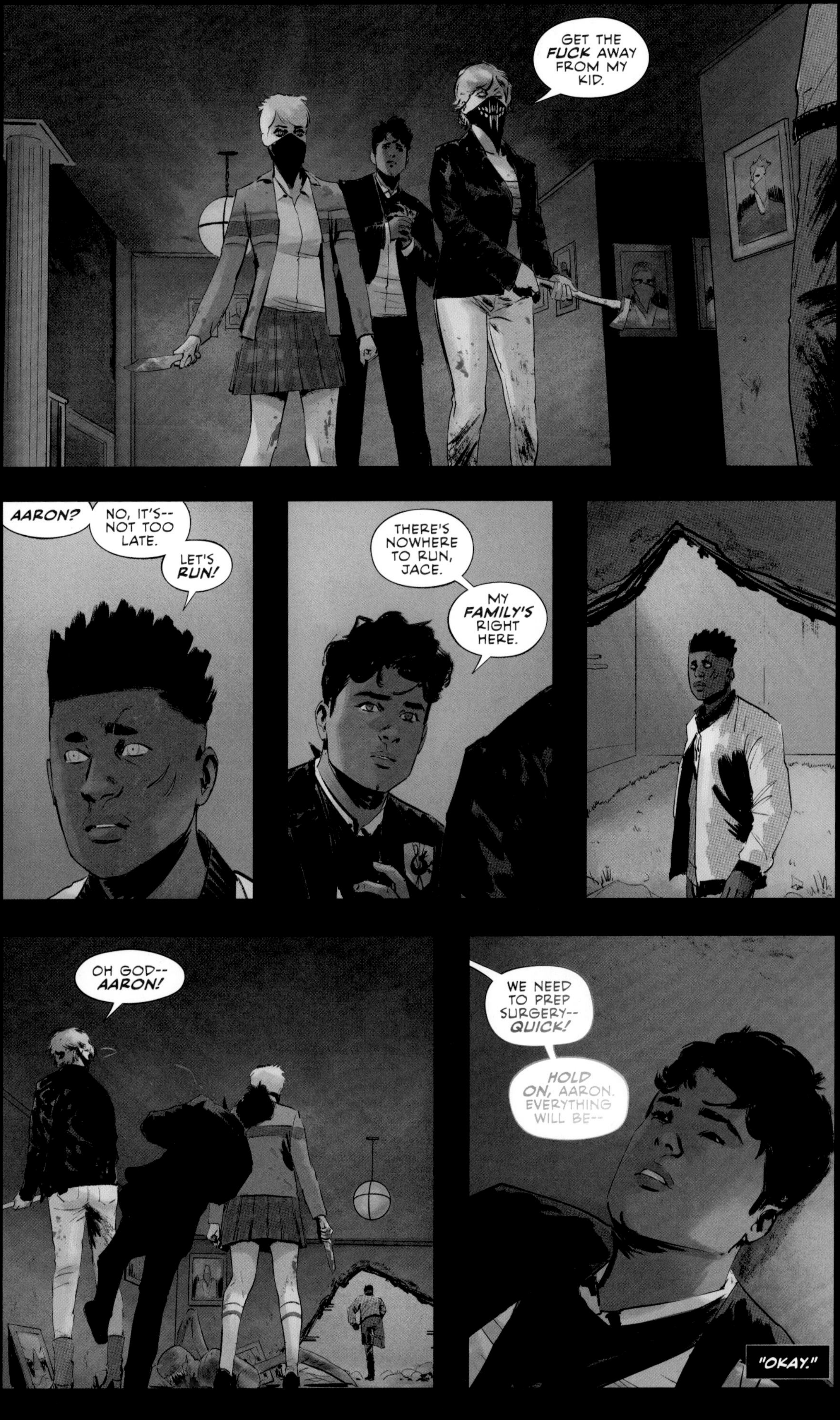
GET THE FUCK AWAY FROM MY KID.
AARON?
NO, IT'S-- NOT TOO LATE.
LET'S RUN!
THERE'S NOWHERE TO RUN, JACE.
MY FAMILY'S RIGHT HERE.
OH GOD-- AARON!
WE NEED TO PREP SURGERY-- QUICK!
HOLD ON, AARON. EVERYTHING WILL BE--
"OKAY."

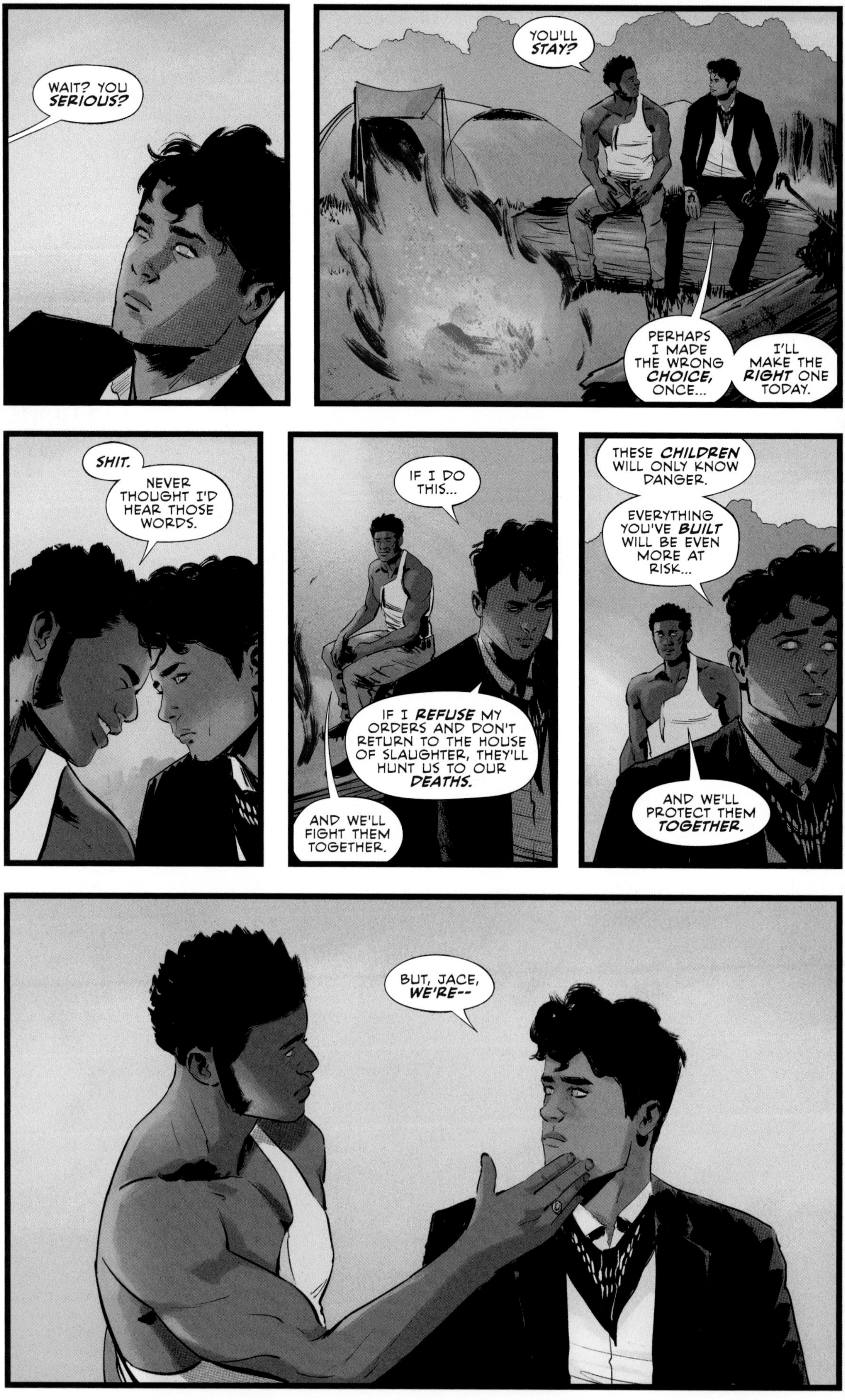
WAIT? YOU SERIOUS?
YOU'LL STAY?
PERHAPS I MADE THE WRONG CHOICE, ONCE...
I'LL MAKE THE RIGHT ONE TODAY.
SHIT.
NEVER THOUGHT I'D HEAR THOSE WORDS.
IF I DO THIS...
IF I REFUSE MY ORDERS AND DON'T RETURN TO THE HOUSE OF SLAUGHTER, THEY'LL HUNT US TO OUR DEATHS.
AND WE'LL FIGHT THEM TOGETHER.
THESE CHILDREN WILL ONLY KNOW DANGER.
EVERYTHING YOU'VE BUILT WILL BE EVEN MORE AT RISK...
AND WE'LL PROTECT THEM TOGETHER.
BUT, JACE, WE'RE--

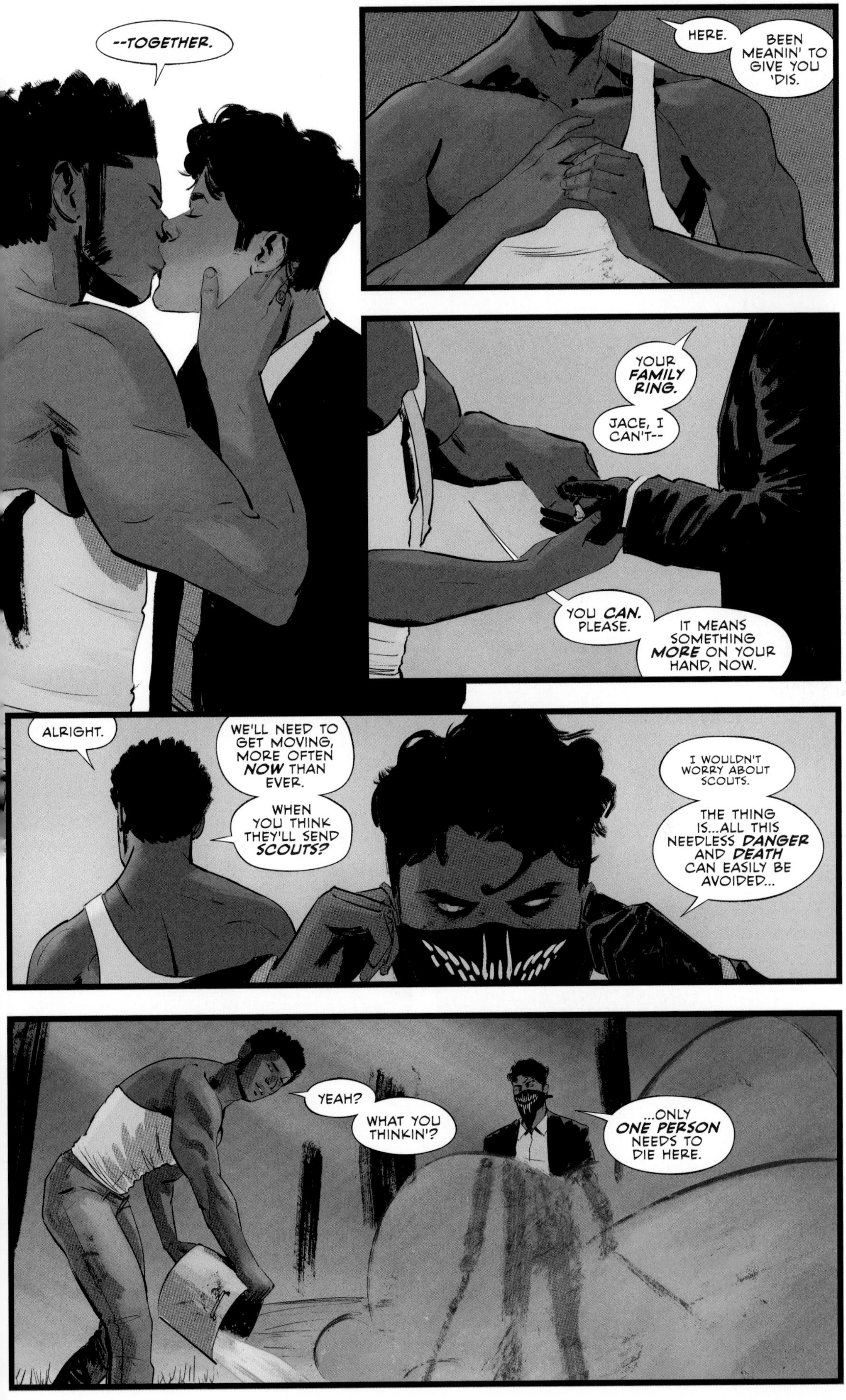
--TOGETHER.
HERE.
BEEN MEANIN' TO GIVE YOU 'DIS.
YOUR FAMILY RING.
JACE, I CAN'T--
YOU CAN. PLEASE.
IT MEANS SOMETHING MORE ON YOUR HAND, NOW.
ALRIGHT.
WE'LL NEED TO GET MOVING, MORE OFTEN NOW THAN EVER.
WHEN YOU THINK THEY'LL SEND SCOUTS?
I WOULDN'T WORRY ABOUT SCOUTS.
THE THING IS...ALL THIS NEEDLESS DANGER AND DEATH CAN EASILY BE AVOIDED...
YEAH?
WHAT YOU THINKIN'?
...ONLY ONE PERSON NEEDS TO DIE HERE.

...and just like that, the Butcher is dead.

After what he did to our House, to my *family*, he needed to be put down.

A vengeance of my own, you could say.

But I'm sure you're questioning all of this.

TELL ME, HOW'S *AARON* DOING?

"Aaron? Kill a Legacy Hunter?" I know, I know...

THAT BOY FACED A *MONSTER* AND SAVED US ALL.

...but I've always known how to set a *good trap.*

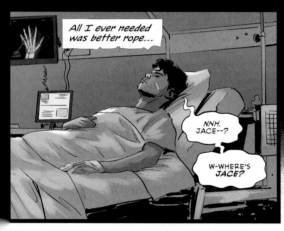

All I ever needed was better rope...

NNH. JACE--?

W-WHERE'S *JACE?*

...the perfect bait...

...and a monster to *hunt.*

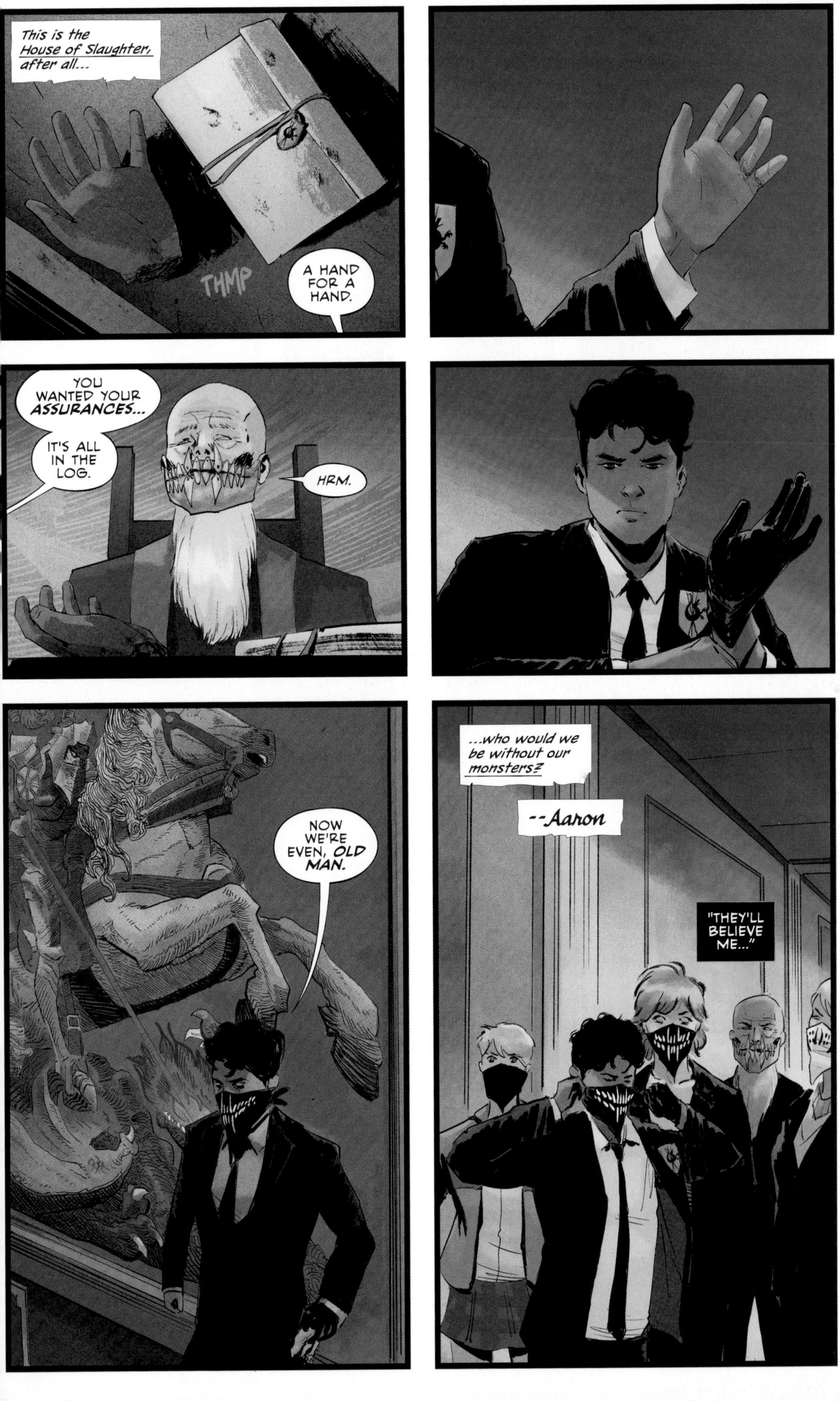
This is the House of Slaughter, after all...
THMP
A HAND FOR A HAND.
YOU WANTED YOUR ASSURANCES...
IT'S ALL IN THE LOG.
HRM.
NOW WE'RE EVEN, OLD MAN.
...who would we be without our monsters?
--Aaron
"THEY'LL BELIEVE ME..."

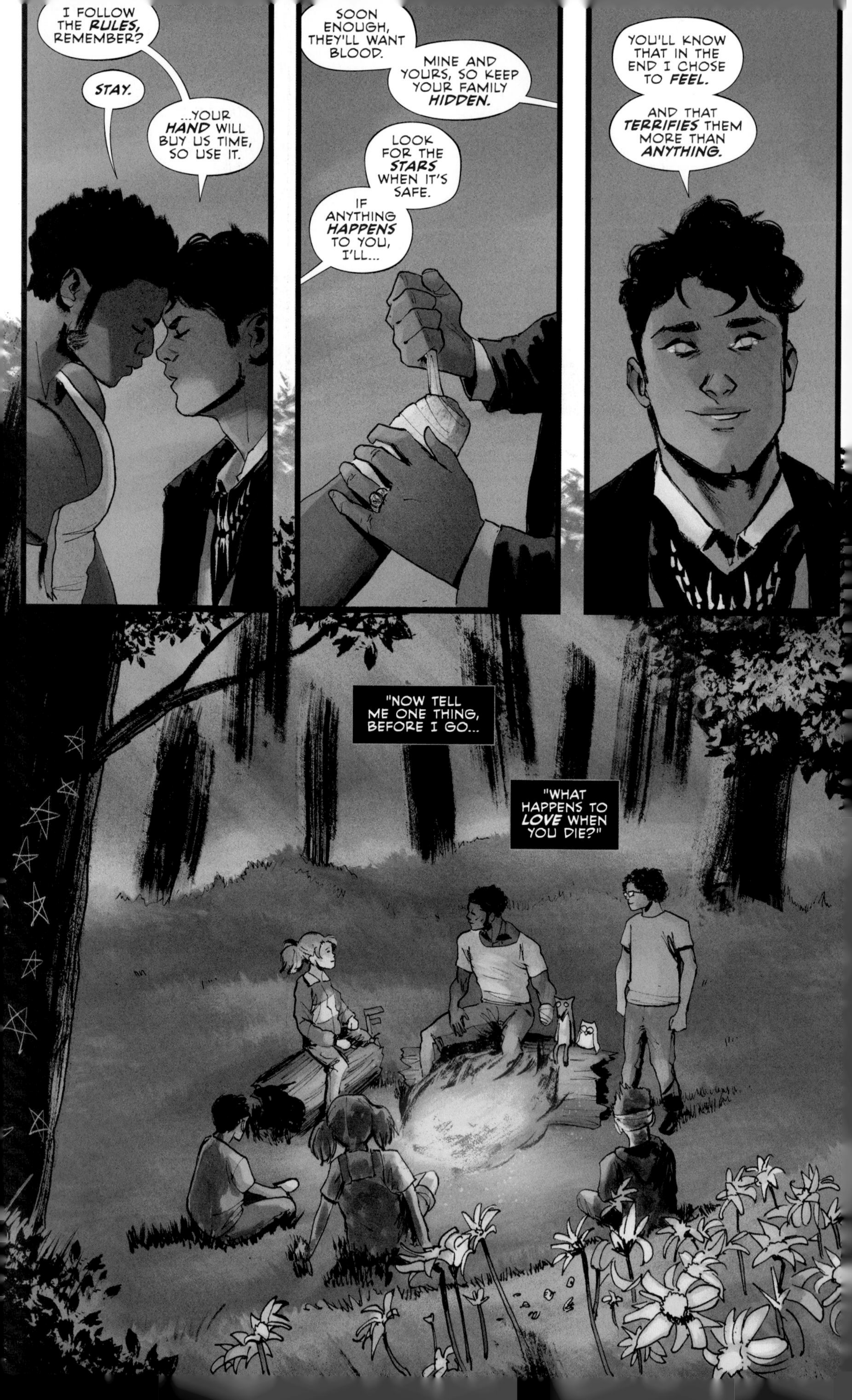
I FOLLOW THE RULES, REMEMBER?
STAY.
...YOUR HAND WILL BUY US TIME, SO USE IT.
SOON ENOUGH, THEY'LL WANT BLOOD.
MINE AND YOURS, SO KEEP YOUR FAMILY HIDDEN.
LOOK FOR THE STARS WHEN IT'S SAFE.
IF ANYTHING HAPPENS TO YOU, I'LL...
YOU'LL KNOW THAT IN THE END I CHOSE TO FEEL.
AND THAT TERRIFIES THEM MORE THAN ANYTHING.
"NOW TELL ME ONE THING, BEFORE I GO...
"WHAT HAPPENS TO LOVE WHEN YOU DIE?"

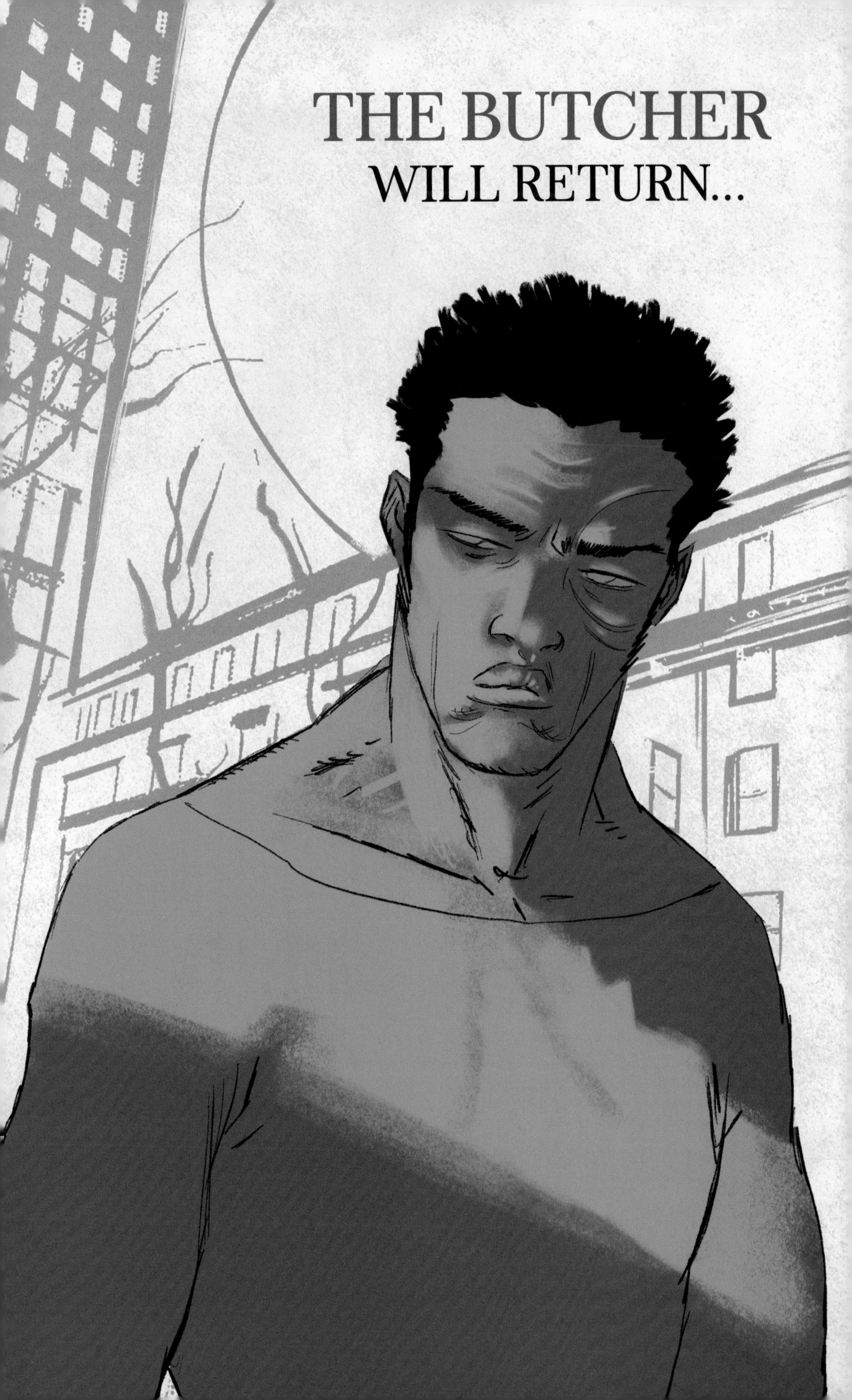
THE BUTCHER
WILL RETURN...

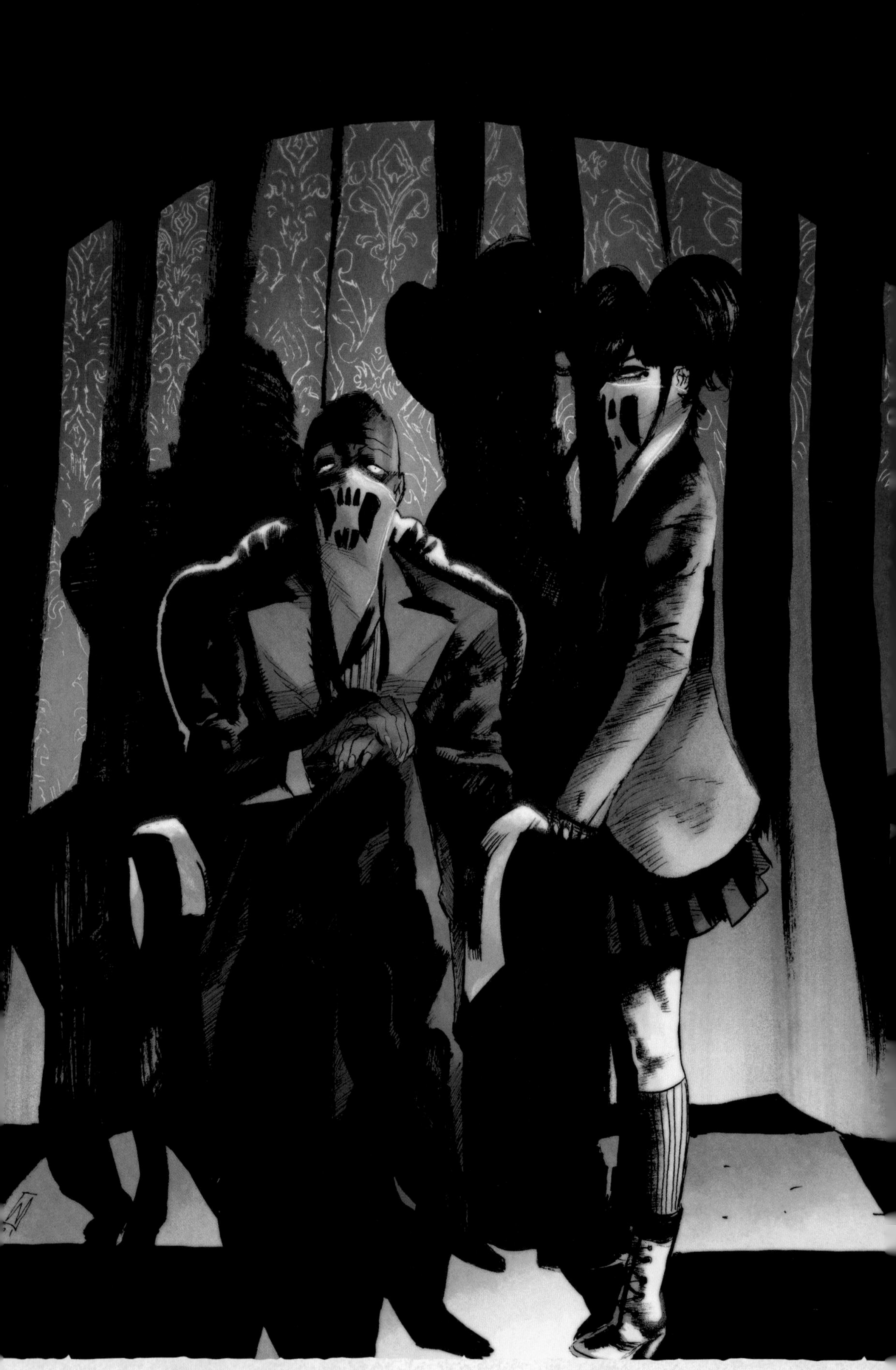

ISSUE FIVE COVER BY WERTHER DELL'EDERA WITH COLORS BY MIQUEL MUERTO

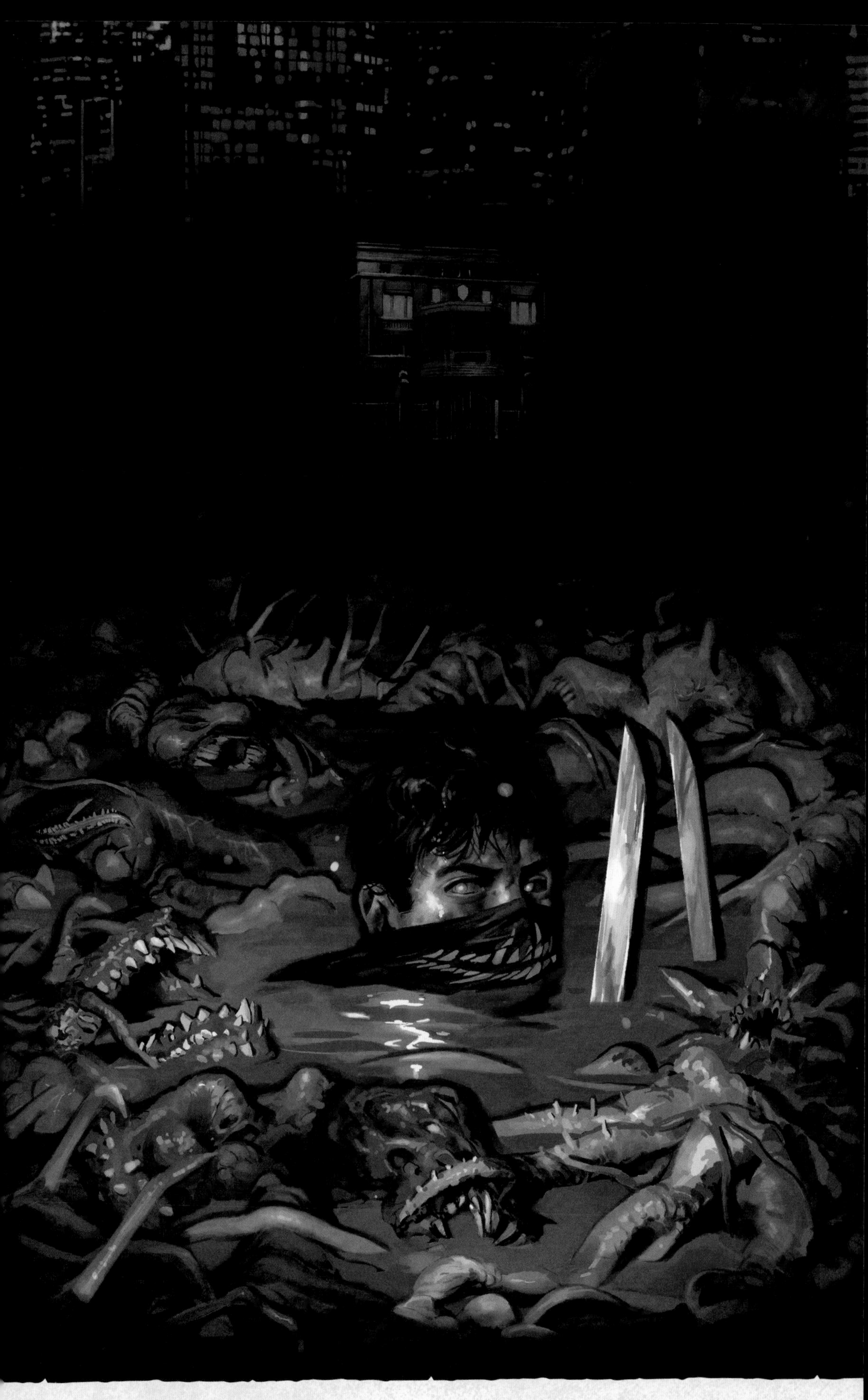

ISSUE ONE VARIANT COVER BY ÁLVARO MARTINEZ BUENO

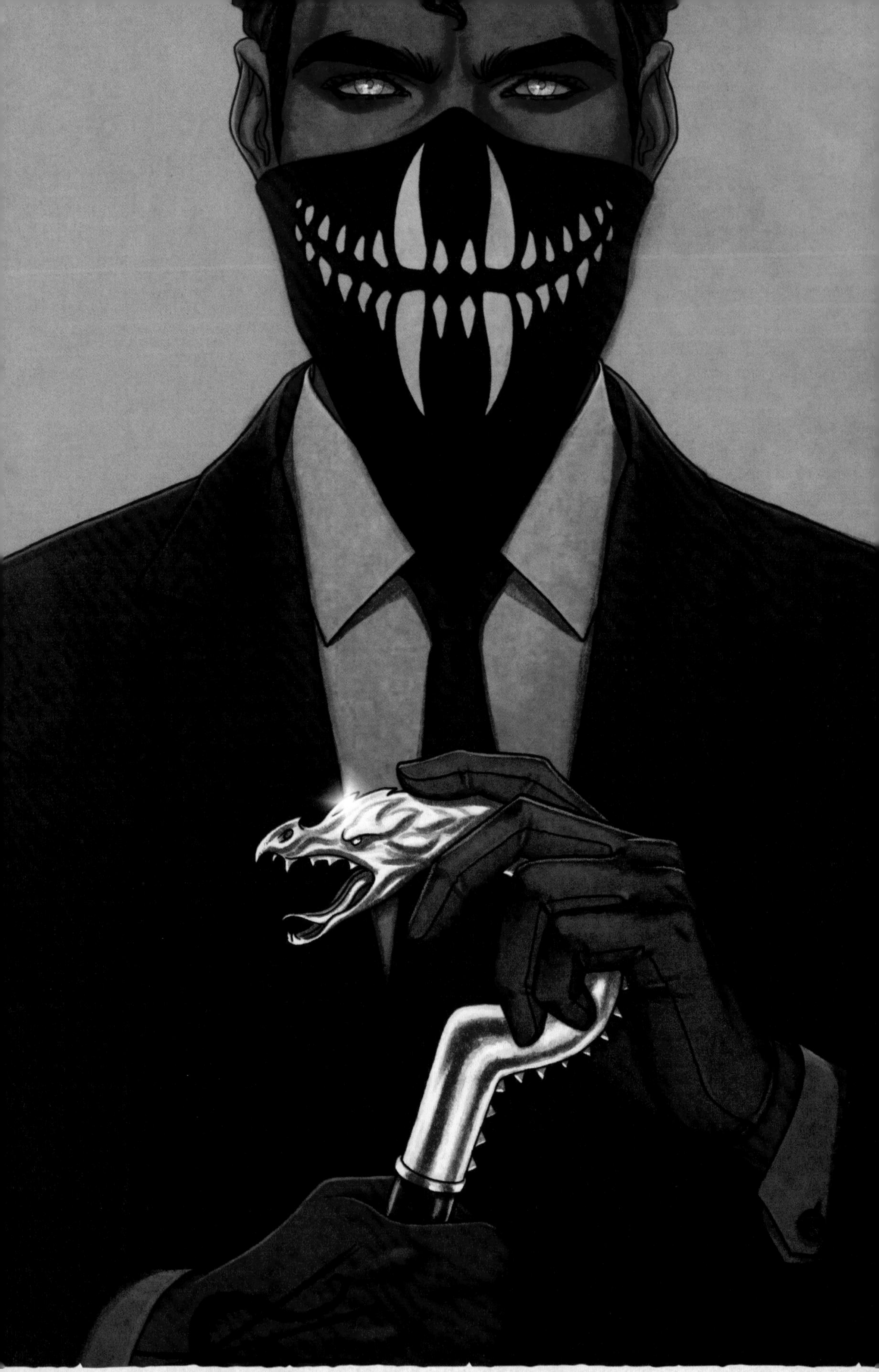

ISSUE ONE VARIANT COVER BY JENNY FRISON

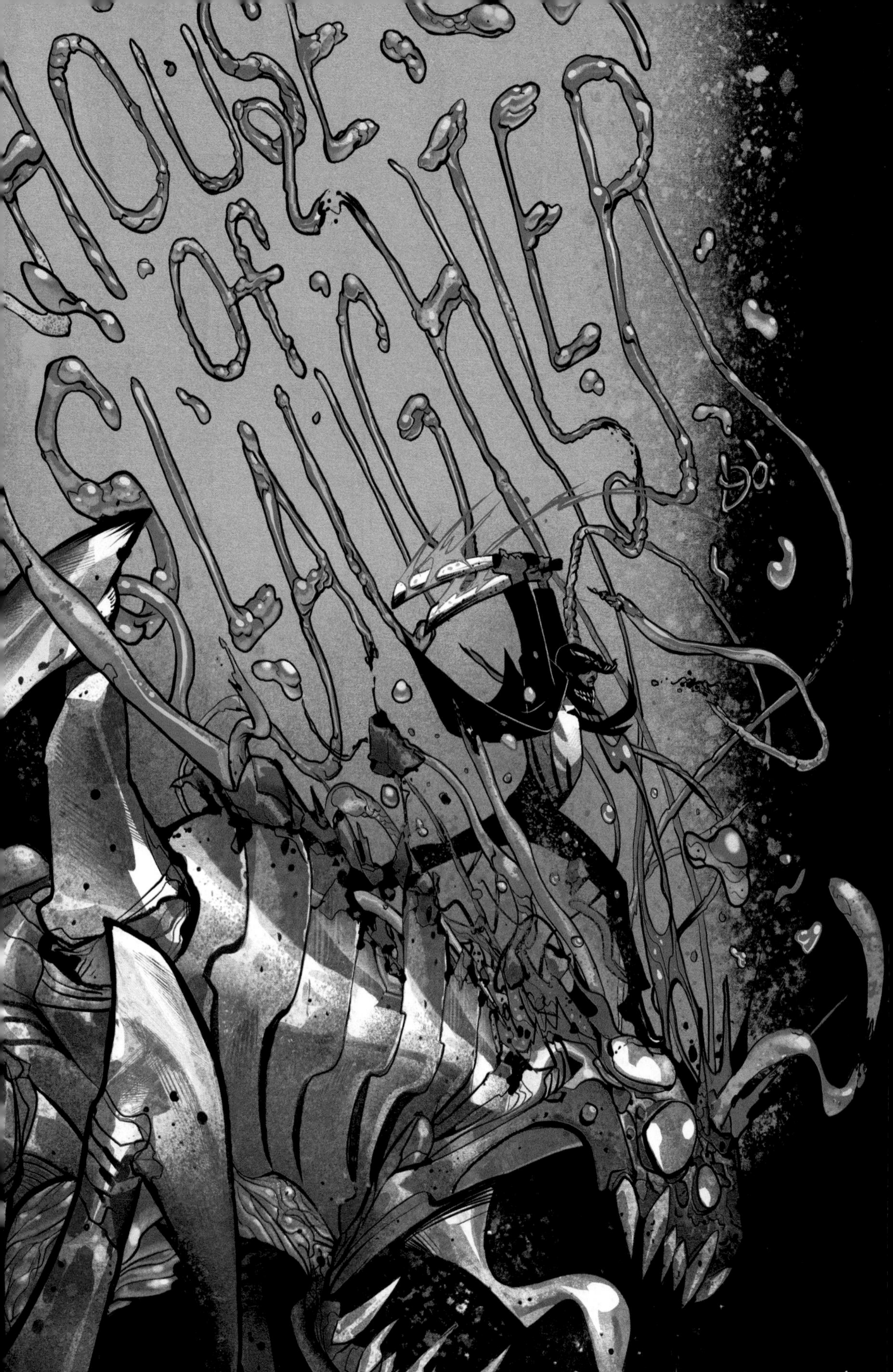
HOUSE OF SLAUGHTER

ISSUE ONE VARIANT COVER BY MIKE DEL MUNDO

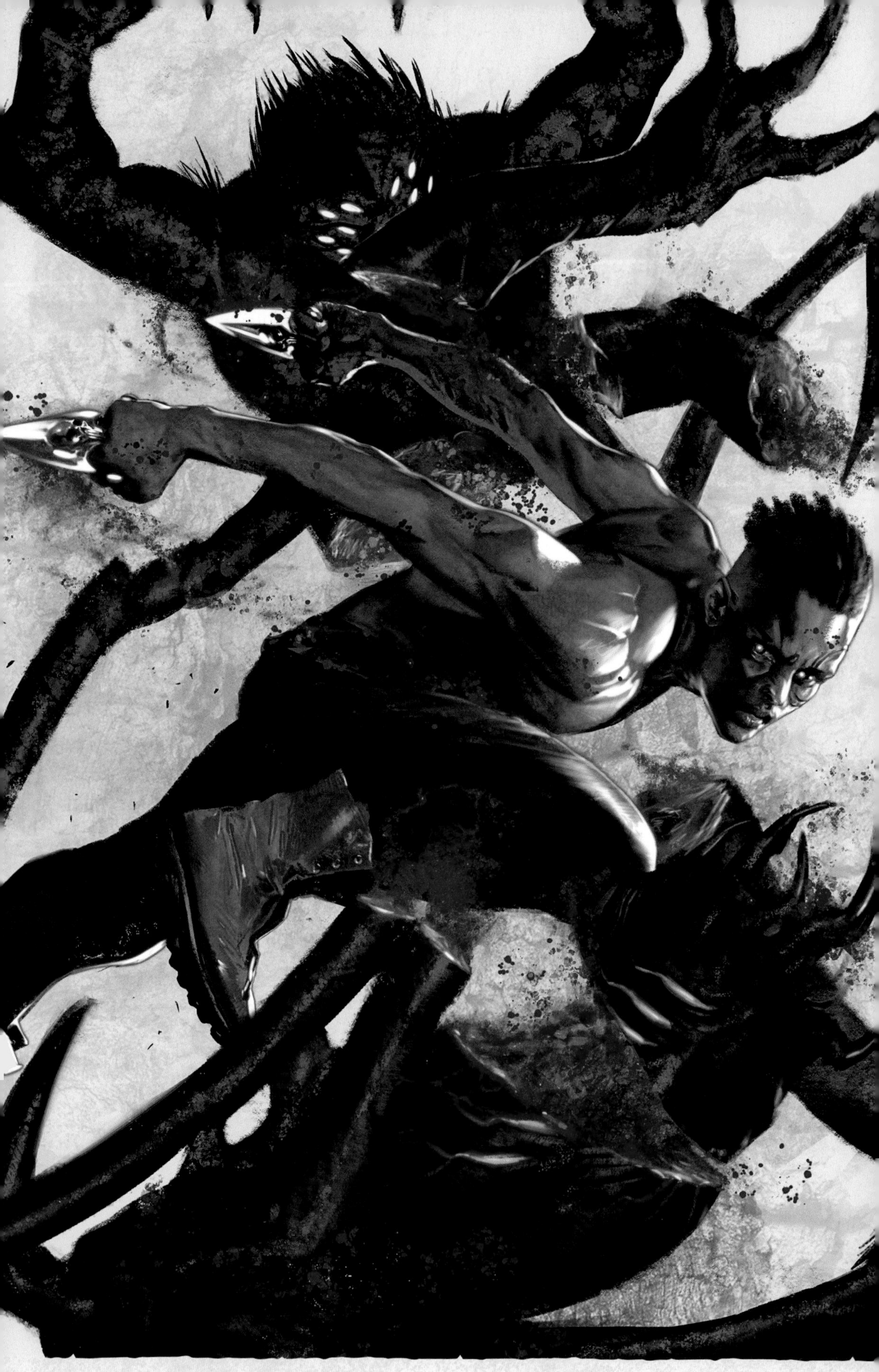

ISSUE ONE VARIANT COVER BY GABRIELE DELL'OTTO

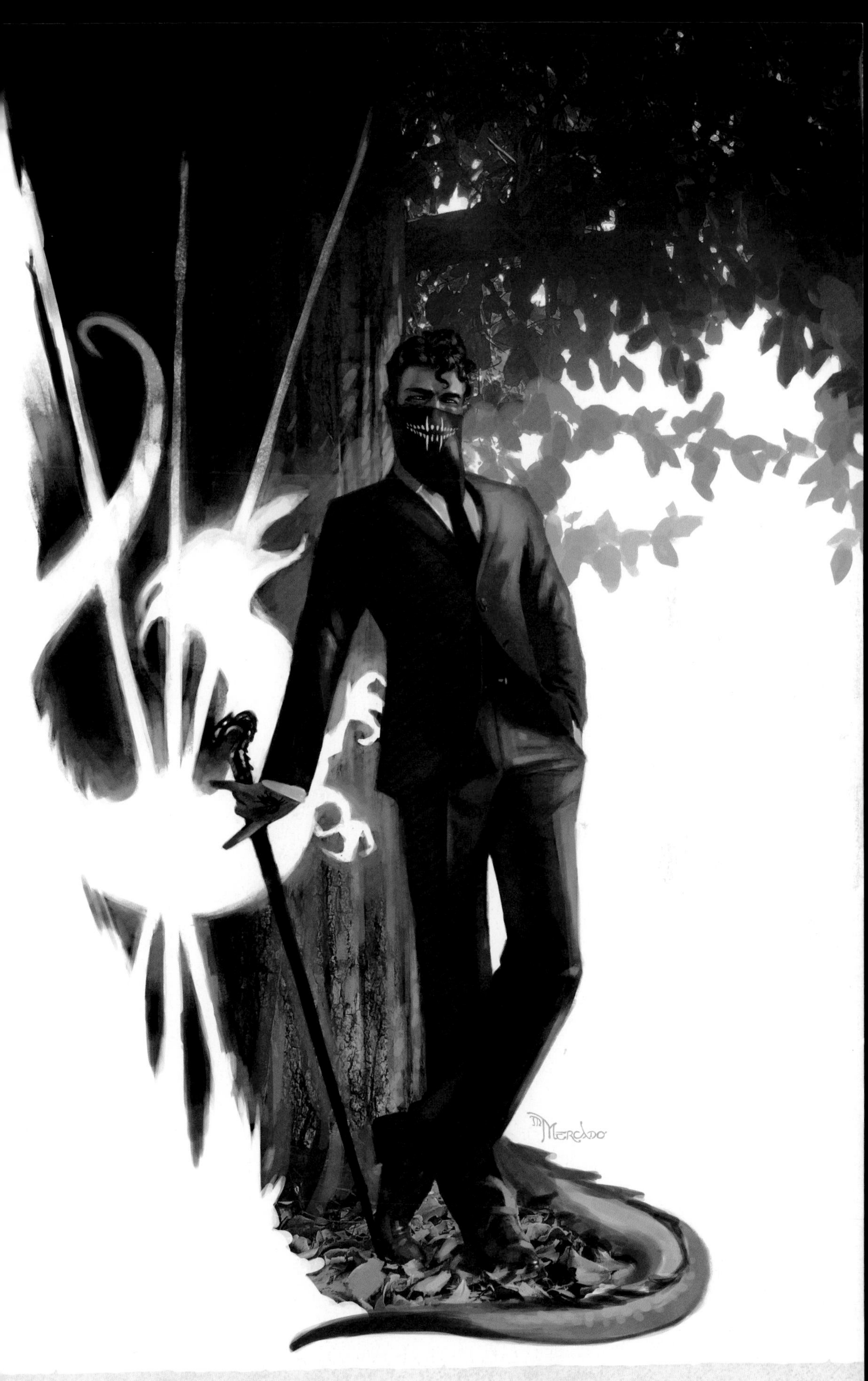
M. MERCADO

ISSUE ONE VARIANT COVER BY MIGUEL MERCADO

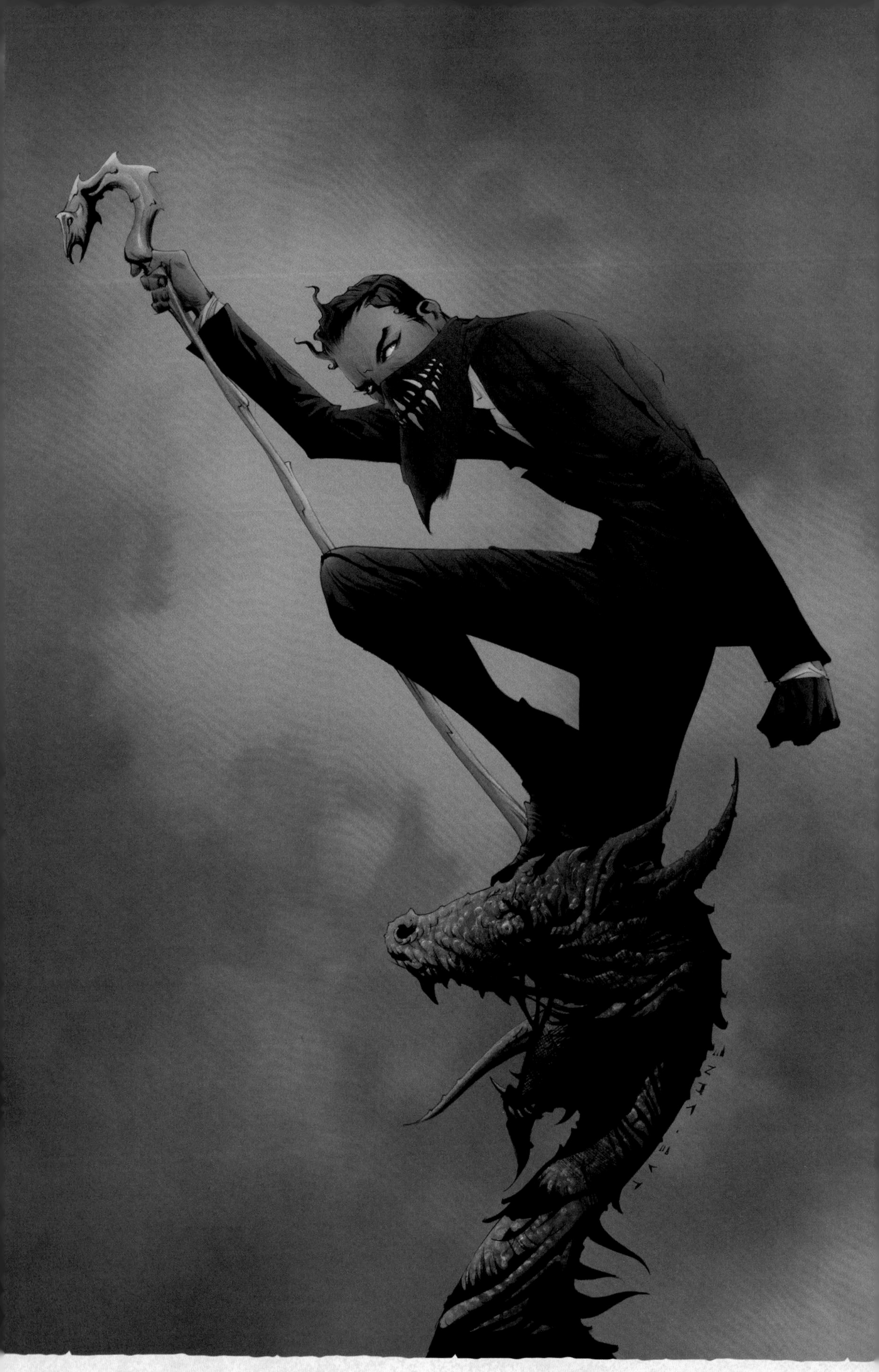

ISSUE ONE VARIANT COVER BY JAE LEE WITH COLORS BY JUNE CHUNG

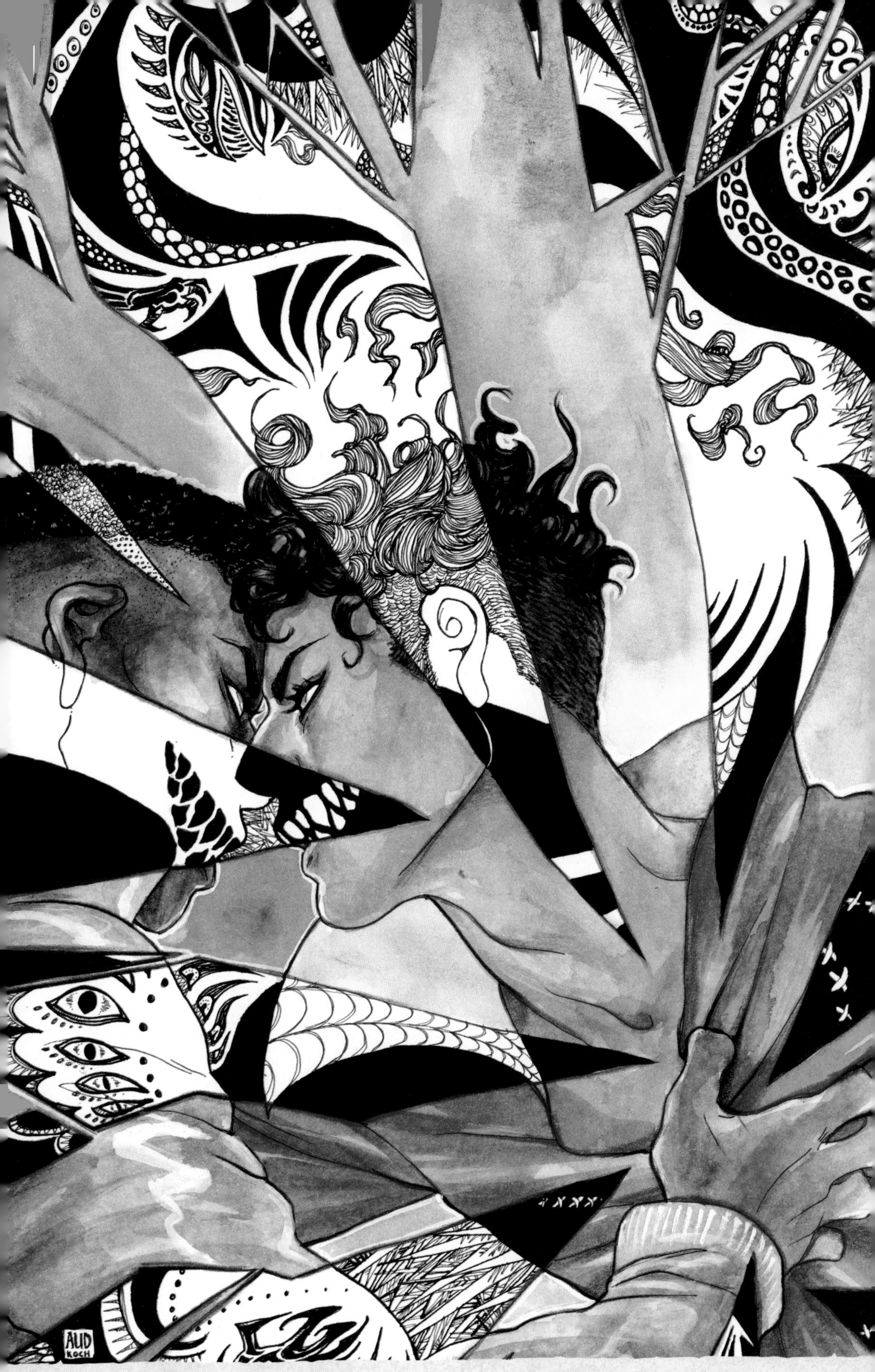
AUD
KOCH

ISSUE TWO VARIANT COVER BY AUD KOCH

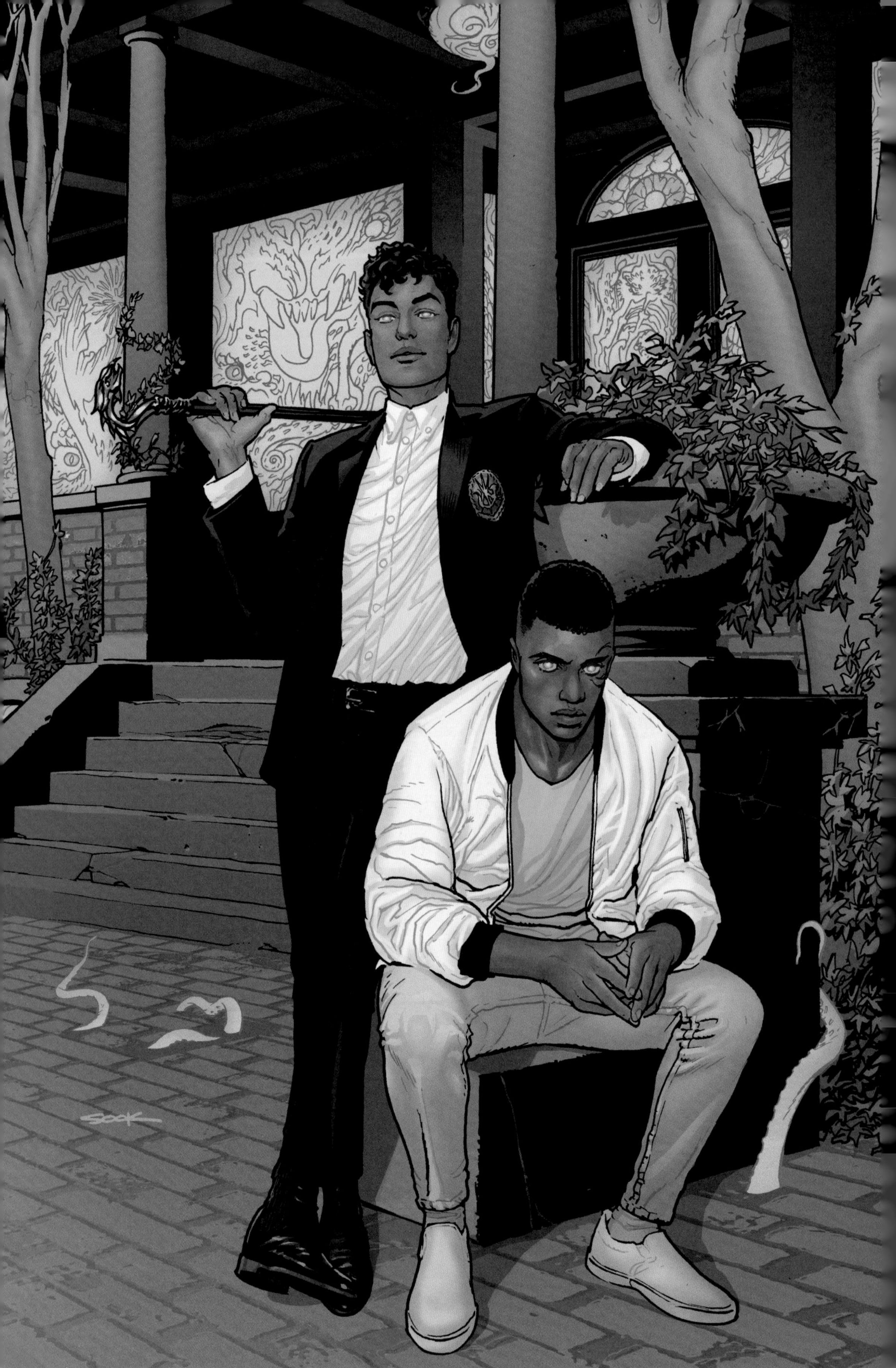
SOOK

ISSUE TWO VARIANT COVER BY RYAN SOOK

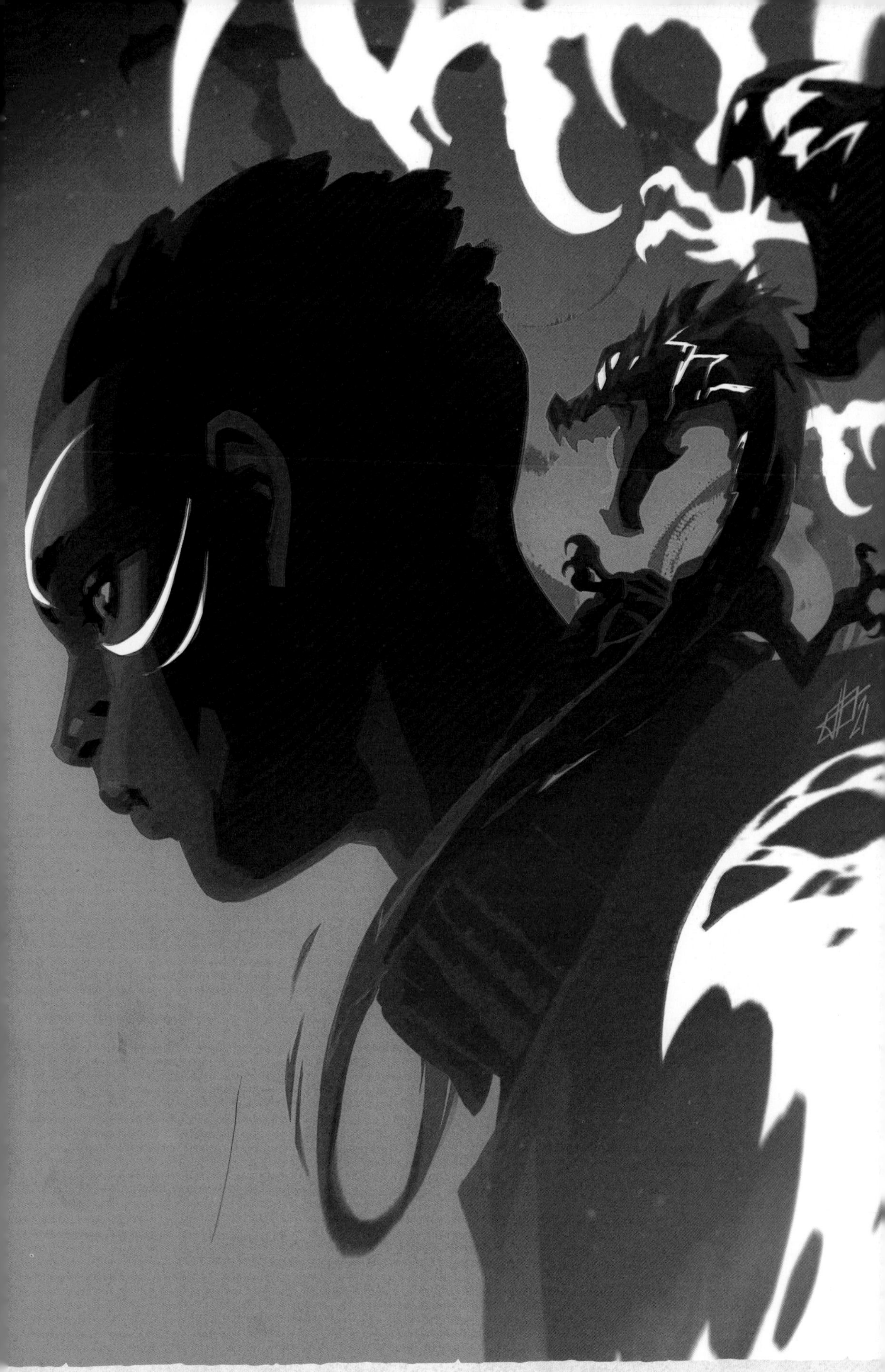

ISSUE THREE VARIANT COVER BY TONI INFANTE

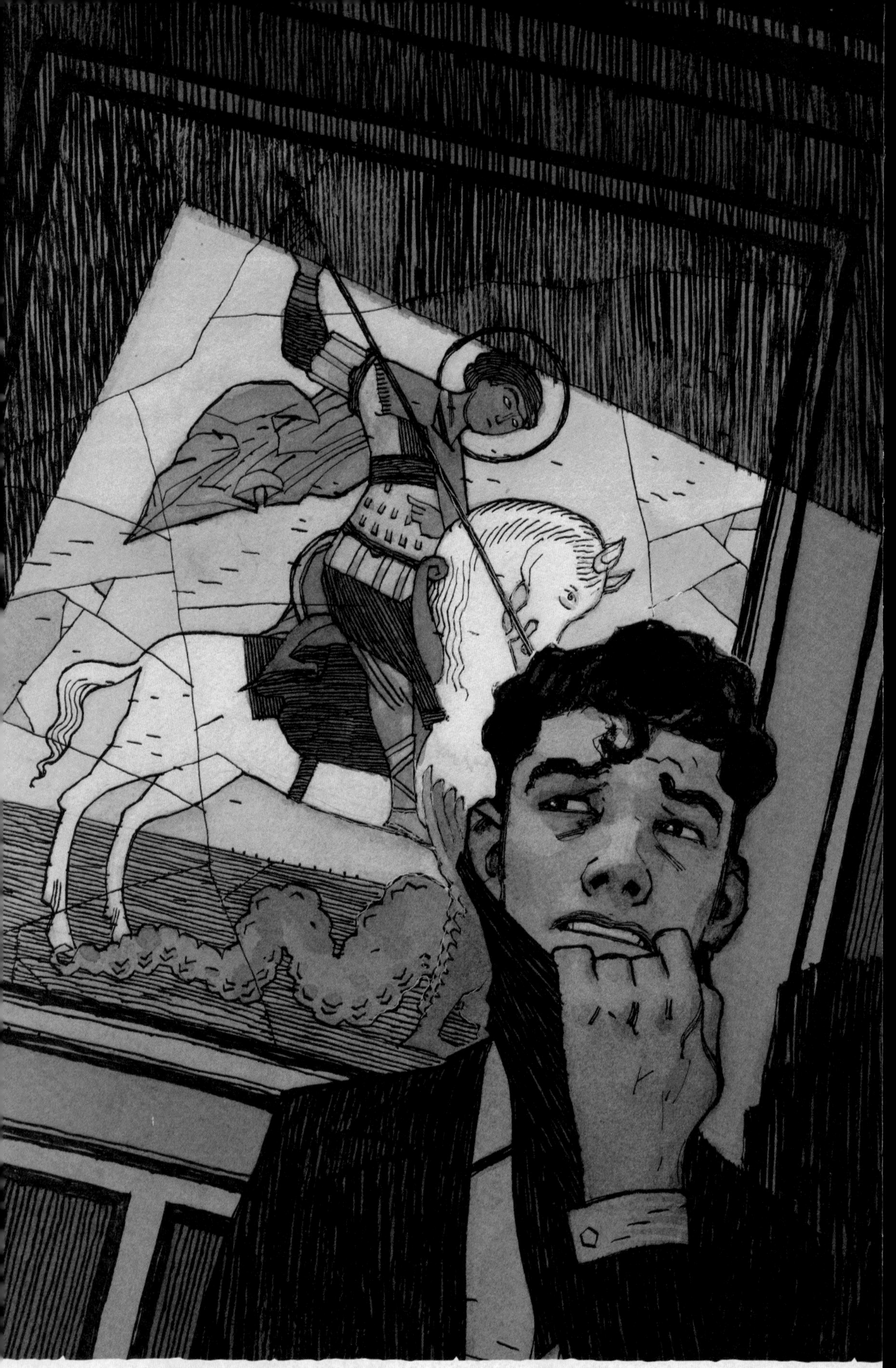

ISSUE THREE VARIANT COVER BY GABRIEL HERNANDEZ WALTA

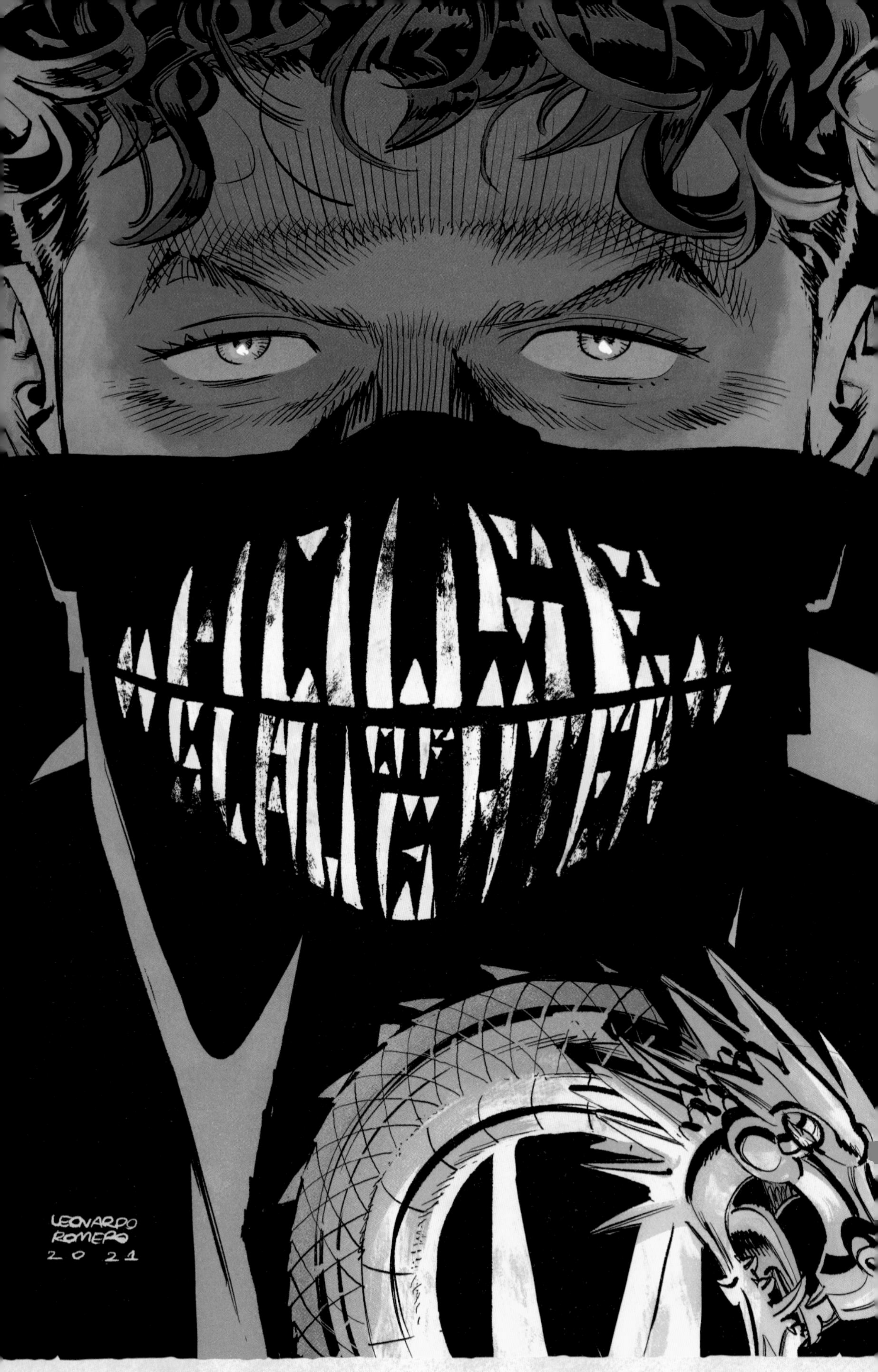
LEONARDO
ROMERO
2021

ISSUE FOUR VARIANT COVER BY LEONARDO ROMERO WITH COLORS BY JORDIE BELLAIRE

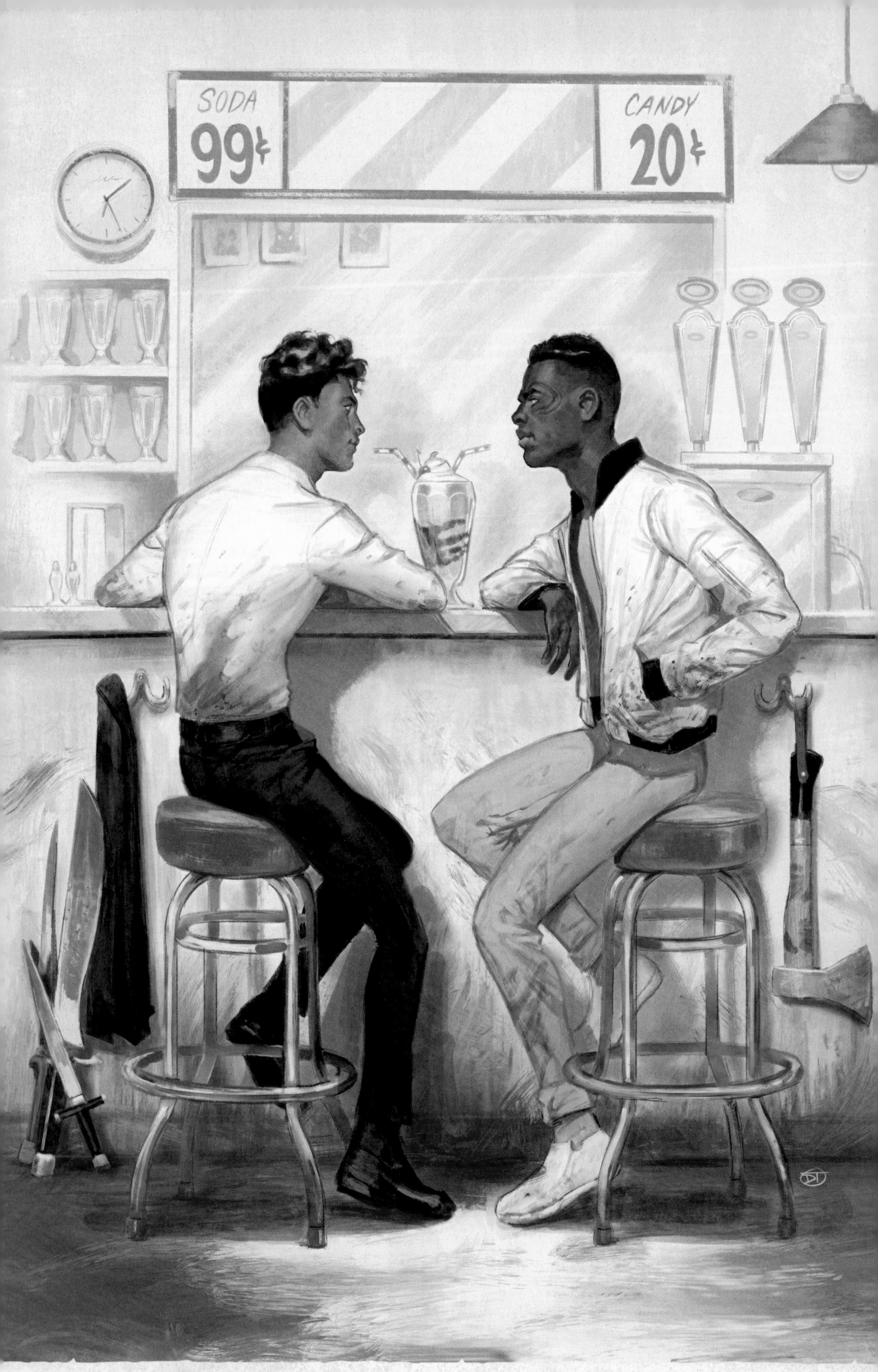
SODA
99¢
CANDY
20¢

ISSUE FOUR VARIANT COVER BY DAVID TALASKI

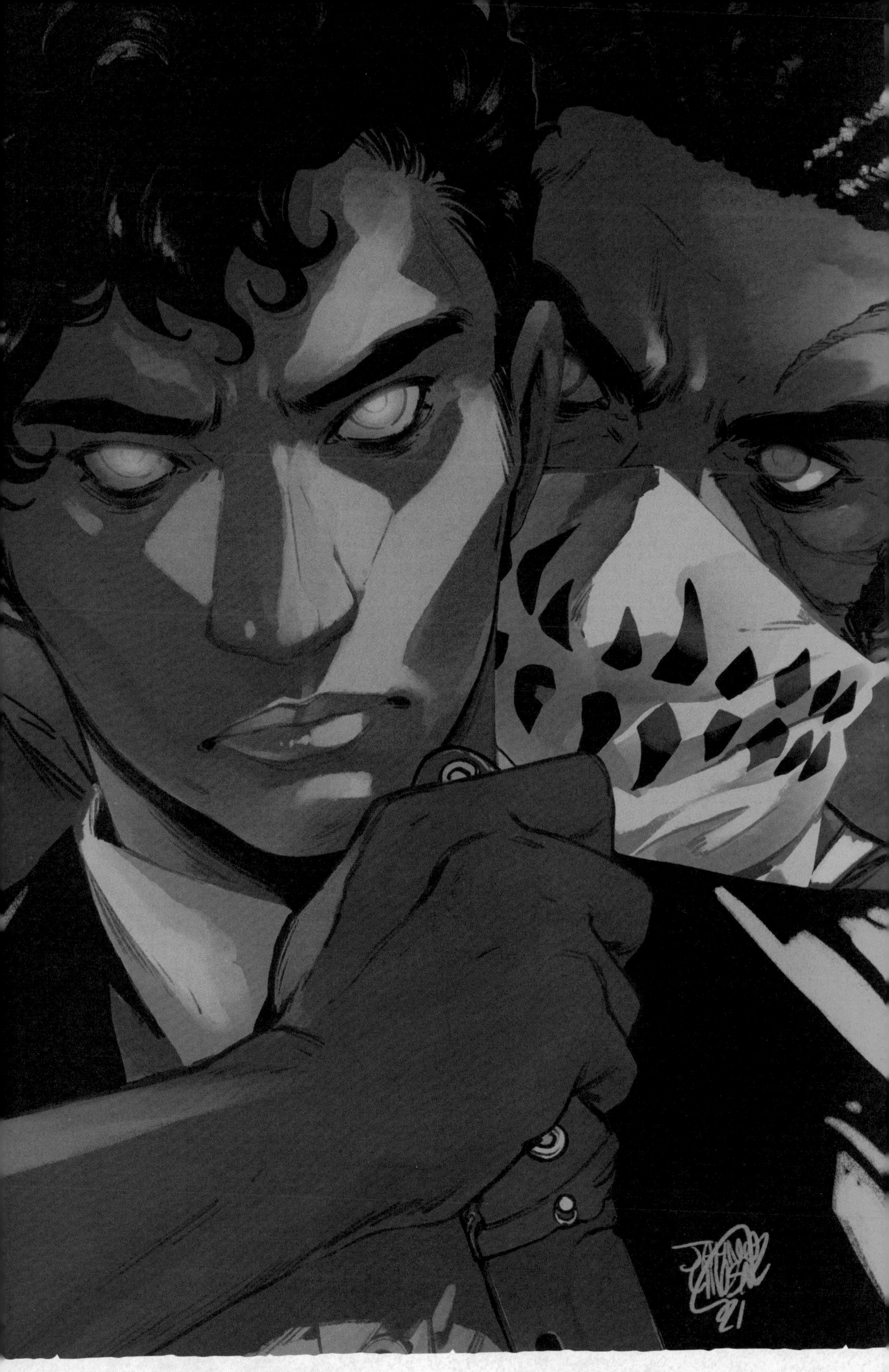

ISSUE FIVE VARIANT COVER BY JAHNOY LINDSAY

JAMES TYNION IV is an Eisner Award-winning, *New York Times* bestselling author and publisher of comic books of all shapes and sizes. Best known as a writer of horror comics, James is the co-creator of *Something is Killing the Children* with Werther Dell'Edera for BOOM! Studios, *The Department of Truth* with Martin Simmonds for Image Comics, and *The Nice House on the Lake* with Álvaro Martinez Bueno for DC Black Label. James also writes manga-infused genre stories for teens, like the fantasy epic *Wynd*, co-created with Michael Dialynas for BOOM! Studios.

TATE BROMBAL is a comic book writer from Toronto, Canada. Tate is best known for his work in Jeff Lemire and Dean Ormston's Black Hammer Universe at Dark Horse Comics, most notably for writing the Eisner-nominated *Barbalien: Red Planet.* You can find Tate on Twitter and Instagram @TateBrombal

WERTHER DELL'EDERA is an Italian artist, born in the south of Italy. He has worked for the biggest publishers in both Italy and the U.S., with his works ranging from *Loveless* (DC Vertigo) to the graphic novel *Spider-Man: Family Business* (Marvel). He has also worked for Image, IDW, Dynamite, and Dark Horse. In Italy, he has drawn Sergio Bonelli's *Dylan Dog* and *The Crow: Memento Mori* (a co-production between IDW and Edizioni BD), for which he has won awards for Best Cover Artist, Best Series, and Best Artist.

CHRIS SHEHAN is an American comic artist living in Austin, TX. He's been published by Vault Comics, Black Mask Studios, Scout Comics, A Wave Blue World, and Titan Books. He is also the artist and co-creator of *The Autumnal* from Vault Comics. He can be found on Twitter and Instagram @ChrisShehanArt

Not dead, **MIQUEL MUERTO** has lived in Barcelona since 1992, where he studied illustration, ran a small press, and worked as a graphic designer until feeling entitled to chase his dream: doing comics! *The Druid's Path* (2016) was his comic book debut as a full artist, a traumatic experience he swore would never happen again. Coloring comics was the first good step he has taken in his career and he has been happily following that path ever since.